Diplomat Heroes of the Holocaust

Diplomat Heroes of the Holocaust

by

Mordecai Paldiel

Preface by
Rabbi Arthur Schneier

Introduction by
Ambassador Richard Holbrooke

Rabbi Arthur Schneier Center for International Affairs
of Yeshiva University
in Association with
KTAV Publishing House, Inc.

Library of Congress Cataloging-in-Publication Data

Paldiel, Mordecai.
  Diplomat heroes of the Holocaust / by Mordecai Paldiel ; introduction
by Richard Holbrooke; preface by Arthur Schneier.
     p. cm.
  Includes bibliographical references and index.
  ISBN 0-88125-909-8
  1. Righteous Gentiles in the Holocaust—Biography. 2. Holocaust,
Jewish (1939-1945)—Personal narratives. 3. World War,
1939-1945—Jews—Rescue. 4. Diplomats—Biography. I. Title.
  D804.65P347 2006
  940.53'180922—dc22
  [B]

                                   2006032449

Distributed by
KTAV Publishing House, Inc.
930 Newark Avenue
Jersey City, NJ 07306
www.ktav.com

"Visas! We began to live visas day and night. When we were awake, we are obsessed by visas. We talked about them all the time. Exit visas. Transit visas. Entrance visas. Where could we go? During the day, we tried to get the proper documents, approval, stamps. At night, in bed, we tossed about and dreamed about long lines, officials, visas. Visas."

Leo Spitzer, *Hotel Bolivia*,
New York: Hill & Wang, 1999; 35

Whoever who has not gone through a country shaken by internal troubles, by war or foreign occupation, does not know the significant role that an identity card or an administrative rubber stamp can play in a person's life. In general, it is about a ridiculous piece of paper or an unimportant rubber stamp that a certain clerk had mindlessly affixed on a document. But, there are tens of thousands of persons, hundreds of thousands, perhaps millions who seek desperately to acquire such a rubber stamp. How many thousands of lists, how much money, patience, vital energy were expended by thousands of persons to take a hold of such a rubber stamp! How many swindlers manage to make a living by illegally fetching these rubber stamps and identity cards from those who need it? So much happiness and unhappiness are involved in the legal or illegal possession of this type of paper.

Lion Feuchtwanger, *Le Diable en France* (translated from the German *Der Teufel in Frankreich*),
Paris: Belfond, 1996; 73-4

All photos are courtesy of Yad Vashem Archives, Jerusalem.
Also, Franklin D. Roosevelt Library, Hyde Park, New York—
for documents of Angelo Roncalli
Cheminements, Macouard, France—
for photos of Valdemar Langlet.

Diplomat Heroes of the Holocaust

Preface

Rabbi Arthur Schneier

It is said that one who saves one life saves the world. How much greater are those who saved thousands while putting their own lives in jeopardy. As a child growing up in Vienna, I experienced first hand the horrors of *Kristallnacht* on November 10, 1938. My mother and I realized our situation was dire (my father died in 1936). We had to leave our hometown and country. Shanghai was the only destination that did not require a visa. However, there was a one year waiting period for a boat passage. As an alternative, we fled to Hungary, where my grandparents had been living and which, up until March 19, 1944, stood outside the clutches of Nazi Germany.

By May 1944 almost all of the Jews living in Hungary had been rounded up, including my grandparents and close relatives. and thrown into ghettos where they languished until their deportation to Auschwitz and other concentration camps. With the exception of Budapest, the Nazis and their Hungarian fascist collaborators cleansed the countryside of 435,000 Jews. Whereupon some of the diplomats we hail in this book moved into action working to save the remnant of Hungarian Jewry. They held out the promise of diplomatic recognition to the radical Arrow Cross government that came to power in exchange for a limited number of safety passes.

I was issued a Swiss Safety pass from the office of the Swiss Consul General, Carl Lutz. The pass offered me Swiss protection and entry into the International Red Cross Safety House. Ironically, this building used to be my Jewish Gymnasium (1940–44). What was once my school now became home, providing me with shelter and security.

The passes provided protection for thousands of Jews in Budapest. These diplomats of action and compassion violated their own governmental policy in order to save human life. They risked their careers and their lives to rescue the remaining Jewish population of Budapest.

Judaism teaches that in every generation there are Thirty Six Righteous Individuals who uphold the world. They represent the finest of humanity, dispensing justice and kindness to all who come their way. This book bears witness to such righteous people. It gives an account of those who spoke up and provided a life-line when much of the world stood by silently as six million Jews perished.

I am grateful to see this volume published by The Rabbi Arthur Schneier Center of International Affairs at Yeshiva University. If not for the humanity, courage and generosity of Carl Lutz and his diplomatic colleagues, I, and many others would not have survived. They are heroes of compassionate diplomacy and serve as an inspiration for public officials in the future. May their memory be blessed.

Arthur Schneier, Budapest, May, 1941

Arthur Schneier's mother, Mrs. Gisela (Gisa) Schneier, with Yellow Star, May, Budapest, 1944

Arthur Schneier's Grandfather, Chief Rabbi Moses Bergmann of Körözomezö and the Region, 1942. Deported to Auschwitz, May, 1944.

Arthur Schneier, first grade, Jewish Gymnasium, Budapest, 1940

Introduction

Ambassador Richard Holbrooke

You are a consular officer, in the early years of a diplomatic career that you hope will lead to an ambassadorship. On your desk sit two rubber stamps. Use the one that says "APPROVED," and the person in front of you can travel to your country legally. Use the other stamp which says "REJECTED", and the visa applicant in front of you might die or go to prison—simply because he or she is Jewish.

Sounds simple, but there is a catch—a very big one. Your government does not want you to use the stamp that will save a life. Your boss does not want these people—these desperate people waiting outside your office, milling around in the street, hiding in their houses—in your country. Stamp too many visas "APPROVED", and your career will be in danger. Follow your instructions, and people will die.

What would you have done, if you were stationed in Bordeaux or Marseilles in 1940? Or if you faced a modern version of the same situation, with a different cast of characters, say refugees from Vietnam or Darfur?

In the movies, the hero stares out the window, the music swells, and he does the right thing. (Think of Humphrey Bogart in *Casablanca*, with the famous "letters of transit.) But in the real world, it is not so easy; there are few heroes in such situations. Government service is based on the well-founded principle that officials must carry out their instructions; otherwise, anarchy would prevail. But what happens if your instructions have horrible—literally fatal—consequences? And your boss is watching you? And your career is on the line?

We heard, and mocked, the defense of many Germans after World War II; they were just following orders. But the same rationale was used by the majority of non-German diplomats in Europe during the 1930s. For every Wallenberg there were hundreds of consular officials who played it safe – or were themselves determined to use their power to keep Jews out of their country. As a result, many thousands of Jews whose lives could have been saved were left to fend for themselves; most later died in the camps. This was not always simply officials passively following instructions; some were rather enthusiastic in their rejection of Jewish visa applicants. Take, for example, the Brazilian consul in Lyon, France, in 1940, who proudly wrote his foreign minister that the people swarming around his office were "almost all Jewish or of Semitic origin, and only a very few of them may be of interest to us. I therefore believe that by my categorical refusal to grant the visas that they request, I will have done Brazil a great service."

Yet a few risked everything to save the lives of people, mostly Jews whom they did not even know, simply because they knew the policy was wrong. Tens of thousands of lives were saved by these heroes. If it were not for the work done by the Commission for the Designation of the Righteous at Yad Vashem, in Jerusalem, we would probably not even know the names of most of them. But this invaluable effort has not only brought belated recognition to many unsung heroes, it also provides a continuing lesson about the need to think not only about one's day-to-day duties and the rulebook, but also to the larger context of one's life.

As Mordecai Paldiel points out, it was not the Germans who punished these brave men and women, it was their own governments. Yet in the face of such risks, a few ordinary men suddenly showed great moral courage, knowing full well that they might pay with their careers. They came from many countries, although so far, Yad Vashem has not honored any American officials, and only one, Hiram Bingham, appears to be under serious consideration. (Bingham defied Breckinridge Long, who headed the European Bureau of the State Department and had out-maneuvered Eleanor Roosevelt when she tried to get State to issue more visas to Jews. For his actions, Bingham was removed from his post, and replaced by a hand-picked officer who enthusiastically carried out Long's infamously anti-Semitic policies.)

Yet a handful of Chinese, Spanish, Portuguese, Romanians, Swiss, Brazilians, Dutch, Turkish, Italian, Vatican, Yugoslav, and even Japanese and German diplomats risked everything—their careers, their reputations, even their lives—to save Jews. The most famous, of course, was Raoul Wallenberg, whose fearlessness, courage and creativity approached nearly insane levels, and who did pay with his life—at the hands not of the Nazis, but the Soviets, who thought he was an American spy.

Wallenberg, from an aristocratic family in Sweden, had been sent to Budapest on a special mission by Franklin Roosevelt. But most of the others had been given routine assignments only to find themselves in an unexpected moral dilemma of historic dimensions. Take, for example, the astonishing story of Aristides de Sousa Mendes, the Portuguese consul-general in Bordeaux. After the Portuguese dictator Antonio de Oliveira Salazar prohibited the issuance of transit visas to refugees, singling out Jews, Mendes, a devout Catholic, visited the stranded Jewish refugees on the streets, then retreated to his house, tossing and turning on his bed for three days, sweating profusely, according to his son. Then he emerged, "flung open the doors to the chancellery, and announced in a loud voice, 'From now on I'm giving everyone visas.'" Mendes later told his sons that he "had heard a voice, that of his conscience or of God."

For a few weeks in June 1940, Mendes was in a frenzy of activity, issuing visas as fast as possible, even going to the Spanish border to make sure that they would be honored by skeptical border police. He knew he was racing against his own government. In July he was removed from his post, and put under a nasty investigation supervised personally by Salazar. He was unrepentant: "My desire is to be with God against man rather than with man and against God," he told his superiors, one of whom told the investigating tribunal that Mendes had gone crazy. He was dismissed from government service, and, although supported by some of the Jewish community in Lisbon, died in poverty. Not until after the fall of the Salazar regime did the Portuguese restore his good name and honor him, and today, there are schools and streets named after him in Portugal.

Mendes's story was typical of those remembered in this book. Given the risks and costs to those who defied their governments, it is not surprising that there were so few. But every age will present such difficult choices. The details will vary, but the challenge will be similar. As a former Foreign Service Officer, I hope this book will be required reading for all aspiring young diplomats—so that they can ask themselves, "What would I have done?" And so that they can be better prepared if they have to face such a challenge, in whatever form, during their career.

Chapter 1

Why Diplomats?
The Significance of Their Action

It is a fantastic comment on the inhumanity of our times that for thousands and thousands of people a piece of paper with a stamp on it is the difference between life and death.
—Dorothy Thompson, American journalist

During the Nazi period, before and during World War Two, the two sides seemingly squared off against each other as the Bad Guys—Nazi Germany and its supporters, and the Good Guys—the democratic Allies and their supporters. While it is true that the survival of the Jewish people in the face of the genocidal Nazi onslaught against them depended on an Allied victory, the sad fact is that the Allies were not so much concerned with the survival of the Jews as with stopping Nazi Germany and its partner nations from their mad race to conquer ever more lands and countries, and thereby upset the fragile balance of power in the world. When it came to the Jews, the Allies found one excuse after another to shirk responsibility from an active involvement in rescuing them. The Evian and Bermuda conferences of 1938 and 1943, convened to discuss the plight of Jewish refugees, ended without any practical decisions, nor any readiness to admit into their countries the few who escaped from the Nazi inferno. In 1944, deep in the war, and with victory in sight, the United States and Great Britain nev-

1

ertheless came up with excuses for declining to bomb the railroads leading to the death camps, although by then they had gained supremacy over Europe's air space.

Saving the Jews trapped in German-dominated Europe was left to individual non-Jewish rescuers, many of whom have been honored by the Yad Vashem Holocaust Memorial in Jerusalem as Righteous Among the Nations. Among them may be counted some select individuals, serving in various diplomatic capacities, who thanks to their official positions were able to save many Jews, and they deserve special attention. Whereas most rescuers could save only one or a handful, diplomats, if they so wanted, could do a lot more in terms of number of persons helped, using their power to issue visas or protective passes not only to a few but to many—to dozens, hundreds, if not thousands. To many fleeing Jews, at the end of their wits in their effort to escape the closing dragnet, a visa became a magic word and a life-line to freedom from deportation and death. Thus the stampede for such documents. For diplomats, on the other hand, the issue was their country's policy on issuing visas on a mass scale to fleeing Jews. Was it permitted or not? In most cases, it was not.

When acting on their own, diplomats faced two choices: either to disobey instructions from their superiors that forbade them to issue visas or other documents that would protect the bearer against persecution, or to reinterpret the instructions from above in such a way as to make it appear as if they were carrying out their country's immigration policy even though they were, in fact, turning it upside down. Either way, diplomats faced the possibility of serious consequences to themselves, from reprimands to dismissals and further punitive measures. In this study, we shall tell the stories of the relatively few diplomats who faced up to this moral challenge, and responded to the appeals for aid. Some paid a heavy price—punished not by the Germans, but by their own governments.

In a significant development, the Nuremberg Tribunal that tried the surviving top Nazis immediately after World War Two rejected the claim of the accused that their obligation to blindly follow orders from above excused their wartime behavior. The question remaining open was not whether not to obey, but of taking it a step forward—of disobeying by acting contrary to orders and instructions that were clearly a violation of universal principles of human rights. The diplomats in this study took this additional step when they acted contrary to government immigration policies that prohibited the admission to Jews to their countries. Their legacy to future generations is the example they present of administrative behavior by top civil servants bound to universal principles of humanity and not merely to narrow bureaucratic obligations; of official conduct at its humanitarian, as opposed to technocratic, best.

In 1962, Yad Vashem established the Commission for the Designation of the Righteous, a public agency headed by a Supreme Court judge, to choose non-Jewish rescuers of Jews to be awarded the honorific title of Righteous Among the Nations, as provided by the 1953 Yad Vashem law of the Israeli parliament. One of the fundamental criteria was and still is risk to the life and safety of the rescuer when extending assistance to a Jewish person during the Holocaust. However, when dealing with help by diplomats, two different criteria were applied. In other instances, the requirement was help even to a single Jewish person. With diplomats, it was not a question of sheltering and hiding fugitives from the authorities in one's own home. Instead it has to be shown that the person in question extended help, in the form of visas or other life-saving documentation, to more than one or several individuals; in fact, to many more. In addition, it has to be established that the diplomat acted either in violation of clear instructions or in such a way that his action, while not a clear violation, nevertheless in the end amounted to acting against the spirit of his instructions. A diplomat meeting these two qualifications would be awarded the Righteous title even if there had not been any immediate danger to his personal safety from the Germans and their allies in the country where he was posted, but only of punitive administrative measures from his own government.

In the case of Raoul Wallenberg, who was active in Budapest, the risk element was not totally absent. SS Colonel Adolf Eichmann warned him that an accident could always be engineered. Fearing for his safety during the phase of Arrow Cross rule in Budapest, Wallenberg was careful to always spend the night in a different location. His diplomatic status, in this instance, was no sure guarantee against physical harm. It was otherwise for the Portuguese diplomat Aristides de Sousa Mendes, in Bordeaux, France. He clearly disobeyed instructions from above not to issue transit visas to Jews; in fact, he distributed these life-saving documents in the thousands. As a consequence, Mendes was victimized by his government with punitive measures that included dismissal from the diplomatic service and annulment of all retirement benefits. The Swiss diplomat Carl Lutz, also in Budapest, went beyond the mandate given by his government in issuing protective letters to Jews. Likewise for Francis Foley, a British diplomat in Berlin, whose far-reaching reinterpretation of British immigration laws, at times in contradiction to their spirit, made it possible for many Jews to leave Nazi Germany.

These stories took place in a time when a piece of paper, usually a visa or a diplomatic protective document, could spell the difference between life and death for a fleeing Jew anxious to escape the Nazi web of destruction. Diplomats posted to various European capitals understood this well, and some took note of what their conscience dictated in the effort to save innocent lives, even and in spite of immigration regulations that restricted their scope of operation. To their credit, the total number of people saved runs into the thousands, even several tens of thousands.

The narratives in this book will illustrate the methods employed by diplomats in securing the lives of innocent Jews during the Nazi reign of unrestricted terror. Their humanitarian acts are testimony to the wide latitude available to persons in high places in the cause of universal principles—if, of course, they are prepared to obey the dictates of their heart and conscience, during periods of emergency, instead of the more narrow administrative requirements of their official post. They represent the best and the bravest in terms of human behavior during one of the darkest chapters of civilized life and its moral values.

Chapter 2

Nazi Germany
Where It All Began

Introduction

Germany is the country where it all began; the avalanche and downward slide, engulfing and burying in its sway a centuries-old heritage of human values. When Hitler assumed power on January 30, 1933, the 522,000 Jews of Germany, comprising fewer than 1 percent of the population, were not only in the process of full acculturation, but held influential positions in the country's life, especially in journalism, the theater, and schools of higher learning, in proportions much higher than their corresponding share in the non-Jewish population. This was, tragically, to change drastically. The first months of Nazi power saw physical attacks on Jews, many of whom were subjected to public humiliation, with the police standing by. A climax was reached with the anti-Jewish boycott of Jewish-owned stores of April 1, 1933. This went hand in hand with laws excluding Jews from influential positions, such as the Law for the Restoration of the Professional Civil Service, now reserved only for Aryans (a term henceforth applied to those who were "racially" non-Jews). All Jews were automatically fired from public service positions.

Very quickly Jews were excluded from cultural life, journalism, and academic institutions. On April 7, 1933, all professors of law who were Jews were driven from their universities in humiliating circumstances. This was followed by the suspension of all Jewish judges. Martin Heidegger, Germany's most famed philosopher, joined the Nazi Party, and as head of Freiburg University dismissed Jews from the faculty, including his own mentor, declaring: "The Fuehrer himself, and he alone, is the German reality of today, and of the future, as of its law." Cities and towns vied with each other in pronouncing that "Jews were not wanted in this place."

While all this was happening, the country's civic and religious leaders kept their silence. Stunned by the unexpected turn of events, the Jewish response was, in general, to seek immigration possibilities in other countries. Some 300,000 left in the following years, and well into the first two years of World War Two. In September 1935, the Nuremberg laws were promulgated, annulling the citizenship of the country's Jews, and prohibiting marriage and sexual relations between Jews and non-Jews, as racially defined. In October 1938, passports held by Jews were marked with a large *J*; the same for personal identification cards. A year earlier, Jews were required to add "Jewish" middle names on their ID cards: Israel for men and Sarah for women. Jews were also ordered concentrated in special "Jewish" houses, and were forced to sell their holdings in real estate, as well as other large enterprises, at prices a fraction of their real value, a process euphemistically termed Aryanization. Jews were eventually prohibited from leaving their homes after dark, and certain sections of the cities were placed out of bounds for them.

With the start of the war on September 1, 1939, further restrictive decrees followed one another in quick succession, such as the requisition of personal goods: jewelry, radios, cameras, electrical appliances, and any other valuables. In September 1941, all Jews aged six and above were ordered to wear the Jewish Star. Jews "fit for work," practically everyone, were assigned to the most menial and difficult tasks. A year before the start of the war, on the evening of November 9–10, 1938, several hundred synagogues, thousands of small-scale Jewish enterprises, and Jewish homes were either torched or vandalized throughout Germany (which now included Austria and the Sudeten region of former Czechoslovakia as part of the Greater German Reich), in a government-orchestrated orgy of horror that came to be known as *Kristallnacht*, or "Night of Broken Glass." Close to 100 Jews were murdered and 35,000 were carted off to the concentration camps (at this stage, most were released upon the presentation of transit visas to other countries).

Here, too, civic and religious leaders kept their silence, only voicing concern at the economic losses caused by these destructive acts. This time, there was a stampede to consulates for visas to emigrate to any destination possible, including places as distant as the international compound in Shanghai, China. About 164,000 Jews (of the 215,000 counted in September 1939) were still living in the expanded Reich on October 1, 1941 (the date of the ban on further emigration). Large-scale deportation of Jews began in October 1941. By then, over 300,000 had managed to leave the country, some to neighboring countries, and these people fell victim to the Germans when their host countries came under German occupation. The remaining Jews faced the final murderous brunt of the regime.

As the war expanded, with the invasion of the Soviet Union on June 22, 1941, special killing units known as *Einsatzgruppen* carried out mass exterminations of Jews in the newly conquered territories. In Germany, the fall of 1941 saw the start of mass deportations of German Jews to killing sites in the East, including Auschwitz. The more privileged were initially deported to the "model" camp of Theresienstadt, established to fool the deportees and international agencies, such as the Red Cross, into believing that the camps were created with the sole purpose of separating Jews from the rest of the population but nothing worse. After the Red Cross team left the scene, the inmates they had met were dispatched to the gas chambers in Auschwitz. In sum, a total of 137,000 Jews were deported from Germany, of whom only 9,000 survived the depredations of the camps. Between 10,000 and 20,000 Jews survived inside Germany (an estimated 7,000 in Berlin alone), some protected by their marriages to non-Jewish spouses.

In neighboring Austria, annexed to Germany in March 1938, the Jewish population was 185,000—170,000 in Vienna alone. Following the annexation, the Gestapo (state political police) launched an organized campaign of looting Jewish apartments and confiscating Jewish-held valuables. Jews were dismissed from most important posts, and synagogues were desecrated (this took place before the infamous *Kristallnacht* in November of that year). All major Jewish enterprises were closed and taken over. Up to the start of the war, some 126,000 Jews managed to emigrate. The rest were deported to concentration camps in Poland, where most perished. At the end of the war, only 1,000 Jews were to be found in Vienna; some were partners in mixed marriages, and others had gone underground. A total of 65,000 Austrian Jews perished at the hands of the Nazis, with only 1,700 surviving the horrors of the camps and death marches.[1]

Francis Foley

In 1919, Lieutenant Francis ("Frank") Foley, after distinguished service in the British army in World War One, arrived in Berlin as an agent for the MI6 section of British intelligence, to observe and report on the activities of the communist-led organizations that were so strong and active at the time in Germany, such as Rosa Luxemburg's Spartacist movement. As a cover for his spy work, he officially was chief passport control officer in the British embassy, where he had wide latitude to judge and decide on the admission of foreigners to the various parts of the British Empire—all, of course, in accordance with the relevant immigration laws and regulations governing the United Kingdom, the dominions, and the various colonies, protectorates, and mandated territories of the British Empire. Foley continued in this post until the outbreak of World War Two in September 1939. Earlier, with the Nazi rise to power in 1933, Foley's attention had shifted to the rearmament of Germany, and he simultaneously began to be more preoccupied with helping Jews to emigrate, a need which became urgent after the staged pogrom of November 8, 1938, the notorious *Kristallnacht*. Foley utilized legal means whenever possible and in other instances exploited loopholes in Britain's immigration rules. For instance, British regulations at the time forbade the issuing of entry visas to persons liable to compete with certain professional categories in England, as well as to the very aged, the sick and handicapped, and members of the Communist Party. As for entry to Palestine, then a

Francis Foley,
the British diplomat in Berlin, Germany.

British-mandated territory, the applicant had to have £1,000 on hand in order to obtain a "capitalist" visa. This was a sizable sum at the time, the equivalent of £40,000 today, and unavailable for many Jews whose bank accounts and other assets had been frozen by the Nazi authorities. The following examples will illustrate how Foley helped people overcome these obstacles.[2]

Elisheva Lernau (born Elsbeth Kahn in 1913) is one of the many people who credit Foley with facilitating her exit from Nazi Germany. In 1935, her father, attorney Bertholt Kahn, opened an account with the Deutsche Bank in the amount of 20,000 marks as required by the British in order to get a capitalist visa for Palestine, but Nazi regulations blocked the money for many years, and she had only £10 in cash.

A certain Mr. Walbach suggested she see Captain Foley. Wallach in the meantime informed Foley that Elisheva knew enough Hebrew to be able to be self-sufficient in Palestine right from the start. Foley then decided that the balance of £990 would be available to her the minute she landed in Haifa, and on the strength of that decision issued her a capitalist visa for Palestine even though the capital was not available at the time. This was in August 1935. "Next month, I landed in Haifa with 10 marks. The capital, incidentally, was transferred to me only shortly before the outbreak of the war." In her words, "I am convinced that without the 'unlawful' help of Captain Foley I would not have reached Palestine in time. . . . I have always been deeply grateful to this unknown man."

Foley similarly bent the capitalist visa rule in the case of Wolfgang Meyer-Michael, who could not raise the £1,000 required for a visa. To overcome this obstacle, Foley suggested finding the money through someone who would guarantee it. "Just get a promise; you don't have to use it," Foley told the surprised Meyer-Michael. As told by Wolfgang's daughter, Sabina, "My father then looked up a cousin in Holland, who understood the dilemma. They drew up two documents. In one the cousin promised to lend my father £1,000 when/if he needed it. In a second my father declared the first one invalid and promised not to make use of it. Mr. Foley knew, of course, that this was a ploy but issued the visa immediately." The result? Meyer-Michael landed safely in Palestine. "This was truly a good man," my father wrote in his memoirs. "It is thanks to Mr. Foley that I am alive today."

Similarly for Zeev Estreicher, whose funds were blocked by Nazi laws, and in 1935 was given a capitalist visa on the basis of a letter from a bank certifying that the man had the required £1,000 on deposit. At that, Foley took Estreicher's passport and stamped a British visa for travel to Palestine. "He probably saved my life." Likewise for Heinz Romberg, born 1909, who desperately needed to leave Germany in October 1935, as a result of a foolish decision he had made several months earlier in returning from Spain. He was referred to Foley, who immediately gave him a capitalist visa for travel to

Palestine, although Romberg did not have the required £1,000. Thanks to this, Romberg was able to leave Germany on the deadline date specified by the German authorities. "I have not and shall never forget this man," Romberg emphasized in his testimony to Yad Vashem. "He enriched my life with a wife, three children, eight grandchildren, and five great-grandchildren (so far)."

Others helped by Foley to leave the country included Adele Wertheimer (born Neumark) who tried through various Jewish aid organizations to leave the country, but to no avail. At a loss what else to do, one of the Jewish organizations referred her to Foley "as the last possible source of help." Adele saw Foley, who granted her a visa to Palestine "for the sake of the child," her 8-year-old son Siegbert Simon, and both left the country in August 1938, several months before *Kristallnacht*. As for Ida Weisz, who was almost without means, she too went to see Foley as a last resort, traveling from Vienna to the British Passport Office in Berlin in 1939. "Mr. Foley let me stay at his house for a few days and then he came home late one night with the necessary exit visas and papers. I left for Belgium and then onward to England on the early train the next morning. The last time I saw Mr. Foley was at the station."

Amalia Arian was another person saved by Foley. After she arrived safely in Palestine in May 1939, her son, Dr. D. Arian, penned a letter of thanks to Foley with the words: "Destiny has placed you in a position where you daily come in touch with sorrow and despair, and where a man like you always feels the restrictions of power to help those who suffer. However, I know that whenever you find a possibility to assist the oppressed you do all you can to help them and by doing so you find happiness and satisfaction. . . . It may also please you to hear that wherever your name is mentioned 'from Dan to Beer Sheva' you are talked of with the greatest respect and devotion, and that you and a few other persons effect as a counterweight where the evils of everyday politics suppress and destroy the faith in honesty and humanity." To which, Francis Foley responded from Berlin in July 1939: "You must be very happy to have your mother with you again. . . . Conditions are getting worse and worse for the Jews. I dread to think of the misery and suffering they—especially the older people—will have to face next winter. Their funds are running low, and they do not know where they will find accommodation. The quota is a calamity, especially in these days of rabid persecution and permanent cold pogrom. The courage and fortitude of the Jews are beyond praise. They have our profound admiration."

A most extraordinary story is that of Gunter Powitzer. He had been jailed for violation of the Nuremberg laws of September 1935, which forbade illicit relations between Aryan and Jew—a very serious offense in Nazi Germany, known as *Rassenschande* ("race soiling"). Gunter had such an amorous relationship, which produced a son, Zeev (his current Hebrew name). Arrested and tried, he was jailed for 21 months. Upon the completion of his sentence, in December 1938, he was taken by an SS man to the Sachsenhausen concentration camp, where he was assigned to hard labor in a brick plant. One day, an SS guard came to Gunter's workplace and ordered him to take a shower, then go to the dispensary for treatment of the wounds inflicted by beatings. "What happened?" Gunter asked. "Shut up," the SS man shouted back at him. "He threw on me a long gray coat, and said: 'Shut up and put it on. You have a visitor.' I was very skinny, . . . I thought to myself, 'Who in the world knows that I'm here? Who can it be?' " Dressed in civvies, neat, clean, combed, and shaven, Gunter was taken to the camp's office. "There sat a short man with eyeglasses, who told me in English: 'My name is Foley, and I am from the British consulate in Berlin.' " Gunter asked the SS man for a translator, so as to have him leave the office. "'I understand English,' I told Mr. Foley. He smiled and said, 'Tomorrow you will be freed and papers are waiting for you in the consulate for travel to Palestine.' I asked: 'And what about the child?' Foley answered, 'Don't worry, your brother in Palestine took care of everything.' " That child was Zeev. On February 1, 1939, Gunter Powitzer was released from the Sachsenhausen camp. A car was waiting for him outside. After 12 days, he and his son left Germany for Italy, then to Palestine.

Foley was aided in his rescue efforts by Hubert Pollack, a Jewish communal worker who told him about individuals in desperate need of help to leave the country, such as Gunter Powitzer. One case involved a twenty-year-old woman (identified only as H.H. in Pollack's postwar account) imprisoned because of her membership in the outlawed Communist Party. She had given birth to a child while in jail, and the father, who had already left for Rhodesia (then a British colony), now wished her to join him. The Gestapo had released her on condition that she leave the country within two weeks. Pollack placed her documents on Foley's table. Following is the conversation between the two men, as reported by Pollack.

Foley: "How old is the young lady now?"

Pollack: "Twenty."

Foley: "She has spent two years in prison; thus she was eighteen when she was sentenced. How do you say 'youthful enthusiasm' in German? At least, this is my impression. Or do you think that in Rhodesia the young lady will become an active communist?"

Pollack: "Hardly."

Foley: "Then please send her to me."

Pollack: "Is the child also to be entered on the passport?"

Foley: "Yes."

Pollack: "Excellent; goodbye!"

After a long conversation with Captain Foley, Miss H.H. returned to Pollack with a visa in her passport, and twelve hours before the end of the deadline she had left on a ship from Bremen.

In another difficult situation, the police record of a man who wished to go to England showed that he had been imprisoned for performing an abortion, an offense that automatically cancelled entry into any of the British Empire's territories. Pollack suspected that this was a trumped-up charge to annul the Jewish man's medical qualification, and went to consult with Foley. Foley examined the application documents, then asked Pollack whether he thought the man had practiced abortions. Pollack answered in the negative. Two days later, Foley told Pollack: "That is a clearly antisemitic verdict without any definite proof. I want to see your client, but alone." A few weeks later, the man received a visa, and headed to Palestine. In the words of Pollack, "Again and again I faced the situation that people who thanked me effusively in the *Hilfsverein* [Jewish assistance office] for a life-saving visa to Trinidad, Southern Rhodesia, India, or Great Britain—that I had to tell them, full of shame: Go to Tiergartenstrasse 17 [the British consulate] and thank Captain Foley. For the visa you are getting, you have to thank him, not me."

After the war, Pollack testified that "the number of Jews who were saved in Germany would have been ten thousand times—yes, ten thousand—less, if a 'competent official' had occupied that post instead of Captain Foley." Benno Cohn, head of the Zionist Federation in Germany, testified at the Eichmann trial in 1960 that immediately after *Kristallnacht*, he frantically called his superiors in Jerusalem to find ways to save the Jews of Germany, adding: "Nevertheless, we succeeded in getting a sizable number of Jews to Palestine. That was thanks to a man who is to my mind to be counted among the Righteous Gentiles. . . . Captain Foley did all he could to enable Jews to immigrate to Palestine. He helped a lot of people of every category ['capitalists,' students, etc.]. . . . One may say that he saved thousands of Jews from death."

Foley's wife Katharine, in a 1961 interview, related that during the *Kristallnacht* pogrom period, she and her husband hid Jewish fugitives in their Berlin home. "They would ring up and ask for help, and Frank would slip down to the door late at night and let them in. . . . There was one young Jew whom we sheltered many nights. He had always left the flat by the time I got up for breakfast. But he never failed to leave something on my plate as a token of his gratitude . . . a little box of chocolates . . . sometimes a solitary rose. . . . I do not know what the Nazis would have done if they had discovered we were hiding people. We had to remember that we had our young daughter, Ursula, with us."[3]

Foley worked long hours to help fleeing Jews, especially after the November 1938 *Kristallnacht* pogrom, when many flocked to the British Passport Control Office, hoping for the miracle of a visa. To help him with the work backlog, Foley had additional British workers from the British embassy building, located on Wilhelmstrasse, brought over to regulate the flow of people into the consulate. In order to facilitate the exits of these people, Foley made use of a British plan to temporarily house refugees in England in what became known as the Richborough Camp. When the permits for the camp arrived, Foley and Pollack, on behalf of the still-functioning Jewish aid organization, established an effective and reliable high-speed procedure for the issuance of visas that did not require the presence of the applicant. "That," in Pollack's words, "was an extraordinary concession, significant for the high degree of confidence Captain Foley showed us." All these people and, in Pollack's estimation, thousands of other Jews as well as non-Jews owe their rescue to Captain Foley and his team.

Days before the start of the war, on August 24, 1939, Hanan Baram, a Zionist operative in Berlin who had been in touch with Foley on matters pertaining to emigration to Palestine, was told by a Gestapo official to find himself a way out of the country or else—threatening words that could only mean that Baram was in danger. He was soon informed that Foley, who was also packing to leave, had left a message for him to quickly pick up eighty immigration certificates for England, before the closure of the British consulate at 4 o'clock, in the afternoon of the following day (August 25). And so it was. A week later, England was at war with Germany.

Returning to England by way of Norway, where he also helped fleeing refugees (Jews and others) during World War Two, Foley's intelligence work included the interrogation of Rudolf Hess, Hitler's misguided deputy, who landed in Scotland in May 1941, hoping to strike a deal between Germany and Britain. Foley's nephew, William L. Kelley, in the United States, related in a letter to Yad Vashem that on his eighteenth birthday his mother told him about his uncle's achievements: his espionage mission (evacuation of the king of Norway in 1940, interrogation of Hess when he defected to England, a year later, his collaboration in the plot to fool the Nazis into believing that Sicily would not be invaded in 1943). "But what they were most proud of was Frank's efforts to save Jews from the Nazi concentration camps. He and Aunt Kay hid Jews in their Berlin home; issued visas; went to camps to personally get them out."

In April 1945, as Allied troops were liberating the concentration camps in Germany, Frank Foley wrote to Dr. Senator, "We are reading about and seeing photographs of those places the names of which were so well known to us in the years before the war. Now the people here really and finally believe that the stories of 1938–1939 were not exaggerated. They were understated in fact. It is all too horrible. Looking back, I feel grateful that our little office in Tiergartenstrasse was able to assist some—far too few—to escape in time. . . . I am particularly sympathetic towards children because my only child is very ill and is causing my wife and me a great deal of worry and anxiety. . . . I have often hoped that as I helped so many doctors, fate would arrange for me to meet *the* doctor who would cure her. We feel that some such man exists." His daughter suffered from epilepsy. Unfortunately, she could not be cured, and died of an epileptic fit in 1982. Francis Foley died in 1958, at the age of seventy-three, followed by his wife, Katherine (Kay), in 1979.

On July 10, 1959 friends and work colleagues of Foley gathered in a forest near Harel, in the hilly region outside Jerusalem, to dedicate a forest in remembrance of him. Benno Cohn spoke in praise of Foley: "By a lucky stroke, a man had been put into this position [passport control officer] who didn't only know the regulations, but also had a big heart for the people crowded there with requests." During the *Kristallnacht* period, "the rooms of the consulate were transformed into a shelter for Jews looking for protection from persecution. Thirty-two thousand men were in prison in concentration camps during those weeks, their wives besieging the consul for a visa that meant liberation for their husbands. It was a question of life or death for several thousands. During those days, Captain Foley's great humanity became obvious. Day and night he was at the disposition of those seeking help. He generously distributed every kind of visa, thus helping the liberation of many thousands from the camps." Benno Cohn then recalled asking about his motivation. "The basic factor was—he was a *Mensch.* It was really a rare experience to meet a person like him behind a desk in a German [-located] office. . . . He often told us that, as a Christian, he wanted to prove how little the Christians then governing Germany had to do with real Christianity. . . . He hated the Nazis and, as he told me once in a conversation, considered them as the realm of Satan on earth. . . . Today, on the first anniversary of his death, we look back to his deeds and recall the fact that in those gloomy days he gave back to some of us a belief in mankind."

In 1999, Yad Vashem awarded the late Francis Foley the title of Righteous Among the Nations.[4]

José Ruiz Santaella

Berlin was also the locale where the Spanish cultural attaché José Ruiz Santaella helped several Jews at the height of the Holocaust. Our main source is Ruth Gumpel (born Arndt, in 1922). She graduated in 1941 as a pediatric nurse, and in April 1944, after hiding in various places, was referred to Santaella, who was looking for a nurse for his children. She met him at the Adlon Hotel in Berlin, and he took her by diplomatic car to his home in Diedersdorf, where he and his family had been evacuated because of the Allied air raids on Berlin. There she took care of the four children of the diplomat and his wife, Carmen, was paid regularly, and had a peaceful few months. "I was treated with love and respect and taken care of when I was ill. They took me along on summer vacation to the Harz Mountains. They also sent food stamps to Berlin for my family, who were also in hiding. In May 1944 they sent for my mother, whom they employed as a cook, with pay. . . . My mother was introduced as 'Mrs. Werner.' My name was 'Nurse Ruth Neu.' My mother ate in the kitchen with the staff, and I of course spent all my time with the family. I shared a room with the older children. My mother and the 'sewing lady' shared a room in the servant quarters." The Santaellas also gave shelter to Gertrude Neumann, a Jewish woman, who as a seamstress did all their sewing in return for pay, and who had earlier been a patient of Ruth Gumpel's physician father. In fact, it was Mrs. Neumann who had recommended Ruth as a nurse for the Santaella children. The Santaellas were very religious Catholics and attended church services regularly.

In September 1944, Santaella was transferred to Switzerland. Ruth Gumpel recalled that "he wanted to take me along, but that proved impossible. So we tearfully parted. . . . Mrs. Santaella gave me some clothing and they continued to send food packages from Switzerland to Berlin via a trusted secretary at the embassy and another rescuer." In her testimony to Yad Vashem, Ruth Gumpel added: "They certainly knew that I, as well as my mother and the 'sewing lady' were Jews, and furthermore they were aware we had already been living in hiding for more than a year when they took us in." After the war, Ruth visited her benefactors twice in Spain; in 1971 and 1986. The Santaellas now had seven children and thirteen grandchildren. "Most amazing to me, all the children, including their spouses, knew of me and the circumstances surrounding all of us. Santaella's religious beliefs and their basic human kindness compelled them to help persecuted Jews." In 1988, Yad Vashem awarded the Righteous title to José Ruiz and Carmen Santaella.[5]

Constantin Karadja

The story of Constantin Karadja also begins in Berlin and continues in Bucharest, Romania. Karadja, who served as consul general of Romania until 1941, was born in 1889 in The Hague, Netherlands, and moved to Romania before World War One, where he worked for the Ministry of Foreign Affairs. He was accredited as a consul general in Budapest and then in Stockholm, and from 1931, was assigned to Berlin. While there he worked to protect Jews who were Romanian nationals from Nazi persecution and facilitated their emigration back to Romania. Danger threatened Romanian Jews living abroad when, on March 7, 1941, the Ministry of Foreign Affairs ordered Romanian consulates to stamp the word "Jew" on passports held by Romanian Jews. At the urging of Karadja (who cited as an excuse the need to assuage public opinion and "Jewish interests" in Great Britain and the United States), the Romanian dictator, Marshal Ion Antonescu, rescinded this order but had the word "Jew" replaced with a special notation Romanian officials would easily recognize as referring to Jews.[6] Returning to Bucharest, where he worked in the Ministry of Foreign Affairs, Karadja reportedly managed to obtain the return home of Romanian Jews in France, thus preventing their deportation.

The official Romanian policy at the time (especially after it slowly dawned on the country's rulers that the Axis alliance, to which Romania belonged, would not necessarily win the war) was to instruct its diplomats to protect Romanian Jews abroad from persecution, but not to encourage their return to Romania proper. In August 1942, before the tide of war began to change, Prime Minister Mihai Antonescu (not to be confused with the country's dictator, Ion Antonescu), declared that Romania was washing its hands of any obligation to protect Romanian Jews living in areas under German control, but insisted that their assets be turned over to the Romanian treasury. This declaration released nearly 1,600 Romanian Jews living in Germany and Austria for deportation, as well as an unknown number in other countries, and 3,000 more from France. Most of them perished in concentration camps.

In 1943, now faced with a possible defeat, Romania changed its policy and allowed its diplomats to extend diplomatic protection to the remaining Romanian Jews under Nazi control.[7] On April 6, 1943, Mihai Antonescu approved a request from Karadja at the Ministry of Foreign Affairs for permission to repatriate Romanian Jews from Germany, France, and other occupied countries. A week later, in Berlin, the Romanian legation requested that Romanian Jews arrested after March 31 be allowed to return to Romania, and the Germans complied. Recently revealed documents indicate that once the deportation of the Romanian Jews from France began, Karadja wrote several strong memos asking for them to be protected; he specifically pointed out that this protection was to prevent them from being killed. In his efforts to repatriate Romanian Jews in France, Karadja entered into a conflict with General Constantin Vasilu, the first deputy minister of the interior, who opposed these attempts. It estimated that more than 4,000 Romanian Jews in France survived as a result of these diplomatic interventions, several hundred being repatriated on a train that crossed German territory. Furthermore, bowing to pressure from Karadja, on December 17, 1943 Mihai Antonescu, who seconded as foreign minister, instructed the Ministry of the Interior to accept repatriated Romanian Jews from France, Greece, and Italy, otherwise threatened with deportation to German concentration camps.[8]

Karadja subsequently gained Mihai Antonescu's acceptance for a new policy with regard to Romanian Jews living abroad. He wrote: "Having ascertained that Romanian citizens of the Israelite race settled or residing in Central Europe under German occupation are today threatened with the loss of property, freedom, and life in defiance of conventional rights, the royal government considers it only proper to bring them back to our country, whenever necessary and whenever the persons concerned desire it." Karadja added soothing words to placate the strongly held antisemitic feelings of the Romanian leadership. "Having no emotional bonds with our people, and not even knowing the Romanian language, [the returning Jews] will find, it is true, only a temporary asylum in Romania, where they will be treated well. Soon they themselves will realize that current conditions in Romania—quite apart from the wishes of the Romanian government—are hardly favorable for a long stay. [Therefore,] it may be safely predicted that the majority of these Jews will not be capable of making a livelihood and of leading worthy and honest lives in Romania. . . . The Romanian Jews who arrive under these conditions [will] be able to find, as soon as possible, a country for their final destination—that is, as far removed from Europe as possible—where they can live in peace by contributing through the qualities peculiar to them to the general progress of humanity. The permanent duty of all Romanian diplomatic and consular agencies is to cooperate in reaching this goal, henceforth exploiting every opportunity to facilitate the emigration of Romanian Jews"[9]

Karadja showed great courage and resolve in protecting Jewish lives, within the constraints of a government that officially embraced an antisemitic policy, including the killing of thousands of Jews in certain areas under Romanian control, and the expulsion of tens of thousands of Jews to Transnistria in the newly conquered territories, where many were put to death. In all of his efforts, Constantin Karadja based his arguments on the principles of human rights and international law. He also astutely warned of the consequences of violating these laws in the event that Romania found itself on the losing side in the war. In November 1941, as the head of the consular department in the Ministry of Foreign Affairs, he instructed Romanian diplomats to extend protection to all Romanian nationals without exception.

As for the risks to Karadja, Romania's slow exit from the war on the side of the Axis, culminating in August 1944 with its joining the Allied camp, probably saved him. In one of his memorandums to Mihai Antonescu, Karadja wrote: "I know I am risking myself in writing this way"— in other words, in such strong language, when arguing in favor of Jews. Karadja died in Bucharest, in 1950. In 2005, Yad Vashem honored his memory by bestowing on him the title of Righteous Among the Nations.[10]

Jean-Edouard Friedrich

Still in Berlin, we also note the life-saving work of Jean-Edouard Friedrich, a Swiss with diplomatic credentials working for the Geneva-based International Red Cross. A good part of the story comes from Dr. Herbert Strauss's deposition to Yad Vashem. Strauss was studying at the Hochschule für die Wissenschaft des Judentums in Berlin, hoping to obtain a student certificate for the Beth Hakerem Teachers Seminary, in Jerusalem, when the war intervened. In the early 1940s, he and his companion and future wife, Lotte Schloss, were conscripted to forced labor—Lotte in an electronics shop, Herbert as a street cleaner. On October 24, 1942, forewarned of an arrest, the two fled their Berlin-Charlottenburg flat. For the next six or seven months they moved from place to place. In the meantime, Lotte's uncle and aunt in Lausanne, Switzerland, Ludwig and Ilse Schoeneberg, were able to communicate with Lotte through a friend, Ellen Christel Simons, and urged them to see a certain Friedrich, who was at that time a delegate of the International Red Cross, in charge of liaison with Allied prisoners-of-war in German camps.

When Herbert and Lotte made contact with Friedrich, up to then a total stranger, he invited them to his Berlin Red Cross office on Ballenstedter Strasse. Lotte was overcome by fear on the eve of her first meeting with Friedrich, but this dissipated when he greeted her warmly. In Lotte's words: "I realized that he came from a different world. He had the bearing of a diplomat; his good manners and disposition were evident, . . . He appeared to have all the time in the world, as he sat across from me and listened to the story of our flight and the deportation of my parents. I had the feeling that only he could understand the great terror that had befallen my family." She pleaded for him to inform her uncle in Switzerland of the situation, for that would somehow ease a bit her anxiety. Friedrich promised to help.

Lotte continues: "I took a deep breath. . . . I was convinced that in this desperate situation, I could rely on him and his help." Friedrich, however, would not let her go before she described to him the various hiding places she had used, her contacts, and whether she could fend for herself in the coming days. "I remained silent for a while, aware that I had not prepared myself for these specific questions." Could she reveal such secret details to this stranger, and risk jeopardizing herself and her clandestine colleagues? She dared not. She only minced a few words: "We have nothing, zero! . . . Yet, my fears were unfounded. Herr Friedrich reacted appreciatively, and maintained his friendly demeanor." He told her that for the moment he could suggest no solution to her plight, but asked her to compose a letter for her uncle in Switzerland, which he would dispatch via diplomatic mail. Toward the end of the meeting, he asked her to return in two days' time with the letter. He then asked Lotte to write a detailed report of her parents' deportation as well as her and Herbert's miraculous escapes, and he forwarded it in his Red Cross mail pouch to Lotte's relatives in Lausanne.[11]

Friedrich himself then went to Lausanne, where he gave the Schoenebergs a comprehensive picture of the Nazi persecution of Jews and urged them to do everything they could, whether legal or clandestine, to save Lotte and Herbert. When he returned from Switzerland, he brought them some money from the Schoenebergs. In Herbert's words, "Mr. Friedrich now took a leading role in our survival and escape. He acted as an intermediary to secure the funds for our survival and to buy the fake documents needed for our trip to the frontier."

In the meantime, Friedrich got to know Luise Meier, who lived in Berlin, and who had befriended a former secretary of Ludwig Schoeneberg. Luise Meier had successfully helped two Jewish women to flee to Switzerland. Luise and her friends declared themselves willing to help Lotte escape across into Switzerland with the help of a local guide. Friedrich consequently made his office available for meetings between Herbert, Lotte, and Mrs. Meier, an act certainly not consistent with his mandate as a functioning Red Cross official in Berlin. Ironically, two of Luise Meier's sons were serving in the SS and fell in the war; a third son was taken prisoner by the English. After Friedrich contacted her, he brought her greetings and news of the two women who had safely arrived in Switzerland, including details of how they had made the crossing, information that would be of help to other people willing to make such a dangerous journey. Friedrich then asked Luise to take upon herself the flight of Lotte, with all attendant costs to be defrayed by Friedrich himself. Friedrich gave Lotte and later Herbert vital information on the German police controls they would face during the half-day train ride to the frontier. He also took a photograph of Lotte to pass on to the frontier contacts, and organized the time and place of Lotte's meetings with the frontier guide in Singen, on the German-Swiss border.

In Lotte's words, "We met frequently at Ballenstedter Strasse where, he told us later, he also had temporarily sheltered other Jews sought by the Gestapo. He also informed us of problems we would meet after we were stopped by Swiss frontier guards." In September 1942, the Swiss had instructed their frontier personnel that fleeing Jews would not be considered "political refugees" and thus would be refused admission unless they pleaded extreme danger to life and limb in Germany. "We used the formula proposed by Mr. Friedrich to suggest the mortal danger we were in," and thus hoping to benefit from refugee status. With the help of another underground colleague, who lived in the border town of Singen and helped people over the border, Lotte Schloss successfully crossed into Switzerland in the spring of 1943.[12]

In helping Lotte Schloss and Herbert Strauss, as well as others, Jean-Edouard Friedrich acted on his own, without the explicit backing of his Red Cross superiors. His colleagues in the Berlin Red Cross office viewed Friedrich's activities with some trepidation, fearing that a disclosure would interfere with their ability to carry out the Red Cross mission. In a 1997 interview with Philippe Abplanalp, Friedrich gave a lengthy account of his activity as a Red Cross representative in Germany, where he arrived in July 1942. That year, as part of his duties, he visited prisoner-of-war camps in Salzburg, Silesia, Posen, Nuremberg, Regensburg, Lübeck, and Stuttgart. Later, on a trip to The Hague, he told of secretly meeting a certain Mrs. Ross or Rosen, who handed him a list of 2,000 deportees to the camps—Jews and political offenders. Returning to Berlin, Friedrich set himself to get the precise camp addresses of these people and send them packages on behalf of the Red Cross.

The head of the International Red Cross (IRC), Burckhardt, had once told him: "Listen, everything that you do for the Jews— do it! But at your own risk and peril. So do it, but don't talk about it."[13] This, according to Friedrich, was the green light that cleared the way for his resolve to help Jews in Berlin, such as the above-mentioned Strausses, as well as others. "I dealt with passing Jews to Switzerland. It is probably as a result of this that my colleagues learned of this, especially Dr. Schirmer . . . who was furious that I was handling Jews. I hid them in the cellar of the delegation [building], and he rightfully felt that this would compromise our work with the Wehrmacht High Command, the Gestapo, and the [German] Foreign Office. Dr. Schirmer complained about me to Geneva." This resulted in Friedrich's being called back and given a different assignment in the IRC office in Geneva.

As for the fate of the Jews deported to camps outside Germany, Friedrich recalled that people generally knew they were being sent to the East, apparently for work-related purpose, such as in agriculture. "However, it never crossed our mind, that such horrible things as gas chambers and extermination could have been devised by human beings. . . . No one ever told us 'Pay attention, something unusual is happening!'. . . I did not know what was really happening." He considered his work in Berlin "the most active when it revolved to help

Jews." For example, "if a Jew approached us saying that he no longer had a ration card, and if we could not give him something, we gave provisions that we received from Geneva, and it happened that we also distributed meat to Jews in the region. Many delegates complained about my activities in Berlin, in particular with regard to hiding Jews in the cellar, and the help I gave them later on." This included complaints about his going to Singen am Rothwil, on the German-Swiss border, when in April 1943 he accompanied a Jewish woman from Berlin, "and I wanted to lead her to the spot indicated to me by my Berlin contact." On that occasion, he sent the woman ahead of him, so in case he was arrested for being in a frontier town without a special permit, he would keep the guards busy with explanations while she crossed safely the border. This is what indeed happened; Friedrich was apprehended and made to spend a night in jail. "When I returned to Berlin and stupidly related this to my colleagues, they said to one another, 'Oh, this one is going to cause us problems.' That is why I was recalled to Geneva."

Following this incident, on May 7, 1943, Friedrich was ordered back to Geneva. However, Red Cross officials in Berlin stated that the recall would make the Germans suspicious about the activities of the IRC people in Berlin, so they asked for a postponement. The recall was temporarily rescinded, but was finally activated several months later. On July 29, 1943, Friedrich returned to Switzerland, and reassigned to a desk job. A year later, in December 1944, he was asked to submit his resignation. A. R. Rigg, an assistant director of the IRC, in a private memo to a colleague on December 21, 1944, wrote with regard to Friedrich: "I've repeated to Mr. Friedrich the charges made against him and I warned him that, in light of the difficulties which have already arisen during his activity as a delegate in Berlin, his position within the IRC is quite a delicate one. Mr. Friedrich . . . especially is conscious that he no longer has the trust of his superiors. He is in agreement with me that, under the circumstances, his departure is the only possible solution." It was therefore agreed that he retire on December 26, 1944. The IRC, nevertheless, agreed to give him time to seek another job, but only until the end of February 1945, or at the latest, the end of

March. As a disobedient official, he no longer fitted the bureaucratic criteria of the IRC organization even if he acted strictly out of human-itarian considerations—strangely, the very principle that supposedly guided the work of the IRC. In 1999, Yad Vashem awarded Jean-Edouard Friedrich the title of Righteous Among the Nations.[14]

Aracy De Carvalho-Guimaraes Rosa

North of Berlin, in Hamburg, Mrs. Aracy De Carvalho served in the Brazilian consulate under Consul-General Antonio Guimaraes Rosa (whom she later married). As the person responsible for the visa section, she aided Jews to obtain visas to Brazil. As told by Dr. Gunter Heilborn, he and a group of fifteen Jews approached the Brazilian con-sulate in Hamburg and asked Mrs. De Carvalho for visas to Brazil. At the time, Brazil's president, Getulio Vargas, was known to be sympa-thetic to the Nazis and had prohibited the issuance of immigration visas to Jews. Nonetheless, Mrs. De Carvalho decided to act otherwise. In Heilborn's words, she "listened to us with much patience and friendliness, and gave us advice on the necessary documents, and how to obtain them." Heilborn's group returned to her and were told when to come for the visas. The group left for Brazil on the *Monte Sarmiento* on February 18, 1939. In token of gratitude for the great help afford-ed him by Mrs. Carvalho, Heilborn named his first-born daughter Marion Aracy.

Maria Margarethe Levy (born Bertel, in 1908) similarly described Mrs. De Carvalho's special "manipulations" to help her obtain a tourist visa, "thereby saving our lives." According to Mrs. Levy, "I was witness that she helped many Jews with visas." During the *Kristallnacht* pogrom, on November 9, 1938. Mrs. De Carvalho hid Mrs. Levy's husband, Hugo, a medical doctor, in the consulate for a while, then took him to her home, where she lived with her mother and her son. Later on Mrs. Levy was able to arrange an alternative hiding place for her husband. During all this time, until the Levys' departure by ship on November 24, 1938, Mrs. De Carvalho made her car (flying the Brazilian flag) available to them, so that Mrs. Levy could visit her hus-band in his new hiding place. She also arranged for the Levys to take their household goods including the furniture on their voyage to Brazil. In addition, she took the Levys' jewelry and delivered it in person to them on the ship. She remained aboard until moments before the ship's actual departure to make sure that the Levys were not given any difficulties. Others who benefited from De Carvalho's visa generosity included Albert Feis, Grethe Jacobsberg, Tuch, Katzenstein and others. In Mrs. Levy's words, "we owe her our thanks for saving our lives." In 1982, Yad Vashem awarded Aracy De Carvalho-Guimaraes Rosa the title of Righteous Among the Nations.[15]

Feng Shan Ho

Moving south of Berlin to Vienna, the capital of Austria, annexed to Nazi Germany in March 1938, we have the story of the Chinese diplomat Feng Shan Ho. Born in Yiyang, Hunan province, in 1901, into a poor family, he was named Feng Shan, which means "Phoenix on the Mountain." His mother, Yala, had been converted to Christianity by the Norwegian Lutheran Church, where Feng Shan completed his elementary and middle schooling, and then attended the College of Yale-in-China, established by Yale University. He continued his studies in Munich, where he earned a scholarship for doctoral studies in 1929, and three years later, a Ph.D. in political economics. Returning to Hunan in 1932, he was sent to Turkey, then to the Chinese embassy in Vienna, under Ambassador Tung Degang. Because of his mastery of German, he had a wide-ranging circle of friends in Vienna, especially among the intelligentsia, many of whom were Jewish. After the German takeover (the *Anschluss*), Tung was transferred to Turkey, and with the change of the Chinese legation into a consulate in May 1938, Ho was appointed his country's consul-general in Vienna. His appointment coincided with a severe persecution of the city's Jews by the newly installed Nazi regime.

The 185,000 Jews then living in Austria were subjected to a reign of terror unprecedented in its swiftness even when compared to Nazi Germany, as noted by historian Saul Friedlander. Public humiliation was more blatant and sadistic, expropriation better organized, forced emigration more rapid. The Austrians seemed more avid for anti-

Chinese diplomat in Vienna, Feng Shan Ho.

Jewish action than their northern German neighbors, and the popu-
lace relished the public shows of degradation.[16] Less than a month
after the annexation, the first Jewish prisoners were sent to the Dachau
and Buchenwald camps. They were told that they would be released if
they emigrated immediately. To leave the country, the Nazis required
them to present an entry visa or a ship ticket to another country. Many
wanted to leave for the United States, but it had long filled its Austrian
quota. As for Palestine, under Arab pressure, Britain had severely
reduced the quota for Jewish emigrants there. At the Evian
Conference, convened in July 1938 to discuss ways to alleviate Jewish
refugee suffering, the thirty-two nations represented there refused to
budge from their restrictive immigration policies. Meanwhile, the Jews
of Vienna besieged the foreign consulates day after day in a desperate

Chinese visa issued by Feng Shan Ho, consul-general in Vienna.

search for visas. In contrast to other diplomats in Germany (with the notable exception of the British consul Francis Foley in Berlin), Feng Shan Ho issued Chinese visas to everyone who applied, even people who wished to go elsewhere but needed to show an end-visa to be able to get out of Nazi Germany. Many of those Ho helped did indeed reach Shanghai, either by ship from Italy, or overland via the Soviet Union. Many others availed themselves of the visas to go to other destinations, including Cuba and the Philippines.

One typical case involved Norbert Lagstein, who rushed to the Chinese consulate with the passports of his family only to find a throng of people waiting on line. He went home and with his fountain pen carefully copied onto a clean envelope a series of Chinese characters gleaned from the family's encyclopedia. He returned and told the policeman on duty that he had a special delivery for the consul. The policeman immediately let him in. Once inside, Norbert stuffed the envelope into his pocket, took out the passports, and applied for the visas. Thanks to Ho, the five younger members of the Lagstein family were able to leave Vienna in time and were saved.[17]

Nineteen-year-old Hans Kraus also tried desperately to bypass the long line waiting in front of the Chinese consulate. One day, as he lined up again, he saw the consul-general's car about to enter the consulate compound. The car's window was open, so he thrust his visa applications through the window. Soon after he got a telephone call to come and pick up his visa. Hans Kraus and his four family members left Vienna for Shanghai. Likewise for the four Hugo Seeman family members, who before the Nazi takeover owned a department story in Vienna. On October 12, 1938, after obtaining visas for Shanghai, they left on the Trans-Siberian railroad, which took them there by way of the Soviet Union.[18]

In China itself, following the Japanese invasion in 1937, which included the conquest of Shanghai, the Chinese Nationalist government under Chiang Kai-shek moved to Chungking. From there, the Chinese maintained very close diplomatic relations with Germany. Chiang asked Germany for military assistance, and Hitler obliged by sending two military advisers: the former chief of staff of the German

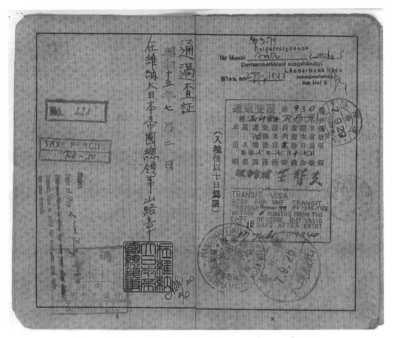

Chinese visa issued by Feng Shan Ho, consul-general in Vienna.

army, General Hans von Seeck, and Lieutenant General Georg Wetzell. The Nationalists also bought German weapons from the Krupp industrial conglomerate, and Chiang sent his son, Chiang Wei-kuo, to Germany for military training. In Berlin, the Chinese ambassador was concerned that helping Jews would damage the good diplomatic relations between China and Germany.

No visa was required for entry into Shanghai, because it was under Japanese control at the time. The Chinese government had no jurisdiction there at all, and a Chinese visa would have been useless if the Japanese had required an entry visa. In issuing visas to Shanghai, Ho knew that there was nothing the Chinese government in far -off Chungking could do to stop the emigration of Jews to that city. The visas to Shanghai were in reality "exit visas" for Jews to escape from Nazi Austria and find their way to other destinations. Jews who were detained or sent to concentration camps could be released with the Chinese visas as proof of emigration. The visas named an "end" destination, so that countries like Italy, which required such proof, were able to issue transit visas through their territory. Ho himself said that the visas were "to Shanghai in name only." The Japanese allowed relatively free entry into Shanghai until the latter part of 1939.

Eric Goldstaub's father was another recipient of one of Ho's Shanghai visas. As told in Eric's account, after the *Anschluss,* "I spent days, weeks, and months visiting one foreign consulate or embassy after another trying to obtain a visa for me, my parents, and our near relatives, numbering some twenty people." Finally, on July 20, 1938, he received for all of them from Ho visas. Then, during *Kristallnacht,* Eric and his father were arrested and sent to concentration camps. "The fact that we had a visa for China as well as ship tickets for the end of December [via Genoa] enabled us to be released within a few days and we were on our way by train to Italy and liberty in China." The whole party left Vienna for Genoa by train on November 12, 1938, and then sailed for Shanghai on an Italian steamship. Eric's uncle and aunt, thinking nothing would happen to them, decided to stay in Vienna. By the time they changed their minds it was too late and they perished in the Holocaust.

During *Kristallnacht,* Karl Lang was one of the many Austrian Jews hauled to Gestapo headquarters and from there to the Dachau camp. His wife Katerina began making the rounds of the consulates. In the words of their daughter, Marion: "Word got out that the Chinese consulate was issuing visas. [Mother] got a visa for my father with an end-destination visa to Shanghai. Armed with this, she went and bought a temporary transit visas from the consulate of Monaco. I took our passports to the Gestapo headquarters to get them stamped. My father was in Dachau from November 1938 to February 1939. He was released and had to sign a paper that said he would leave Austria within 48 hours. My father left and went to Monaco. From there, to Trieste, and then to England."

Karl's brother-in-law, Erwin Hostovsky, also got a Chinese visa, and left for Shanghai. His wife, Helene, sadly did not make it and perished in a concentration camp. As for daughter Marion, she left on the last *Kindertransport* (children transport) to England right after her father's release. Her mother joined her later, on a domestic-help visa, and her father came a bit later. In a touch of irony, when the war broke out, Karl was for a while interned by the British as an enemy alien on the Isle of Man, due to his German passport.

Bernard Grossfeld and his parents, in Vienna, were also granted visas by Feng Shan Ho for travel to Shanghai, thanks to which his father, Morris, was released from Dachau. In July 1939, Bernard and his parents took a train from Vienna to Genoa, where they boarded the *Count Rosso*, one of the ships of the Lloyd-Trieste Shipping Company, making the run from Genoa to Shanghai. It was a two-month voyage. Bernard's grandmother as well as her two other sons stayed behind and perished in the Holocaust. Another story takes us to Fritz Heiduschka. After his arrest in mid-June 1938, his wife, Margarete, obtained a visa from Ho for travel to Shanghai. At first both headed for Trieste, then together with their daughter Hedy they boarded an Italian ship bound for Shanghai. When it stopped at Colombo, Ceylon, Margarete changed her mind and decided that it would be better to go to the Philippines. Indeed, they remained there through the Japanese occupation, and until the end of the war.

We continue with the story of Lotte Lustig, born in 1928, who led a life of relative comfort until the arrival of the Nazis. On October 18, 1938, her father went to the Chinese consulate and obtained three visas—" 'just in case,' he told us." At this, Lotte's mother exclaimed: "*Schanghai? Ja wo ist das doch* (Where is that?) *China?*" The mother's friend had told her that Shanghai was a place where "*Ja da toeten sie doch alle weisse Menschen?*" (That's where they kill all white people). When Lotte's uncle was brought back from Dachau for burial in December 1938, "it was then that Shanghai became an immediate necessity." Lotte left Vienna on January 11, 1939, with about twenty of her relatives. Eighteen members of her extended family did not make it and were engulfed in the Holocaust. "We parted from our 78-year-old *Grosspapa* [grandfather] who would die in Theresienstadt in 1942. . . . I am one of the 4,500 to 6,000 Viennese who arrived in Shanghai between 1938 and 1941."

Finally, there is one more story linked to Ho's magnanimity. Lilith-Sylvia Doron, in Israel, related that she met Ho accidentally as both watched Hitler's entry into Vienna on March 10, 1938, which was accompanied by physical assaults against the city's Jews. "Ho, who knew my family, escorted me home. He claimed that thanks to his diplomatic status, they would not dare harm us as long as he remained in our home. Ho continued to visit our home on a regular basis to protect us from the Nazis." When Lilith's brother Karl was arrested and taken to Dachau, he was released thanks to a visa from the Chinese consulate. Lilith and her brother left for Palestine in November 1939 on the strength of Chinese visas that were, of course, meant for another destination—Shanghai. As for Leya Vardi's family, they used the Shanghai visas to leave and head north to Sweden.

Ho's charitable behavior did not meet with the approval of his superior, the Chinese ambassador in Berlin, Chen Jie, who ordered him to desist. Ho countered by claiming that the Foreign Ministry's orders were to maintain a liberal policy in this regard. On hearing this, Chen snapped: "If that is so, I will take care of the Foreign Ministry end, you just follow my orders!" Ho stuck to his guns. This so angered the ambassador that he sent a subordinate, Ding Wen Yuan, to Vienna on the pretext of investigating rumors that the consulate was "selling" visas, a charge which proved unfounded. On April 8, 1939 Ho was reprimanded, and a "demerit" was entered in his personal file. It is assumed that the "demerit" was linked to his insubordinate behavior on the issue of the visas toward his immediate superior, the ambassador in Berlin. He reportedly had issued hundreds of visas, perhaps a whole lot more, in spite of contrary instructions. Recha Sternbuch, a Jewish activist working out of Switzerland, claimed that in 1939 at least 400 Jewish refugees used Chinese visas to make their way to Palestine via Switzerland. As for Ho, in May 1940, he was removed from his post in Vienna and left with his wife, and 11-year old son, Monto. For a year, he spent time doing political analysis in the United States. In 1941, through the efforts of Henry Luce and the China lobby, the United States edged close to Chiang's China, and began to deliver large-scale military material to support its military struggle against the Japanese Empire. When China broke off relations with Germany and closed ranks with the Allies, Dr. Ho was recalled to China to lend a hand in the war effort against the Japanese.

In the meantime his successor in Vienna, Yao Ding Chen, adhered strictly to the rules laid down by the ambassador in Berlin and reduced the number of Chinese visas to "the utmost minimal number." On May 29, 1940 he reported: "In the period of April 1938 to 1939, the monthly number of visa applicants was extremely high . . . [about] 400 to 500 [each month] and even higher. . . . [However], I have adhered strictly to regulations. Presently, this kind of visa has already been reduced to the utmost minimal number." Up till the start of the war, in September 1939, nearly 70 percent of the 185,246 Jews in Austria managed to emigrate, of which an estimated 18,000 made their way to China. In August 1939, the Japanese overseers of Shanghai began to close the doors to further Jewish immigration.

After the war, Ho served his country as ambassador to Egypt, Mexico, Bolivia, and Colombia. He retired to San Francisco in 1973 and died in 1997 at the age of 96. It was only after his passing, through the efforts of his daughter, Manli Ho, that the story of his help to Jews was made public, through evidence submitted by some of his beneficiaries. In 2000, Yad Vashem declared Feng Shan Ho a Righteous Among the Nations. He had once written: "I thought it only natural to feel compassion and wanted to help. From a humane standpoint, that is the way it ought to be."[19]

Ernest Prodolliet

We end this chapter with the Swiss diplomat Ernest Prodolliet, who was stationed in the Austrian-Swiss border town of Bregenz. Born in Amriswil, Switzerland, in 1905, Prodolliet entered his country's foreign service in 1927. From April 1938 to April 1939, he was a secretary in the Bregenz consulate on the Austrian side of the border with Switzerland. From April 1939 to the end of 1942 he was posted to Amsterdam, and then served in Berlin and Paris until the end of the war. In 1968 he retired as consul in Besançon, France.

In December 1938, the consul in Bregenz, K. Bitz, complained to his superior (Dr. R. Stucki, in the Swiss Foreign Ministry's Political Department) about certain aspects of Prodolliet's behavior which were inconsistent with the activities of a diplomat and in opposition to standard operating procedures. Bitz then spelled out what he had in mind with accusations that Prodolliet had overstepped his mandate as the responsible person for the issuance of visas. More "seriously," he had shown "a too great interest in the Jewish question," so that much of his time is spent in "negotiations with Jews." Bitz asked Stucki to remove Prodolliet from Bregenz. On December 15, 1938, Swiss police chief Heinrich Rothmund added his positive recommendation to this request, but added that Prodolliet transgressed "out of humanitarian considerations."

Even more troubling, Prodolliet sometimes illegally escorted parties of fleeing Jews across the frontier. For instance, on December 7, 1938, at a time when persecutions of Jews in Nazified Austria had reached a pitch after the November 10, 1938 *Kristallnacht* pogrom, Prodolliet arranged for two Jews, Wortsmann and Udelsmann, to illegally cross into Switzerland. On February 9, 1939, Prodolliet was ordered to appear before the judicial department of the Swiss Foreign Office to respond to the charges against him.

Responding to each of the charges, Prodolliet pointed out that he had issued only a very few visas, in fact only 50 visas, even though at least 1,000 people had requested them. Prodolliet claimed he had sacrificed himself in the interest of refugees, to which came a sharp rejoinder from the questioning officer: "Our agency is not here in order to benefit the Jews." Prodolliet admitted facilitating the passage of Herbert Rektor from the Diepoldsau refugee camp in Switzerland across the border to Bregenz, but this was only in order for him to meet his mother there. As for Dr. Tauber, including the man's two companions, Wortsmann and Udelsmann, whom Prodolliet helped to cross the border into Switzerland illegally, this was done without any financial remuneration. Prodolliet further elaborated on this incident. Tauber was a Viennese gynecologist forced by the Nazis to give up his practice. Looking for a way out of the country, he met a certain Maria Stefan who had promised to arrange the doctor's family's passage to Switzerland in return for a substantial payment, based on a fabricated claim that he needed urgently to visit a sick patient in Zürich. However, the Swiss consulate in Vienna turned down Tauber's request. The contact person then advised Tauber to try the Swiss consulate in

Bregenz. In the meantime, Mrs. Stefan contacted Prodolliet, who arranged an entry permit for Tauber with the Swiss police in St. Gallen. He and his wife entered Switzerland on September 26, 1938. Prodolliet was accused of having facilitated this even though they did not have proper visas. The Taubers were arrested in Zürich on October 3, 1938. In his defense, Prodolliet was only able to say that he had informed his superior, K. Bitz, of this undertaking, but he did not refute the charge itself.

In the case of Max Wortmann, originally from Stuttgart, his wife and two children had reached Switzerland and were residing in St. Gallen. Through the mediation of a police captain, Paul Grüninger, a meeting was arranged between Wortmann and Prodolliet, who promised that Wortmann's entry to Switzerland would present no complication, since the family possessed a visa for the United States. The problem, however, was that Mr. Wortmann did not have a travel permit as required by the German authorities. To overcome this bureaucratic obstacle, Prodolliet urged Wortmann to cross the border illegally in the Diepoldsau region. More damaging to Prodolliet's case was his consent to accompany Wortmann on the illegal crossing. This took place on the night of November 23, 1938, but both were discovered by German border guards, who opened fire on them. Prodolliet was able to reach the Swiss border, but was caught by Swiss guards at 11:15 P.M., whereas Wortmann fled into Austria and made his way back to Stuttgart. However, a few days later, Wortmann reappeared in Bregenz and was given a visa by Prodolliet, without the obligatory *J* on it. Again, Prodolliet accompanied Wortmann to a border crossing, near Hoechst. Here, again, trouble awaited the two. The German customs officials forbade Wortmann's passage when he refused to answer their question whether he was an Aryan. In this incident, Prodolliet stated that he acted without any personal gain. His only object was to help this man to get out of hell and be reunited with his children. "I was motivated to help him solely out of humanitarian considerations."

In another case that caused trouble for Prodolliet, a Swiss soldier, Ernst Kamm, testified that in March or April 1939, Prodolliet had asked him to allow certain persons to enter the country, a request turned down by Kamm. Prodolliet also gave a certain Mrs. Mindel Schottenfeld a 24-hour permit to visit her sick son in the Diepoldsau refugee camp. However, Kamm stated that she actually extended her stay with Captain Grüninger's complicity.[20] Another serious charge involved the case of Josef Udelsmann, whom Prodolliet took across the Swiss border by car on September 26, 1938. Udelsmann was then arrested by the Swiss police.

After the war, Eliezer Levin testified to Yad Vashem that Prodolliet had helped him and a large group of Jews to cross into Switzerland in February 1939. Originally from Germany, Levin had a visa for Shanghai and he asked for a 48-hour transit visa through Switzerland. While in Bregenz, he met the Jewish activist Recha Sternbuch, who negotiated directly with Prodolliet the visas for Levin and the other Jewish fugitives who had arrived there. After crossing into Switzerland, Levin continued to Italy and from there was able to reach Palestine. Holocaust historian Yehuda Bauer stated that he had learned from Gertrude van Tijn, who dealt with emigration in the Netherlands, of Prodolliet's help to her (while stationed there in 1942), in several ways, including money loans.

Luckily for Prodolliet, the verdict against him by the Swiss Foreign Ministry's judicial board in May 1939 was limited to "a strong reprimand" without further punitive steps. In fact, Prodolliet continued his diplomatic career in various stations, and honorably left the diplomatic service when he reached the retirement age. In 1982, Yad Vashem awarded Ernest Prodolliet the title of "Righteous Among the Nations.[21]

Prodolliet's case is unique in the annals of help to Jews by diplomats, in that he not only facilitated their passage to a safer haven, but also, in some cases, even joined them in the illegal border crossing, so as to ensure their safe passage. This was clearly a non-diplomatic act, but done in consideration of an overriding principle—responding to the pleas of innocent victims of persecution, to help them assure their survival.

Chapter 3

Lithuania
Where Is Curaçao?

Jan Zwartendijk

Very few people in Lithuania had ever heard of Curaçao, a small Dutch-controlled island in the Caribbean Sea, off the coast of Venezuela. Originally held by the Spanish, it was acquired by the Dutch in 1634, and in 1659 the first Jews arrived there, seeking a haven from persecution in areas of South America under Spanish and Portuguese control. There were some 2,000 Jews in the early 1700s. In 1732, the Mikve Israel–Emanuel synagogue was built in Willemstad town, and it remains the oldest still-functioning synagogue in the Western Hemisphere. In 1914, oil was discovered in Venezuela, and a refinery was built in Curaçao to process this important natural resource. The reader may ask the point of all these details. The answer lies in the name and place of Curaçao, which became a magic word for thousands of Jews in far-distant Lithuania, who first heard of the island in 1940 without actually knowing anything about it—even its precise location. The man who quite accidentally made Curaçao a household term for thousands of Jews seeking a way out of war-torn Europe was a Dutch businessman turned diplomat named Jan Zwartendijk.

Shortly before the war began, Zwartendijk arrived in Lithuania to represent Philips, a Dutch electronics firm. Opening an office in the capital city of Kaunas in mid-1939, he soon befriended some of the city's few Dutch residents, including several Dutch-Jewish men study-

39

ing in its world-renowned talmudic seminaries (yeshivot). As war clouds gathered over Europe in the fall of that year, Zwartendijk was busily selling the products of his company. In the meantime, when war broke out in September 1939 and Germany occupied Poland, thousands of refugees streamed into Lithuania, adding to the burdens of this small country wedged between two giants—Nazi Germany and the Soviet Union. When Germany invaded the Netherlands on May 10, 1940, the Dutch ambassador for the Baltic region, L. P. J. de Dekker, stationed in neighboring Riga, Latvia, discharged the pro-German Dutch consul in Kaunas and looked for a replacement. Learning of Jan Zwartendijk's anti-Nazi credentials, he turned to him to fill the post of honorary Dutch consul-general. Zwartendijk procrastinated for a while but finally, on May 14, consented. The following day, the Soviet Union invaded Lithuania, and for all practical purposes the country ceased to be independent.

The Soviets moved immediately to incorporate Lithuania and its two sister Baltic states (Latvia and Estonia) into the Soviet Union, a process that was swiftly accomplished in the summer of that year. One week after the Soviet invasion, on May 21, Zwartendijk cabled his superiors in the Netherlands about the virtual stoppage of commercial activity in the country. "The banks are closed . . . the general mood is rather nervous. . . . The coming weeks look rather somber. What exactly is going to happen is not entirely clear yet, but I'm convinced that there will no longer be an independent Lithuania. . . . Commercially we are finished here, whatever the further developments may be. It can only become bad or still worse." He then waited for instructions from his head office, in now German-occupied Holland, about wrapping up his business. He also waited for a word from his diplomatic senior, Ambassador De Dekker in Soviet-occupied Latvia, as to the future of the Dutch consulate in Kaunas, which Zwartendijk had recently taken over and operated out of his business office.

While Zwartendijk was pondering on his future stay in Lithuania, events on the Jewish refugee side were unfolding in the summer of that year that were to immerse him in a rescue operation of great magnitude. It all began when Pessia Lewin applied to Ambassador De Dekker for a visa to the Dutch East Indies on her Polish passport. Although originally a Dutch citizen, she had by Dutch law forfeited her nationality in 1935 when she married a Polish citizen, Isaac Lewin, a leader of the Agudath Israel religious movement and a Polish national. Mrs. Lewin asked for her case to be reconsidered in light of her Dutch nationality and because of the precarious status of herself and her husband as Polish refugees in a country not too happy to have them. There was a clear and persistent danger that Lithuania would expel all Polish nationals back to the Poland, now divided between Nazi Germany and the Soviet Union.

The Dutch ambassador politely responded that the issuance of such visas had been terminated. Not taking no for an answer, Mrs. Lewin wrote back to De Dekker asking him to help in some way, especially since she had once been a Dutch citizen. De Dekker again replied evasively, stating that he did not see how he could be of assistance, since no visas at all were being issued to the Caribbean possessions of the Dutch government. To enter these colonies, the ambassador added, one had to have a permit from the local governor in Curaçao. The ambassador did not mention that the governor was unlikely to issue such documents because of the military importance of the fuel-refining installations on the island. Curaçao was under the control of the Dutch government-in-exile in London, which had vowed to continue the war against Germany side by side with England, in spite of the loss of the homeland.

Attempting one more try, Mrs. Lewin asked whether the ambassador would officially endorse her Polish passport with a statement that no visa was required for entry to Curaçao, and not mention anything about the need for a special permit from the island's governor. She had no intention of going there, she explained, but was simply looking for a way to leave war-torn Europe. De Dekker agreed, and asked her to send him her passport. He returned it with a handwritten statement: "The Dutch Royal Legation in Riga hereby declares that no visa is required for entry by foreigners to Surinam, Curaçao, and the other

Dutch possessions in America. Riga, July 11, 1940." This later became
known as the "Curaçao visa." On July 22, Mrs. Lewin showed this
handwritten visa to Zwartendijk, and he agreed to copy the same
wording on her husband's passport. Four days later, both applied to
Sugihara, the Japanese consul-general in Kaunas, for a Japanese transit
visa, ostensibly in order to reach that distant island via the Pacific
Ocean, through the Soviet Union and Japan.

While Mrs. Lewin was prodding the Dutch ambassador in Riga for
a visa to one of the Dutch Caribbean possessions, another person,
unbeknownst to her, had the same idea in mind. Nathan Gutwirth was
a 23-year-old student at the Telshe Yeshiva and a Dutch citizen. As
such, his situation was better than Mrs. Lewin's, because, as he was
told by Zwartendijk, he needed no visa to travel to any Dutch-controlled territory. Gutwirth nevertheless insisted that a final destination,
or end-visa, be appended on his passport, to avoid bureaucratic red-
tape by overzealous passport control officers en route to these distant
territories. When Zwartendijk was shown De Dekker's statement on
Mrs. Lewin's passport, he saw no reason not to oblige Gutwirth with a
similar one, and on July 23, a day after Zwartendijk had appended the
Curaçao visa statement on Mr. Lewin's passport, he did likewise on
Gutwirth's Dutch passport.

Gutwirth then spread the word of the Curaçao scheme among his
fellow students, and word soon reached Dr. Zorach Warhaftig, a Polish
refugee and Zionist leader, who was frantically seeking ways to spirit
Polish-Jewish refugees out of the country and the European continent,
fearing that otherwise they would be engulfed in the war that many
expected to break out between Nazi Germany and the Soviet Union or
alternatively be exiled by the Soviets for hard labor in Siberia. Without
any other exit possibilities (Western Europe was under German occupation, and in the south, Turkey was unwilling to let Jewish refugees
pass through its territory), and with only a limited number of certificates for entry into British-controlled Palestine, the Curaçao visa
seemed an ideal ploy for thousands to flee the endangered country in
time—even if it meant traveling halfway around the globe.

Warhaftig asked Gutwirth to find out if Zwartendijk was willing to issue the Dekker Curaçao formula to everyone who asked for it. Zwartendijk immediately said yes, apparently without even bothering to check with the Dutch ambassador in Riga. Warhaftig then met with the teachers and students of the Telshe and Mir yeshivot, urging them to take advantage of the Curaçao visa. Some responded favorably; others laughed it off. Most, if not all, of them had never heard of Curaçao and were unable to locate it on a map. In addition, many wondered aloud if it would be possible to eke out a living on this seemingly God-forsaken island? Thus most of them turned a deaf ear to the scheme, not believing that one could find succor by crossing the whole length of the Soviet Union, then transiting Japan, a country on the brink of war, and continuing across the Pacific to an unknown place.

But some people grabbed at this chance—far more than Zwartendijk could handle in the little time left to him before closing his operation in Lithuania. Moshe Zupnik and three other students of the Mir Yeshiva were chosen to collect and deliver 200 passports of their friends to Zwartendijk's office. He promised to append the Curaçao statement within two days, with the help of two aides. Upon receipt of these, Zupnik immediately headed to the Japanese consulate, where Consul-General Sugihara added the Japanese transit visa. News of this quickly spread, and before long hundreds of people were waiting at Zwartendijk's door. During the relatively short period of eight days, from July 23 to August 4, Zwartendijk and his aides wrote and signed up to 2,400 Curaçao visas. They had to hurry, for in the meantime Lithuania had been annexed to the Soviet Union, and Zwartendijk had to close his office no later than August 3.

The Soviets (who bore a special grudge against the Dutch government for never having recognized the Communist regime in Russia) had told Zwartendijk to quickly close his dual-purpose office. To drive their message home, the new masters of Lithuania hung a large portrait of Stalin on Zwartendijk's office display window. The Japanese consul-general, Sugihara, was allowed an extension of three additional weeks until August 25. He phoned Zwartendijk and asked him to slow up the issuance of Curaçao visas, because he could not match the pace with his transit visas (which had to be written in Japanese calligraphy).

During an intense four-day period from July 24 through the 27, the Philips electronics salesman turned diplomat, issued over 1,300 visas. He maintained the same tempo in the days that followed until he had issued a total of between 2,200 and 2,400 Curaçao visas by August 1, two days ahead of the August 3 deadline for winding up his operation.

Now possessing Dutch and Japanese transit visas, the petitioners turned to the Soviet authorities for a transit visa through Russia. Some were immediately allowed to cross that vast country; others had to wait several months before confirmation was received from Moscow. Ironically, none of the beneficiaries of these visas ever reached Curaçao. They wound up either in Japan, Shanghai, or other locations, and not on that distant, unknown, exotic island. Among those saved were the entire faculty and student body of the Mir Yeshiva and several learned rabbis, including Rabbis Hirschprung, Shimon Kalish, and Aaron Kotler, the latter a renowned talmudic scholar, as well as Dr. Zorach Warhaftig, who later was a minister of religious affairs in the Israeli government.[1]

On August 3, 1940, Zwartendijk shut his office and moved his family (wife Erna, daughter Edith, 13, sons Jan, 11, and Peter, 1) outside the city, to await permission from the Soviet authorities for his family to return to the German-occupied Netherlands. This was finally allowed in mid-September 1940, and Zwartendijk returned to his homeland, and to a new assignment with the Philips company.[2] Throughout the German occupation of the Netherlands, he was concerned about the possible fallout against him because of his activities in Kaunas. The Curaçao visa scheme had become public knowledge in Kaunas, a city teeming with Gestapo agents (Sugihara's chief aide, Wolfgang Gudze, turned out to be a Gestapo spy). On one occasion, the fear of arrest became a frightening reality, when Gestapo agents showed up to question Zwartendijk in his Netherlands home. It turned out that they were after someone else, who had been shot trying to elude the Gestapo, and Zwartendijk's name had been found in his coat.

No questions were asked about Zwartendijk's rescue activities in Lithuania.

After the war, Jan Zwartendijk made no mention of his wartime rescue episode. In 1976, through the mediation of Ernest Heppner, a leader of the Jewish community in Indianapolis, he met with the Holocaust historian David Kranzler. Zwartendijk was by then afflicted with terminal cancer and died that same year. Before dying, he learned from Kranzler that he had saved an entire talmudic seminary, and that among those saved was Zorach Warhaftig, a cabinet minister in the Israeli government. In the 1990s an ever-increasing amount of information on the crucial role of Zwartendijk in the Curaçao rescue scheme began to flow to Yad Vashem, and an intensive examination of all the available documentation was launched. In Jerusalem, the children of Jan Zwartendijk were feted by the reestablished Mir Yeshiva, whose hundreds of talmudic students constituted the single largest bloc of seminarians saved by him. Finally, in 1998, Yad Vashem officially accepted Jan Zwartendijk into the ranks of the Righteous Among the Nations.

Writing about his father in 1996, Zwartendijk's son, also named Jan, who was with him during the Kaunas visa episode, explained that his father had engaged in "this eight-day flurry of action on his own, in spontaneous reaction to an overwhelming need. It required an immediate decision and immediate action." To the end of his life, Zwartendijk remained indifferent to any honors. All he wanted to know was: "How many made it eventually along the Curaçao route?" He was told that everyone had managed to escape the Holocaust, although none of them had ever reached Curaçao. But going to this distant island had never been the original intention of the refugees, nor of Zwartendijk; the idea was simply to get a large group of stateless persons, all of them Jews, out of the country in time, before the Nazi conflagration reached them.[3]

Zwartendijk's humanitarian acts took place against the background of his homeland's invasion by Germany, and the flight and disarray of its government. Without any clear-cut guidance from above (his immediate superior, the Dutch ambassador in Riga, was himself in the process of winding up operations and leaving the country), Zwartendijk acted on his own in a drama with moral implications. Whether a firmly established Dutch government, acting under normal and peaceful conditions, would have allowed the issuance of so many visas to a strategically located island in the Caribbean Sea remains an open question.

There is a final note to this extraordinary story. When the former governor of Curaçao visited Israel, Warhaftig asked him what he would have done if a shipload of refugees with Curaçao visas had reached the island. The answer: "Of course, I would have expelled them back to the sea, just as the United States did with the *St. Louis* a year earlier."[4]

Chiune-Sempo Sugihara

The Curaçao saga has one more element. There was another diplomat involved in the scheme, Chiune Sugihara (later in his life he preferred to be addressed as Sempo Sugihara), who represented Japan, a country allied to Nazi Germany. His role was extraordinary for a Japanese diplomat in those days. Born in 1900, Sugihara joined the Japanese Foreign Ministry in 1934. He spent many years in Manchuria, then the Japanese puppet-state of Manchukuo, where, helped by his expertise in the Russian language, he negotiated with the Soviets the control of the Trans-Siberian Railroad route to the port city of Vladivostok. In late 1939, after an illustrious diplomatic career in various postings, he was sent to open a consulate-general in Kaunas, a place with no apparent Japanese interests. But there was one—a quite serious one. As later reported by Sugihara, "General Oshima [the Japanese ambassador in Berlin] wanted to know whether the German Army would really attack the Soviet Union. The point was that the Japanese General Staff was very much interested in such an attack, since it wanted to withdraw the best forces of the Kwantung Army, i.e., the Japanese army, from the Soviet-Manchurian border and move them to the southern islands of the Pacific. My main task was to establish the foreseeable date of the German attack on Russia quickly and correctly."

Briefly put, Sugihara's task was to engage in intelligence work with the help of spies in order to ascertain from troop movements the approximate date of the German attack, a point of great interest to the Japanese, which had its eyes set on a military expansion in the direction of the Pacific islands. The Japanese were interested in an early German-Soviet war so as to free their large army in northern China to other zones of operation. So in November 1939, Sugihara opened an office in Kaunas, a place without a single Japanese citizen, and began enlisting Polish spies. "I soon learned that my main task was to provide to the General Staff, not merely the Foreign Office, information based on hearsay gossip about the concentration of German military on the Lithuanian border, and of Germany's preparations for an invasion of the Soviet Union." Hitler had kept the date of the invasion a secret from his Japanese ally, and had forbidden the Japanese military attaché in Berlin from visiting the German-controlled areas in the east.

Lithuania was overrun and annexed to the Soviet Union in the summer of 1940 (as part of the Ribbentrop-Molotov pact a year earlier) just a few months after Sugihara opened the consulate-general. Like the other foreign diplomatic representatives in the city, he was told by the new Soviet masters to close his office no later than August 31, 1940. It seemed as if Sugihara's mission had come to an end without his having achieved the principal objective of pinpointing the approximate date of a German attack on the Soviet Union. However, as he packed his belongings and terminated his office's operations, he became involved in a new and totally unexpected undertaking which was to leave an imprint on his life and the lives of thousands of others.

As related by Sugihara many years afterwards, "One August morning, I heard an unusual noise on the street near the consulate. I looked out of the window of my home, and saw a large crowd had gathered near the railing of the house." As it turned out, these were people who had escaped from Poland and wished to get out of Lithuania. With tears in their eyes, they begged him to give them Japanese transit visas, in order to be able to get to other countries via Japan. Only a few had entry visas for the United States. Sugihara asked permission from his

*Chiune-Sempo Sugihara, the Japanese consul-general in
Kaunas, Lithuania.*

superiors to allow him to grant visas to hundreds, if not even more, of
these refugees. Days dragged on with pressure mounting from these
people, who had learned that the Japanese consulate was about to wind
up operations. "I don't know where they succeeded in sleeping these
days—in the train station or simply in the streets." Sugihara checked
with the Soviet consulate, and they informed him of their willingness
to provide transit visas, on condition that the Japanese would do so
first, so that the refugees would not be stuck on Soviet territory.
Sugihara claims that on August 10 he decided to take matters into his
own hands and on his responsibility: "this, without paying attention if
a person had the necessary documents. In this work, I was helped by
my only secretary, the ethnic German, Wolfgang Gudze." From other

*Japanese diplomat Chiune-Sempo Sugihara with his wife and children,
during his tenure as consul-general in Kaunas, Lithuania.*

sources, we have learned that Gudze was a German agent, planted in Sugihara's office to report on his intelligence activities. It is not known whether Sugihara suspected this.

Dr. Zorach Warhaftig gave a slightly different version of Sugihara's induction into the refugee fray. As already mentioned in the Zwartendijk story, Warhaftig was a leading official of the Mizrachi, a religious Zionist organization, and himself stranded in Lithuania as a refugee from war-torn Poland. In the precarious position that he and his fellow Polish refugees found themselves, Warhaftig was desperately looking for ways to get as many of his Polish Jewish colleagues out of the country. Even before the Curaçao scheme came to his attention, Warhaftig had alerted Polish Jewish refugees in the country, especially the religious heads of the yeshivot, to make sure to have valid passports, in case exit possibilities would suddenly spring up. For this purpose Warhaftig sounded out one of the leading rabbinical scholars in Lithuania, Rabbi Hayyim Ozer Grodzinski. Warhaftig said: "We are sitting on a volcano between Germany and the Soviet Union, and we must escape. . . . At least we must make an effort to get them passports, to get them visas." The rabbi's response was evasive. He felt that, as in past tribulations, the Jewish people could ride out the coming storm. This was preferable to wandering to unknown distant places and at the same time discontinuing one's religious studies. One was to stay put; "Sit and do nothing" was his advice, and rely on divine grace.[5] This stand was supported by other religious dignitaries, with the exception of Rabbi Eliezer Finkel, head of the Mir Yeshiva. Warhaftig sat up with him for a full day and persuaded him to allow his students to get Polish passports from the still-functioning Polish consulate so that, if a door opened to a safe haven, they would have the necessary documents on hand. "This was the only yeshiva, that everyone received documents, and thanks to this everyone there left and was saved."

Travel possibilities were limited; visas were not available from the United States and other countries in the Western Hemisphere; France had just fallen to the Germans, and England was fighting for her life. Besides, travel in that direction was not possible in light of the war

Jewish persons lining up in front of the Japanese consulate in Kaunas, Lithuania, for obtaining a Japanese transit visa.

conditions throughout Europe. The only escape was to go eastward, through the Soviet Union, not yet embroiled in the conflict. When Warhaftig learned of the Curaçao scheme from Nathan Gutwirth, it lit a spark in his mind. For here was an opportunity, not for a trickle but for many, to leave the country for far and distant places, without necessarily having to go to Curaçao, an island most people were hearing of for the first time. Warhaftig and his colleagues rushed to consult maps. "We saw on the map that Curaçao was a small island; that to get there one had to cross the Soviet Union, until Vladivostok; then to Japan, and from there by boat via the Panama Canal. We needed transit visas from the Soviets and Japan."

With the Dutch consul-general, Jan Zwartendijk, prepared to issue a limitless number of end-visas to Curaçao, Warhaftig felt it was time to look up Sugihara. As part of a delegation, Warhaftig was admitted into Sugihara's office, where he spread out a map, showing the Japanese diplomat the location of Curaçao. The only route to that fabled distant island, Warhaftig continued, in light of the war conditions on the European continent, was by way of the Soviet Union and Japan. As the Dutch diplomat had already given his consent, and the Russians would probably want to hear from the Japanese diplomat before adding their consent, Warhaftig pleaded with Sugihara for a ten-day transit visa through Japan for the many hundreds interested in traveling in that direction. He assured Sugihara that the refugees would pay all fares and costs during their time in Japan, and their presence there would not be a burden on the Japanese economy. Sugihara listened attentively to Warhaftig's argument, and promised a response within a short time.

According to a postwar account by Yukiko Sugihara, the diplomat's wife, her husband listened to the representatives (probably including Dr. Warhaftig), then "came up to the second floor with a worried look. He sat at the table in silence and drank some coffee. He waited until the outside grew silent. Then he stood up and went to the window and looked outside; so did I. We saw a little child standing behind his mother hiding himself in his mother's coat, and a girl with an expression of hunger and terror which made her look like an adult and some

Dutch and Japanese transit visas on Zorach Warhaftig's Polish travel document
(in lieu of passport).

others crouching in fatigue. . . . My husband likes children very much. His happiest time was when he kept our children company at home. He would often tell some Japanese old fairy tales at the bedside of our children to make them go to sleep. . . . That night he didn't talk to the children. It seemed that many cares for the Jewish people occupied his mind. Then Lamentations, a book of the Old Testament, suddenly came to my mind, which was written by Jeremiah, a prophet and poet, when he witnessed the fall of Jerusalem brought about by the Babylonian Army. . . . My husband and I are Christians of the Greek Church, so we desired earnestly to help the Jews."[6]

True enough, even before meeting the Jewish delegation, Sugihara had been issuing transit visas to Jews, but on an individual and select basis; such as the visas issued to a group of Czech nationals on August 7, and dutifully reported to his superior, Foreign Minister Matsuoka: "I am issuing a transit visa on a Czechoslovakian passport." On August 10, Sugihara received a cable from Tokyo, reading: "If the Czechoslovakian passport was issued before March 16, 1939, or was extended, you may issue a visa within the effective date of the passport.

*Japanese transit visas on Zorach Warhaftig's (and wife and son)
Lithuanian travel document (in lieu of passport).*

However, in the case of refugees, you need to be careful that you can issue transit visas only to the ones who already have permission from the countries of their destination. But if they do not have that, please do not issue the visas and please be careful about that." That same day, Sugihara responded: "Mr. Bergman and 15 others are powerful figures in Jewish industrial families in Warsaw. They want to immigrate to South America and they have the visas issued at this consulate to pass through Tsuruga [Japan] for ten days only. But on their way through Tsuruga they would like to consult with Japanese industrialists regarding the capital and experience that they have to offer. Consequently, they would appreciate a visa valid for a month. I see no reason to hesitate about these things and so I want to give permission. Please respond promptly as to whether you agree or not." As one may notice, Sugihara was using his diplomatic expertise to sway the powerful foreign minister with the lure of the economic value to Japan by some of the visa recipients.[7]

However, after witnessing the large crowd outside his home, and the visit of the Warhaftig delegation, Sugihara was moved to expand the granting of visas without necessarily justifying it on economic grounds. In his 1967 memoir, Sugihara stated that August 10 was the day when this transformation took place.[8] Recalling those momentous days long after the war, Sugihara described the struggle in his mind as he groped for a decision. "I really had a difficult time, and for two whole nights was unable to sleep. I eventually decided to issue transit visas. . . . I could not allow these people to die, people who had come to me for help with death staring them in the eyes. Whatever punishment might be imposed upon me, I knew I had to follow my conscience."

August 10 is when Sugihara threw caution to the wind. Having made his decision, Sugihara began to issue Japanese transit visas to anyone asking for one—all told, as many as several thousand. The operation continued until the day of Sugihara's departure from Kaunas at the end of August. He had committed himself to helping these people, who represented no threat to Japan, and without regard to the type of documents in their possession or whether the documents were genuine or forged. As he stated: "However, only a few of them had documents issued by the U.S. government, the majority had no documents, indicating that they would only transit Japan without causing hindrance when traveling to the other country. . . . There were not only male refugees, among them were women, old people and children. They all seemed very tired and exhausted."[9] He significantly added: "I did not pay any attention and just acted according to my sense of human justice, out of love for mankind." And he continued to issue visas right up to the moment of his departure from Kaunas, on the morning of August 31, 1940. Some claim to have seen him stamping visas even at the train station. Was he concerned that by disobeying he could be jeopardizing his carefully sculpted diplomatic career by taking matters in his own hands, in a country not accustomed to such behavior by a public servant? Would he also have to face disciplinary measures? "Of course a dismissal from the ministry could be expected, but anyhow I was to take the train to Berlin together with my family in the morning of August 31, 1940. So I went on issuing visas to any Pole who asked for one."[10]

To help with the stampede of applicants and the limited time available, Yeshiva student Moshe Zupnik was enlisted to help process the voluminous visa requests. When Wolfgang Gudze, Sugihara's secretary, asked him who he was, he replied, "I am a member of the Mir Yeshiva. I have three hundred passports with me. We will go to Curaçao. Help us to get there."

"Three hundred people? The consul gave visas to some people, but how will he give visas to three hundred? The consul will never allow this."

"Let me talk to the consul."

"All right, talk to the consul."

In Zupnik's words, "Sugihara asked me, 'Who are you?' 'We are a rabbinical seminary with over three hundred people and we want to go to Curaçao. 'I am afraid you will come and you will stay in Japan and you won't be able to get out. How could I be responsible to my government giving out so many visas at one time?' "

Zupnik thought quickly. "We have a Rabbi Kalmanovich in the United States. He promised us that we don't have to worry." Sugihara, who had already earlier made up his mind to issue visas, was satisfied with this answer, but there was another problem facing the Japanese diplomat. "I have to make a special stamp in Japanese that says that it is only a transit visa and you will go out," and it would take several days before this stamp was ready for use. When the stamp arrived, and for the next two weeks, Zupnik and Gudze stamped the passports. When people started to crowd outside, they passed their papers through the window to Zupnik and he stamped them with the special rubber stamp prepared by Sugihara.

Looking back at that strange coincidence of working side by side with a Gestapo agent inside the Japanese consulate, Zupnik wondered: "I still can't understand how Sugihara let me in, a boy. He didn't have any records or anything on me. He simply handed over the consular stamp and allowed me to make visas! He wanted to do good. He told me, 'I do it just because I have pity on the people. They want to get out so I let them have the visas.' He had a good heart and he was very outgoing and saved people. . . . And he did it wholeheartedly. And he was not formal. He listened to us and he knew that we were in danger and he did it."[11]

Soon, Sugihara began receiving alarming telegrams from the Japanese Foreign Ministry as well as from the captains of ships making the run from Vladivostok to Tsuruga. The dispatches raised concern about the great number of people crowding the vessels and arriving in Kobe and Yokohama without previously formalizing their upkeep in these two places. Moreover, on August 14, Sugihara received the response about the economically important Mr. Bergmann and his group of 15 persons. "Must complete the procedure for obtaining the entrance visas to the terminal country. Someone who had not finished the procedure we will not permit that person to land. Please consider that." In another cable from Tokyo, on August 16, Sugihara was told: "Recently, we discovered Lithuanians who possess our transit visas which you issued. They were traveling to America and Canada. Among these there are several who do not have enough money and who have not finished their procedure to receive their entry visas to the terminal countries. We cannot give them permission to land... There were several instances that left us confused and we do not know what to do. . . . You must make sure that they have finished their procedure for their entry visas and also they must possess the travel money or the money that they need during their stay in Japan. Otherwise, you should not give them the transit visa."[12]

Sugihara was asked to immediately discontinue issuing transit visas but disregarded this request. As he later stated, "I acted solely out of love for people and humanitarian feeling. I had no doubt that one day I would be dismissed from my job at the Foreign Ministry." By Sugihara's account, he issued around 3,500 transit visas. Some estimates give different figues of visas. Ernest Heppner reports that 2,178 refugees arrived in Japan with forged passports, illegal papers, and Curaçao visas. Among them were 70 rabbis and 350 talmudic students, mostly from the Mir Yeshiva. Dr. Warhaftig estimates the number of refugees who arrived in Japan at 2,800. There were a total of

4,608 in Kobe, the city where the refugees were allowed to stay. Of these, 2,184 were from Germany, 2,111 from Poland, and an additional 313 others who probably were also recipients of Curaçao visas.[13]

The visa recipients, among them hundreds of yeshiva students (notably from the Mir Yeshiva), left the area before the German attack on the Soviet Union on June 21, 1941 and thus were saved. They crossed Russia and Japan and continued on to Shanghai, the Philippines, the United States, Canada, Palestine, and other destinations. Ironically, none of them landed in Curaçao. As early as August 16, refugees from Kaunas were already arriving in the Japanese port city of Tsuruga with ambiguous documents, so it seems likely that Sugihara was neglecting the "customary" procedures even before August 10, the date when he began issuing large numbers of visas. Lucille Camhi reports that she and her sister were detained by the Japanese in Tsuruga because they did not have end-destination visas. "We told them that we expected to get a visa to the U.S. They said they would ask the U.S. Embassy to check." In the end, the Jewish community in Kobe interceded in their behalf, and the two sisters' stay in Kobe was extended for two months, until their American visas came through. Jack Friedman made it to Japan via Korea, where he was joined by his brother. They stayed in Japan for seven months before parting. Jack went to Shanghai; his brother Bernard made it to Bombay. Irene Malowist recalled that the American diplomats in Tokyo initially suspected him of being a Soviet spy because of his passage through Russia. His ten-day Japanese transit visa was also extended for many months, until his departure for America. As for Ludvik Salomon (later Lewis Salton), who held a Curaçao visa, he continued to Panama. There he managed to get off the ship together with some other Jewish refugees and headed for Mexico. Nathan Gutwirth wound up in the Dutch East Indies and was later taken prisoner by the Japanese. Zorach Warhaftig went on from Japan to the United States in 1941.[14]

As for Sugihara, when he arrived in Berlin, Ambassador Kurusu asked him to open a consulate in Koenigsberg (today known as

Kaliningrad, and part of Russia), another ideal intelligence listening post to learn about German military preparations. He visited the city in December, but it was only in March 1941 that he was allowed to stay there. Before then he was stationed in Prague. In the intervening time, at the request of his superiors, he compiled a list of the visas he had issued and sent it to the Foreign Ministry in Tokyo.[15] On June 7, 1941, he was asked to leave Koenigsberg, and a few months later he was stationed in Bucharest, which is where he was captured by the Soviets in 1944 and held in confinement for several years. He returned to Japan in April 1947, to find a defeated country occupied by the United States.

Soon after his arrival back home, Sugihara was summoned to the Foreign Ministry in Tokyo and asked to tender his resignation. It is still not too clear what prompted this. The Foreign Ministry claimed that it was a result of retrenchment, since as an occupied country Japan had no need for an expert on Soviet affairs. Sugihara's family claims that his forced resignation was a punishment for the "Lithuanian incident"; for his stepping out of line by issuing so many visas, contrary to instructions. Sugihara himself believed he was being punished. The years that followed were difficult ones for him as he moved from one job to another; working as a salesperson in a department store, and translating Russian reports into Japanese for a radio station. In 1960, he landed a job as a trade representative in Moscow for a Japanese firm. He remained there for over ten years, before retiring to a Tokyo suburb in 1975.

In order to properly assess Sugihara's significant role in the Curaçao visa scheme, one has to compare his behavior, as an emissary of a dictatorial and militaristic regime, with that of the representative of the United States, the bastion of democracy. While Zwartendijk and Sugihara were issuing transit visas to thousands of Jews, the American consulate in Kaunas kept its doors closed to Jewish refugees. On May 12, 1939, the vice-consul, Bernard Guffler, in a dispatch to Washington, described the consulate's difficulties in granting visas as due to the fact that "insofar as could be judged from indications given by them, [the applicants were] registering out of panic and not because they had a fixed desire to emigrate." To add to the burden of the many applicants, the consulate required of them a "moral certificate" from the local police stating that the petitioner was of good character. This was next to impossible for Polish refugees who had only recently arrived in the country. Dr. James Bernstein, the European representative of HIAS (a New York-based Jewish charitable organization), after speaking with Vice-Consul Tomlin Bailey, reported on the bureaucratic obstacles imposed by the consulate. Many could not present documents from Poland as asked of them, because it was occupied by Germany. Bernstein complained that 5,000 of the 1939–40 quota of visas remained unissued.

In the words of historian Hillel Levine, "The same level of imagination that led Sugihara to give out visas was duplicated at the American Consulate, except here it was used not to give out visas." On August 17, 1940, as the U.S. consulate was closing its doors, Bernard Guffler happily cabled to Washington the following message: "Visas issued by American representatives at Kaunas are useless to 99% of the applicants despite the demand for them, since few can obtain proper travel documents and fewer can obtain exit visas or arrange transportation." They were useless because State Department policy and the U.S. diplomats on the spot had helped make them so. As aptly put by Levine, "What we do now know is that, unlike the American diplomats, Sugihara responded. He took initiative beyond his government's policies, beyond his responsibilities to carry those policies out, reacting as a human being first and an administrator second." As Sugihara ironically put it to Rabbi Eliezer Portnoy of the Mir Yeshiva, "The world says that America is civilized. I will show the world that Japan is more civilized." He gave the rabbi 300 visas. Rabbi Portnoy had gone earlier to the American consulate. "I have my orders," one of the consuls said. "The quota for visas to America has been used up. There will be no more visas issued here."[16]

Asked about his motives, Sugihara had this to say in 1986, shortly before his death.

"You want to know about my motivation, don't you? Well. It is the kind of sentiments anyone would have when he actually sees the

refugees face-to-face, begging with tears in their eyes. He just cannot help but sympathize with them. Among the refugees were the elderly and women. They were so desperate that they went so far as to kiss my shoes. Yes. I actually witnessed such scenes with my own eyes. . . . People in Tokyo were not unified [on a proper refugee policy]. I felt it kind of silly to deal with them. So I made up my mind not to wait for their reply. I knew that somebody would surely complain to me in the future. But I myself thought this would be the right thing to do. There is nothing wrong in saving many people's lives. If anybody sees anything wrong in the action, it is because something 'not pure' exists in their state of mind. The spirit of humanity, philanthropy . . . neighborly friendship . . . with this spirit, I ventured to do what I did, confronting this most difficult situation—and because of this reason, I went ahead with redoubled courage."

In 1985, Sugihara was awarded the title of Righteous Among the Nations by the Israeli ambassador in Tokyo, on behalf of Yad Vashem. A year later, he passed away, aged 86.[17]

Chapter 4

France
To Leave in a Hurry

Luiz Martins de Souza Dantas

When German troops swept into Paris in June 1940, Luiz Martins de Souza Dantas had been the Brazilian ambassador to France since 1922. Born into an aristocratic family, he was close to 60 years old when he married an American Jewish woman named Aliza Meyer, an act not viewed with great favor by his diplomatic colleagues. When he moved from Paris to Vichy, the seat of the new pro-German French government, headed by the aged Marshal Philippe Pétain, his office was soon inundated with Jews seeking to leave the country with the help of visas to Brazil. Dantas was suddenly faced with a most serious problem. Was he to disobey his country's policy, which forbade him from granting visas to fleeing Jews, or would he face up to the moral challenge and grant such visas, thus violating the instructions received from his superiors, and seriously undermining his diplomatic career?

His colleagues stationed elsewhere in Europe left room for no doubt as to their attitude on this question. For instance, on July 30, 1940, Osorio H. Dutra, the consul in Lyon, wrote to Brazil's foreign minister, Oswaldo Aranha, of the many people clogging his office seeking visas. "Almost all of them are Jewish or of Semitic origin, and only very few of them, in my opinion, may be of interest to us. I therefore believe that by my categorical refusal to grant the visas that they request, I will have done Brazil a great service." The ambassador in Berlin, Ciro de Freitas Vale, did not lag behind the general anti-Jewish feelings among Brazilian diplomats, and he worked hard to deny travel permits to Jews. Likewise for the consul in Budapest, Mario Moreira da Silva, who wrote that "Jews when living together are harmful, and in response to their behavior, their countries of origin treat them as pernicious, undesirable elements, against whom a series of restrictive measures is taken with one goal in mind: that they should leave. . . . Almost no European country allows Jews to hold public office. Why, then, should we, out of mere compassion, open our doors to immigrants of this kind?" The same attitude typified Jorge Latour, the secretary of the Brazilian legation in Warsaw, who reported, "All universal problems, for better or worse, sooner or later find a solution. The only unsolvable problem is the Jewish question. It is a cyst that forever persists among nations as they develop."[1] In stark contrast to his fellow diplomats, Dantas decided to follow a different course—the humanitarian one. But he knew it was an uphill struggle, fraught with danger, against the antisemitic bureaucrats behind the desks of the Foreign Ministry during the dictatorship of Getulio Vargas.

On June 7, 1937, a Foreign Ministry classified circular prohibited Brazilian diplomats from granting visas to Jews even if sponsored by relatives living in Brazil, with the exception of persons married to Brazilians and Jews of international repute in certain fields. This allowed the famous author Stefan Zweig to obtain a Brazilian visa. In spite of this ruling, thousands of Jews managed to overcome the bureaucratic obstacles and make their way to Brazil. However, as the war clouds gathered in Europe, Brazil intensified its restrictive measures, and by January 1941, the Brazilian Foreign Ministry extended its discriminatory policy to include not merely Jews fleeing Germany, "but all Jews [*Israelitas*] dispersed around the world." Furthermore, "the fact that a Jew has embraced Catholicism or any other non-Mosaic faith does not change his status for the denial of a consular visa. His ethnicity is the determining factor."

Strangely, as much as Brazil's diplomats in Europe tried to enforce the restrictive measures enunciated by their Foreign Ministry, that same agency allowed exceptions to the rules for various and not always fully explicable reasons, and not a few Jews were still able to make their

Luiz Martins de Souza Danta,
Brazil ambassador in France.

way to Brazil. In a communication from Berlin, Lutero Vargas, the son of Brazil's dictator, wrote of Consul Adolpho de Camargo Neves's frustration at the number of Jews allowed to sail for Brazil. "All of them are equipped with entry permits sent by the Foreign Ministry, because the consul does his best to prevent Jewish immigration and approves it only when he is ordered to do so." At the same time, in 1941 Brazil responded negatively to a request by Pope Pius XII to allow 3,000 German Catholics of Jewish origin to enter Brazil, although it had in principle agreed to view the request favorably when first approached on the subject.[2]

In stark contrast to other Brazilian diplomats, Dantas decided to follow a different course. He shrewdly searched for loopholes in his country's immigration regulations that would make it possible for him to issue visas to as many Jewish refugees as possible. Most of this beneficial action took place in the second half of 1940 in France, a country still hurting from its stinging defeat and torn by despair and disillusionment. Careful not to overstep the formal boundaries of his work, in November 1940, he sent a telegram to Foreign Minister Aranha asking permission to issue visas to persons desperate to leave France who simply wanted to travel to Spain and Portugal, and from there to various others destinations—but not Brazil. It was a straightforward request for a humanitarian gesture, but Aranha brusquely turned it down.

Not taking no for an answer, Dantas decided on a different approach. He would issue visas not to everyone but to a select group of renowned intellectuals whose settling in Brazil would redound to the country's benefit. As he stated in a communication to Aranha: "Alongside the humanitarian considerations, I believe that the work of these intellectuals—many of whom are of unquestionable caliber and have produced outstanding creative works, [but are] groping in the darkness that is descending on Europe—will be of great advantage to our country." Another Foreign Ministry ruling that played into the hands of Dantas was a January 1941 directive which allowed consular officers to issue visas to experts, artists, and capitalists who could transfer more than 400 contos ($20,000) to the Banco do Brasil, and thereby prove beneficial to Brazil's economy.[3]

Deciding to act quickly, before immigration policy changed for the worse, Dantas decided to take advantage of the visas permission and issue travel permits to Jewish refugees on the claim of being economically advantageous to Brazil. He also shrewdly relied on a previous Foreign Ministry ruling in January 1939, which allowed diplomats to issue diplomatic visas in exceptional cases and, upon permission of the Foreign Ministry, to individuals of outstanding renown in their own country. Most of the people to whom Dantas issued diplomatic visas could not claim to be of "outstanding renown" or "economically viable" for Brazil. He therefore strongly urged many of them not to go to Brazil but to seek other safe havens. Thanks to these diplomatic visas, whose official validity expired on November 1940, it is estimated that hundreds of fleeing Jews were able to leave France, therefore escaping the consequences of the Holocaust to their families. A few examples follow.

When the Germans invaded Belgium in May 1940, Raphael Zimetbaum and family had fled to France and landed in Marseilles. In February 1941, with most of France now under German control, Raphael's father, Lejzer, and younger brother, Izak, and a certain Jewish lady took the train to Vichy upon the advice of someone, to look up the Brazilian ambassador. They met him in the hotel where his office was located, but he told them that there was nothing he could possibly do, since he had received strict instructions not to issue visas to Jews or persons of Jewish origin. Then, in Raphael's words, "and all of a sudden, staring at our desperate faces, he asked us to return the next day." And the next morning, saying that he knew he was probably saving their lives, he issued diplomatic visas for the whole family on their Polish passports with a retroactive date of November 21, 1940 (before the non-issuance visa regulation), even though it was late March 1941. There was never any discussion of money or other gifts to be paid in return for this, as was customarily done with diplomats from some Latin American countries. The Zimmetbaum family crossed the Spanish border near Pau, and continued to Portugal. After a considerable delay, they were able to board the cargo ship *Santarem*, and arrived in Rio de Janeiro on June 11, 1941 (Raphael's thirteenth birthday). "We had a hard time explaining to the local authorities how and why we had diplomatic visas, but influential Jews of the local community intervened and ultimately the problem was solved," and the Zimetbaums were allowed to disembark.

Regina Feigl's family were also aided by Dantas. She and her husband and son had earlier fled from Vienna and arrived in Belgium. From there, they continued to France. In late 1940, Regina Feigl received diplomatic visas for her family from Dantas. She planned to somehow continue to the United States. In her words: "I met there [Vichy] the greatest Brazilian that I have ever met—Dantas. [When I met him] he told me: 'Listen, I know what this is about, but I have instructions from my government not to issue visas to Jews.' I spoke to

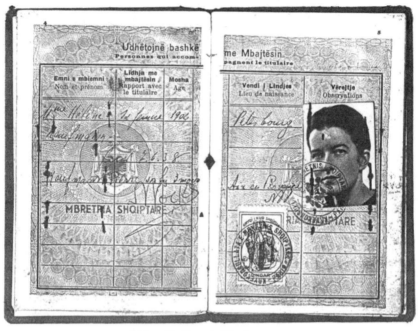

Helene Kaufmann's Albania passport.

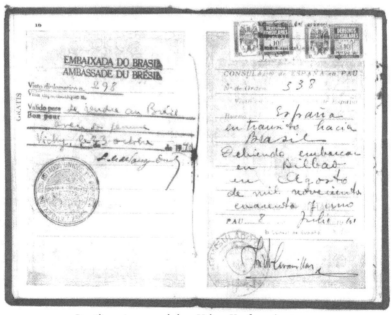

Brazilian visa appended on Helene Kaufmann's passport,
by Souza Dantas, Brazil ambassador in France.

him in French, and told him that the Nazis are hunting us like dogs. He got up from his chair, turned his back, and stood for a while in front of the window, and told me to sit down. I couldn't see whether he wiped his forehead or his eyes. He then went into an adjoining room, had a long conversation with someone I don't know and in a language I could not identify. He came out and told me: 'Go in there and you will receive diplomatic visas.' That is how we arrived in Portugal." From there, the Feigl family boarded the *Serpa Pinto* and arrived in Rio de Janeiro in November 1940.

George Bemski's parents also obtained a diplomatic visa on their Polish passports for travel to Brazil. After crossing into Spain, they were told to leave the country. The family proceeded to Morocco, and while in Casablanca obtained a Spanish transit visa. Heading to Tangier, then Cadiz, they boarded the *Cabo de Buena Esperanza*, which took them to Brazil in December 1940.

As for Lisbeth Forell, she was 14 years old in 1939, and had earlier left Czechoslovakia for Belgium; thence to France. Dantas issued a diplomatic visa to Lisbeth's father and family on their Czech passports. They left by ship, which took them to Dakar, Africa, where they remained for seven months, for part of which the passengers (half of them Jewish) were not permitted to leave the ship. Finally allowed to proceed to Casablanca (where they were also confined for two months in a French Foreign Legion camp), they continued to Tangier. In the meantime, the validity of their Brazilian visa had expired and they were required to renew it. The family finally arrived in Rio de Janeiro on the *Cabo de Buena Esperanza* on September 25, 1941.

The same for Chana Strozemberg's family, of Polish origin, who also obtained diplomatic visas from Dantas in January 1941. He explicitly asked them not to go to Brazil to avoid bureaucratic encumbrances there. Chana said that Dantas dated the documents to November 1940 and explained to her husband and brother Charles that this was because of the prohibition against granting visas after that date. Arriving in Lisbon, they boarded the *Serpa Pinto*, in April 1941. According to Chana's husband Dantas's motivation was humanitarian. "He gave preference to Jews, because he knew that Jews were in danger."

Recently discovered documents in the Brazilian Foreign Ministry and Interior Ministry archives reveal the names of many more recipients of Dantas's diplomatic visas. There are also documents requesting changes in visa status from diplomatic to regular so that the applicant could seek gainful employment on a firmer resident's status. In the above-mentioned Zimetbaum case, a police officer's letter addressed to Foreign Minister Aranha, on February 8, 1943, mentions the inexplicable revelation that these persons deal in diamonds but carry a diplomatic visa, and asks for the diplomatic visa to be annulled.

Some of the Jewish passengers continued to have problems even after they received Brazilian diplomatic visas from Dantas. As a case in point, the Spanish-registered *Cabo de Hornos* arrived in Rio de Janeiro harbor in late 1941 carrying an estimated 95 Jewish refugees, originally mainly from Poland and Czechoslovakia, and including persons with visas issued by Dantas and revalidated by Brazil's consul in Cadiz upon instructions from Dantas. When the ship arrived in Rio de Janeiro in mid-October 1941, the Brazilian authorities refused to admit the Jewish passengers. Representatives of the Joint Distribution Committee asked John Simmons of the U.S. embassy in Rio de Janeiro to exert pressure on Brazil's government to allow the group to enter the country. The Spanish ambassador also lent his support in an appeal to President Vargas, arguing that the refugees were in possession of valid visas issued by a diplomat from Brazil. However, the vessel was towed out of port, and it sailed for Buenos Aires, Argentina, hoping to be allowed to disembark there. Negotiations were simultaneously carried on with members of the Paraguayan cabinet, for it was hoped that in return for a large bribe, the passengers would be allowed there, but nothing came of it. Early on the morning of November 7, 1941, the *Cabo de Hornos* returned to Rio harbor, on its way back to Europe. The ship was scheduled to dock for only 12 hours. In hopes of a favorable decision by the Paraguayan government, this was extended for another day. In the meantime U.S. Congressman Sol Bloom made a personal appeal to Carlos Martins Pereira e Souza, the Brazilian ambassador to the United States, who telegrammed Vargas asking him to allow the people to disembark. Vargas refused, telling U.S. officials that "the Brazilian Foreign Office was not responsible for visas issued against their orders." The *Cabo de Hornos* sailed for Europe, and ten days later the Dutch colony of Curaçao accepted the refugees, pending transfer elsewhere. Their fate had miraculously changed for the best. On December 1, 1941, *Time* magazine carried the story of the *Cabo de Buena Esperanza* and *Cabo de Hornos* passengers, a drama that recalled an earlier one, in May 1939, when the *St. Louis,* with 900 German Jewish refugees carrying valid Cuban visas, was not allowed to dock in Havana, and was forced to return to Europe.[4]

Similar tribulations were experienced by Jewish refugees aboard the *Alsina,* which left Marseilles on January 1, 1941, with 570 passengers, including many Jewish refugees, some with Brazilian visas issued by Dantas. Arriving in Dakar (Senegal), it remained there for over four months before sailing for Morocco on June 6, 1941, where the passengers were interned by the French in Casablanca. In the meantime, the 90-day Brazilian visas had expired. When Dantas learned of this, he ordered the local Brazilian consuls in Casablanca and Cadiz, Spain, (for those refugees who had managed to get there) to revalidate the visas, on August 10, 1941. Some passengers managed to get on board the *Buena Esperanza,* others, on other vessels, and sailed for Brazil, where they again experienced trouble when the authorities refused to allow them to land. Some eventually were allowed to disembark after pressure from relatives and Jewish organizations.

On July 29, 1941, the Foreign Ministry instructed its ambassador in Lisbon, to no longer honor diplomatic visas issued on passports, since they had been granted on false premises, especially to Jews. "We therefore inform you that, in consideration of the means under the law, all diplomatic visas are hereby annulled." Punitive measures were also meted out against the Spanish consuls in Cadiz and Casablanca; the former was reprimanded; the latter was fired. Brazil's consul in Bordeaux, who also had issued some of the visas, pointed an accusing finger at his superior, Ambassador Dantas, claiming he had issued the visas on his instructions. As for Dantas, on November 11, 1941, in a message to Foreign Minister Aranha, he justified his intervention in extending the visas with the excuse that the passengers had valid visas, but their jour-

ney had been held up due to circumstances not of the passengers' voli-
tion, but of exigencies connected with the war. This, however, was not
enough of an excuse to save him from disciplinary measures.

The charges against Dantas stemmed from the privilege granted
him to authorize diplomatic visas to persons who, in the eyes of Brazil's
Foreign Ministry, clearly were not entitled to such prestigious documents. On October 11, 1941, President Vargas ordered the creation of
an administrative investigation committee to consider this charge. The
committee began its work on February 3, 1942. It found that Dantas
had overstepped the mandate given him to issue diplomatic visas.
Moreover, since the authorization was later cancelled, he was in violation of instructions when he continued to issue such visas and back-
dated them to the earlier period. In addition, Dantas was accused of
having issued diplomatic visas to persons definitely not entitled to
them, such as Irena Olipja Stypinska, Halina Wladyslawa Kern,
Waclav Piotrowski, Binen and Regina Grynkaut, Otto and Lisbeth
Forell, Julios Fischel, Arnost and Anna Goldstein—all Jewish-sound-
ing names.

It seemed certain that the committee would recommend punitive
measures against Dantas, but surprisingly, that proved not to be the
case. Having established that Dantas had reached retirement age on
May 5, 1941, but was asked to continue in his post until the arrival of
a replacement, the committee felt that the usual punitive measures
should not be meted out against the insubordinate diplomat, such as
withholding of pension and other benefits accrued after a long career
in the diplomatic service. Thus, even though he had clearly contra-
vened his instructions, Dantas escaped with only a slap on the wrist.
Perhaps the committee's leniency was in part influenced by the fact
that in March 1943, after Brazil joined the Allied camp and declared
war on Germany, the Germans broke into the Brazilian embassy in
Vichy, arrested Dantas, and deported him to Germany, where he
remained incarcerated together with other Latin American diplomats
in Bad Godesburg. Dantas was freed in 1944 following the intervention of Portugal's dictator, António de Oliveira Salazar.

In summary, Ambassador Luiz Martins de Souza Dantas reportedly issued 473 diplomatic visas and authorized the consuls in Bordeaux, Marseilles, Perpignan, Paris, and Lyon to issue 40 additional visas. Most of these visas were issued in October–November 1940, with some as early as August and September 1940; a sizable number was also issued in 1941, mostly in June, but a few even later, with some as late as November 11, 1941. With the tightening of visa restrictions toward the end of 1941 and early 1942, Jewish immigration to Brazil came to a virtual halt.[5]

Upon his liberation, Dantas decided to resign from the Foreign Ministry. With the war over, he returned to Paris, and lived there until his death in 1954. In 2003, in response to requests by many beneficiaries of the diplomat's generous wartime aid, Yad Vashem awarded Luiz Martins de Souza Dantas the title of Righteous Among the Nations.[6]

Aristides de Sousa Mendes

A more vengeful punishment befell another disobedient diplomat, the Portuguese consul-general in Bordeaux, France. Born in 1895 into an aristocratic Portuguese family, Aristides de Sousa Mendes (hereinafter Mendes)[7] chose a diplomatic career. In August 1938, after postings in San Francisco, Zanzibar, and Antwerp, he became consul-general in Bordeaux, France. In May 1940, with the German invasion of France and the Low Countries, thousands of refugees, among them many Jews, headed for Bordeaux, hoping to cross into Spain and continue via Portugal to lands across the Atlantic Ocean. At this critical juncture, the Portuguese government, headed by dictator António de Oliveira Salazar (who also had the post of foreign minister), prohibited the issuance of Portuguese transit visas to refugees, and particularly to Jews.

This prohibition had been spelled out half a year earlier, on November 13, 1939, when Mendes received a memorandum from the Foreign Ministry which altered the country's traditional policy of hospitality and introduced guidelines prejudicial to certain classes of people. It strictly forbade visas to "Jews expelled from the countries of their nationality or from whence they come." Passports and visas were not to be granted to them without prior permission by the Foreign Ministry. In spite of these measures, Mendes already had a record of granting visas not totally consonant with the government's official immigration criteria, and on April 24, 1940, Luiz Teixeira de Sampayo, the secretary general of the Foreign Ministry, reminded Mendes of the irregularities he had committed in issuing visas, warning "that any new fault or infraction in this regard will be considered disobedience and give rise to disciplinary proceedings where it has to be taken into account that you have repeatedly committed acts that merit warnings and reprimands." Willing to brave the risks to himself, Mendes continued to issue transit to people in need, including 17 Belgian subjects on May 28, 1940, and three Polish nationals on June 7, 1940. On the latter occasion the Portuguese police alerted the Foreign Ministry about "the behavior of this consul [Mendes], who has issued visas in passports more than once without receiving the prior authorization of the ministry and sometimes issues them without receiving a reply to requests previously made."[8]

In the latter part of May 1940, against the grim background of France on the verge of collapse, the flow of refugees to Bordeaux turned into a stampede. As the Germans advanced within striking distance of the city, panic prevailed among the thousands of refugees, many of whom were camped out on the streets and in parks. A month earlier, on May 21, Mendes sent a telegram to Salazar requesting instructions on how to deal with the flood of refugees seeking Portuguese transit visas. The answer received was a blunt negative. Several weeks later, on June 13, Mendes asked for permission to issue visas to a group of 30 people, including a certain Rabbi Chaim Kruger. The answer again was a plain and simple no.[9]

Mendes had met Rabbi Kruger during his nightly rounds by car of places where refugees gathered, and he had invited the rabbi to the consulate at 14 Quai Louis XVIII, a street near the docks, which also served as the consul's residence. Mendes listened attentively as Rabbi Kruger related how he had fled from Belgium at the start of the

Aristides de Sousa Mendes, the Portuguese consul-general in Bordeaux, France.

German invasion and was now stranded in Bordeaux together with thousands of other Jewish refugees. At first, as had been his custom in the past in individual cases, Mendes offered Kruger and his family transit visas, but the rabbi turned down this gesture. He gently insisted that the other stranded Jews should also benefit from the generosity of the Portuguese diplomat.

As Rabbi Kruger himself related in a 1967 deposition to Yad Vashem, Mendes had stopped his car in front of the synagogue, where many Jews had assembled, and went up to speak to the rabbi. He invited the rabbi, his family and five children to his home. During the friendly conversation that ensued, Mendes told him that he was a descendant of Marranos (Jews forced to convert to Christianity in the fifteenth century) and the father of 12 children. "He invited us to stay in his home, but I realized I could not do this, since I could not part from the crowd stranded on the streets. . . . I thanked him for his generosity and returned to our brothers stranded outside. I then returned to him and explained that there was only one avenue of rescue—to give all of us visas to Portugal."

This presented Mendes with a formidable moral challenge that entailed grave consequences. Issuing visas to hundreds and thousands of people was a transgression that would not be ignored in Lisbon, unlike the small number of individual visas issued earlier. It should not be forgotten that António de Oliveira Salazar, the dictator of Portugal, styled his regime on the Fascist model. In Portugal of those days, it was unthinkable for a diplomatic official, especially in a sensitive post, to disobey clear-cut instructions and get away with it. Salazar himself had made it clear that no transit visas were to be given to Jews, and for a diplomat to act otherwise would entail grave punitive consequences against him.

For several days, Mendes struggled with himself. He took to his bedroom, tossed and turned on his bed, sweating profusely and occasionally groaning. Despite the agony he was going through, he refused any help from his family. He alternated between intense agitation and passive silence. His son Pedro Nuno noticed the change. "All of a sudden my father seemed terribly weary, as though he had been struck down by a violent disease. He just looked at us and went to bed." Another son, Sebastião, remembered his father looking grave; "his eyes had blue circles around them. His hair had turned completely gray, as white as snow almost." He remained in that state for three days and nights, and had no contact with the outside world. On the morning of June 16, he made up his mind. In the words of Pedro Nuno: "My father got up, apparently recovered his serenity. He was full of punch. He washed, shaved, and got dressed. Then he strode out of his bedroom, flung open the door to the chancellery, and announced in a loud voice: 'From now on I'm giving everyone visas. There will be no more nationalities, races, or religions.' Then our father told us that he had

*Portuguese diplomat Aristides de Sousa Mendes with wife Angelina
and a few of his children in a pre-war photo.*

heard a voice, that of his conscience or of God, which dictated to him
what course of action he should take, and that everything was perfect-
ly clear in his mind." June 16 was also a memorable political date in
France—when Paul Reynaud stepped down as prime minister, thereby
acknowledging France's defeat, and that same evening, Marshal
Philippe Pétain took the helm of a new government. France had capitulated to the Germans. With the German army fast approaching
Bordeaux, Mendes spent the whole day signing visas, no questions
asked. It was a veritable assembly line. Thus began one the greatest rescue operation carried out by a single person.[10]

Rabbi Kruger reported, "I sat with him a full day without food and
sleep and helped him stamp thousands of passports with Portuguese
visas." The rabbi also helped by often stepping outside and collecting

passports from the waiting people. To his staff, Mendes explained: "My government has denied all applications for visas to any refugees. But I cannot allow these people to die. Many are Jews, and our constitution says that the religion, or politics, of a foreigner shall not be used to deny him refuge in Portugal. I have decided to follow this principle. I am going to issue a visa to anyone who asks for it, regardless of whether or not he can pay. . . . Even if I am dismissed, I can only act as a Christian, as my conscience tells me."

Soon the word got out, and there was a stampede to the Portuguese consulate. At this stage of his life, Mendes was 55, the father of 12 children, a monarchist at heart, with financial problems, yet he was challenging his government's immigration policy and confronting the man responsible for it: dictator Salazar. José Seabra, the consular secretary, tried to dissuade his boss from taking this dangerous step. "For the sake of your wife and children, please stop! You're ruining your life and that of your family." Some of his children also feared the consequences from their father's insubordination. His daughter Isabel reportedly told him: "You must stop, Father! Stop taking so many risks! You ought to think of your future and ours."[11]

The consul's nephew, César Mendes, had just arrived in Bordeaux. When he approached the Portuguese consulate, "I noticed immediately that a large crowd of refugees was heading that way. The closer I got to the consulate, the larger the crowd. They wanted desperately to get visas to go to Portugal. Inside, the dinning-room, the drawing room, and the consul's offices were at the disposal of the refugees—dozens of them of both sexes, all ages, and mainly old and sick people. They were coming and going: pregnant women who did not feel well and people who had seen their relatives die on the highways killed by airplane machine-gun fire. They slept on chairs, on the floor, on the rugs. The situation was out of control. Even the consul's offices were crowded with dozens of refugees who were dead-tired because they had waited for days and nights on the street, on the stairways, and finally in the offices. They did not eat or drink for fear of losing their places in the line. They looked distraught; they had not washed or changed their clothes or shaved. Most of them had nothing but the clothes they were wearing. The sidewalks, the front door, the large stairways that led to the chancery were crowded with hundreds of refugees who remained there night and day waiting for their turn. In the chancery, they worked all day long and part of the night. My uncle got ill, exhausted, and had to lie down. He considered the pros and cons and decided to give all facilities without distinction of nationality, race, or religion and bear all the consequences. He was impelled by a 'divine power' (these were his own words), and gave orders to grant free visas to everybody."

An unnamed eyewitness reports hearing Mendes announce to the crowd outside that he was disobeying his government's restrictions on granting visas. He was doing so, he said, because the constitution of Portugal stated that under no circumstances shall the religion or political belief of a foreigner prevent him from seeking refuge in Portuguese territory. "I am a Christian and, as such, believe that I cannot let these refugees perish. A good many of them are Jews, many are prominent men and women who, because their social standing as leaders and such, felt it in their hearts to speak and act against the forces of oppression. They have done what in their hearts was the right thing to do. Now they want to go on where they will be able to carry on their fight for what they think is right. I know that Mrs. Mendes wholly concurs with my views, and I feel certain that my children will understand and not hold it against me, if by giving out visas to each and every one of the refugees, I am tomorrow discharged from my duties for having acted contrarily to orders which, in my estimation, are vile and unjust. And so, I declare that I shall give, free of charge, a visa to whosoever shall request it. My desire is to be with God against man rather than with man and against God."

On June 17, as the news having spread like wildfire, Mendes's apartment was taken by storm, with refugees crowding the drawing-room and dining-room. That same day, Pétain addressed the nation: "I make to France the gift of my person, to attenuate her suffering. . . . It is with a heavy heart that I say to you today the combat must cease." Also that same day, Charles de Gaulle took off for London to continue the resistance against the Germans from there. A chaotic situation prevailed in Bordeaux, with large, dense crowds pressing forward in front of the Portuguese consulate. Suffering from exhaustion, Mendes decided to abbreviate his signature to a simple "Mendes," followed with the invitation, '"Next person please." An indication of the mounting pressure is that after June 22, names were no longer listed, just a note saying that "visas no. 2763 to 2850 were issued by the consul after working hours." His secretary, Seabra, had given up writing the names of all the visa recipients in the consulate's ledger, and stopped asking refuges to pay the visa registration fee.[12]

When Mendes learned that Faria Machado, the consul in Bayonne, a city on the French-Spanish border, was creating problems for refugees asking for Portuguese transit visas, Mendes hurried there to bring the consul in line, since as consul-general, he was superior in rank. Accosting Vice-Consul Manoel Vieira Braga, Mendes asked: "Why don't you help those poor refugees? How would you like to find yourself, your wife and children in the same circumstances as the refugees? You say you're here to carry out the instructions you receive from your superiors. Very well, I am still the consul at Bordeaux, and, consequently, your superior. I order you to pass out as many visas as may be needed."

On July 1, 1940, the Portuguese special envoy Armando Lopo Simeão reported to his government that on June 18 or 19, at the Bayonne chancery, Mendes, "on his superior authority, began issuing visas to everyone who applied, apparently alleging that all these people had to be saved. There was a large crowd in the streets around the consulate and it was only possible to get through with the help of the police force who attempted at great cost to control the traffic. . . . I found it extremely difficult to get into the chancery although accompanied by the consul." Simeão further reported that the days preceding the arrival of the Germans, on June 27, "the tension was such that when told they would not get visas, some threatened to commit suicide, some offered exorbitant sums of money to obtain one, some used cunning, some threats, others attempted bribery. . . . We have only to regret the attitude of the consul in Bordeaux who has really placed us in a discreditable situation that is not above suspicion."[13]

Mendes remained in Bayonne for three days to make sure that the refugees were given visas so that they could cross over into Spain before the Germans reached the area. He went to great lengths to ease the passing of Jews into Spain. Mendes remembered that in the past he had sometimes crossed the French-Spanish border at a less popular point in order to avoid traffic jams on the direct route between Hendaye, in France and Irún, in Spain. Fearing that the Spanish border guards, under pressure from Portugal, might already have received instructions not to honor transit visas issued by the Bordeaux consulate, he decided to help the refugees use this circuitous route. Asking refugees with vehicles to follow his car, he drove slowly to the secondary crossing point. The dumbfounded Spanish soldiers there had no telephone. Mendes told them: "I am the Portuguese consul. These people are with me. They all have regular visas, as you can check for yourselves, so would you be so kind as to let them through." The trick worked well. This was confirmed by Rabbi Kruger, who with his group were held at the border and prevented from entering Spain. Suddenly Mendes appeared on the scene, and after two hours of negotiations with the Spanish border guards, the group was able to proceed. "He himself opened the border fence for us, and they allowed everyone who had a visa from him to pass." This was just in time, for on June 27, German soldiers entered Bordeaux.[14]

While Mendes was still in Bayonne, Salazar decided to take action against the recalcitrant diplomat. On June 21 the Foreign Ministry sent an aide, Armando Lopo Simeão, on a special mission to Bayonne to see if the reports about Mendes's activities were true. He was then to await instructions from the Portuguese ambassador in Spain, Pedro Teotónio Pereira. In the meantime, Mendes had moved to Hendaye, where he continued to sign visas. As reported by two Austrian refugees, Norbert and Heddy Gingold, and a Polish refugee, Nat Wyszkowski: "Suddenly Sousa Mendes appeared in the middle of the square. . . . He continued issuing visas to those who asked him for them. . . . They consisted of a few words indicating that the holder was entitled to enter Portugal and carried Sousa Mendes's signature."

On June 23, Salazar took the first punitive step by stripping Mendes of most of his authority, and especially the right to issue visas. From this point on, any further visas he issued were illegal. For a fortnight, he divided his time between Bordeaux, Bayonne, Biarritz, and Hendaye. While in Hendaye, on June 23, he met the Spanish ambassador to Spain, Pedro Teotónio Pereira, accompanied by two aides (Simeão and Machado), who reminded him: "Orders must be obeyed." Mendes responded: "Not if those orders are incompatible with any human feeling."

Three days earlier, in a communication to Lisbon, special Foreign Ministry envoy Lopo Simeão warned "that if the Portuguese government does not punish Bordeaux consul immediately it would not be able entirely to disclaim responsibility for these acts that should be considered abuse of power." Simeão termed Mendes's behavior an "act of madness" caused by the tragic circumstances of the war. Not wasting any further time, on June 24, Salazar ordered Mendes's immediate recall to Portugal. A day later, the Portuguese ambassador in Madrid, Pereira, declared that all visas granted by Mendes had been declared invalid. In a telegram to his superiors on June 25, Pereira lashed out viciously against Mendes for "giving shelter to the scum of the democratic regimes and defeated elements fleeing before the German victory. I spent time today in San Sebastian watching the border crossing closely and am sure that Spanish authorities are quite clear as to our government's intentions. It is understood that we have declared visas issued by Portuguese consul in Bordeaux as being null and void."[15]

Ambassador Pereira later related what made him decide to void the visas issued by Mendes. Complaints by the Spanish authorities had led him to have a look for himself at what was happening on the Spanish-Franco border. "I decided to travel to the border at Irún to discover what was happening and take the appropriate measures. Once in Irún I saw that the situation was worsening by the hour and that a conflict with the Spanish authorities was imminent on account of the large mass of people wishing to travel to Portugal. I also saw that most of the visas had been issued by the consul in Bordeaux. I then went to

Bayonne, where I was told by the consul, Mr. Faria Machado, that Consul Aristides de Sousa Mendes had arrived in Bayonne two days previously and had continued to issue visas, ordering him, Faria Machado, to do the same without restriction of any kind. Faria Machado had had the good sense to send a telegram to the ministry communicating these instructions. . . . I immediately put a stop to this order. . . . I encountered Consul Aristides de Sousa Mendes the following day and asked him to explain his extraordinary behavior. Everything I heard, coupled with his disheveled aspect, gave the idea that this man was disturbed and not in his right mind. He appeared not to have the slightest idea of the acts committed and said he had no instructions contradicting the procedure he had followed. . . . The behavior of Mr. Aristides de Sousa Mendes implied such confusion that I immediately informed the Spanish authorities that the visas granted by the Bordeaux consulate to a large number of people still in France were null and void, and I had no doubt in stating my conviction that said consul had lost the use of his faculties."[16] Evidently, in the eyes of the Portuguese ambassador to Spain, a diplomat acting solely from humanitarian motivations was to be considered as having stepped out of his mind.

Much worse awaited Mendes after his return to Portugal on July 8, 1940. Settling down with his family on his country estate in Cabanas de Viriato, Mendes awaited further developments in the government's actions against him. He may not have known that four days earlier, on July 4, Salazar had ordered the opening of disciplinary hearings against him. On August 2, Mendes was presented with a bill of indictment, which included charges relating to the period before June 17, 1940, when he was accused of issuing visas to certain persons without prior approval by the Foreign Ministry, as well as to the period after that date, when he issued thousands of visas to fleeing Jews ("these aliens of people of many nationalities to whom it was forbidden to grant a visa"), including his response to Armando Simeão that "to refuse all those poor people visas constituted an effort that was quite beyond his capabilities." This, the indictment charged, constituted "a situation that was dishonorable for Portugal vis-à-vis the Spanish and German authorities." Mendes was also charged with stamping visas on documents that were not even passports.[17]

Mendes was allowed ten days to prepare his defense. On August 12, he submitted a 20-page document explaining his actions on the visas issue. Regarding Harold Wiznitzer, one such beneficiary, Mendes underlined: "He was going to be interned in a concentration camp. . . . I considered that it was a duty of basic humanity to spare him such an ordeal." As to the many others who were granted transit visas, Mendes wrote: "It was indeed my aim to 'save all those people,' whose suffering was indescribable: some had lost their spouses, others had no news of missing children, others had seen their loved ones succumb to the German bombings which occurred every day and did not spare the terrified refugees. How many must have had to bury someone before continuing their frenzied flight! This filled me with commiseration for so much misfortune. There was another aspect which should not be overlooked, the fate of some of the people if they fell into the hands of the enemy. . . . Many were Jews who were already persecuted and sought to escape the horror of further persecution; finally, an endless number of women from all the invaded countries attempting to avoid being at the mercy of brutal Teutonic sensuality. Add to this spectacle hundreds of children who were with their parents and shared their suffering and anguish. . . . Because of the lack of accommodation this multitude slept in the streets and public squares in all weathers. How many suicides and how many acts of despair must have taken place. I myself witnessed several acts of madness! All this could not fail to impress me vividly, I who am the head of a numerous family, and better than none I understand what it means not to be able to protect one's family. Hence my attitude, inspired solely and exclusively by feelings of altruism and generosity." As to the charge of his "strange" behavior, Mendes countered: "It is obvious that the attitude I took could not fail to cause strangeness. However, it should be noted that everything was strange at the time. My attitude was, in fact, a result of the totally abnormal and insuperable circumstances, of force majeure."

Finally, "it may be that I made mistakes, but if I did so it was not on purpose, for I have always acted according to my conscience. I was guided solely by a sense of duty, fully aware as I was of my responsibilities."[18]

Mendes stated about the events in Bayonne that he had gone there at the request of Consul Machado to solve the problem created by "so many thousands of people—about 5,000 in the street, day and night, without moving, waiting their turn, about 20,000 all told in the city, waiting to get to the consulate. I suggested to my colleague Faria Machado that the only way to resolve the momentary difficulties would be to give them the visas they so desired, and as it was materially impossible to charge emoluments and make the respective registrations, the former should be charged by the police on the Portuguese border when the refugees arrived." As to his staying there so long, "It was my intention to return to my post, but as the French police had cut off communications with Bordeaux, I was forced to remain in Bayonne, where I also started issuing visas. . . . On my return to Bordeaux the city was already occupied by German troops." Mendes ended his defense by stating that "I could not differentiate between nationalities as I was obeying reasons of humanity that distinguish neither race nor nationality." He added that to his knowledge "none of the refugees have disturbed the public peace or abused Portuguese hospitality, during their stay in Portugal, which they hope to leave very soon."[19]

Francisco Calheiros e Meneses, the Portuguese ambassador in Brussels, who had withdrawn to Bordeaux as the Germans advanced, gave testimony in Mendes's defense, but strangely excused his "bizarre" behavior as the result, not of wanton disobedience, but lack of stamina and resolve. Meneses stressed Mendes's great physical fatigue and moral distress, all of which were to be regarded as extenuating circumstances, and added words that in retrospect can serve as guidelines for narrow-minded, stiff-necked bureaucratic behavior. "The witness is well aware that a functionary has no need to be humane when it is a question of obeying orders, whatever they may be. Not all people, however, have the same moral resistance that enables them to confront situations such as the one experienced by the witness and the defendant. . . . It would require unusual courage to resist the pleas and implorations of so many unfortunate people, terrified at the approach of the invader and the justified fear of the concentration camp or, worse, the firing squad. These were no isolated cases in a tranquil environment. . . . Panic is contagious, even physically. . . . First the Belgians: politicians, diplomats, civilian and military authorities; then the French. All overcome by events and incapable of reacting or setting any sort of discipline or attempt at order. . . . It is in the light of this environment that the defendant's attitude must be viewed and judged. Others, possibly less impressionable or physically and morally stronger, might have withstood the torment and resisted the vehement and anguished pleas they heard. The witness believes that the consul to Bordeaux allowed himself, like so many others, to be overcome by the horror of the tragedy he was witnessing." Did Meneses mean that Mendes was "overcome," indeed, by human considerations?[20]

Ambassador Pereira's evidence was the most damning for Mendes. Pereira tried to persuade the disciplinary board that the accused had gone out of his mind. "I got the impression of a deeply perturbed man who was not in his normal state. Sousa Mendes's attitude suggested such a degree of disturbance that I hastened to draw it to the attention of the Spanish authorities. And I asked them to regard any visas that had already been issued as invalid. There was not the slightest doubt in my mind when I told the Spanish authorities that the consul had taken leave of his senses."[21]

Count Tovar, the files rapporteur at the disciplinary proceedings, stated that the defendant "glories in having acted the way he did"; that he "does not confess to infractions; he boasts of services that have made him worthy of praise. The defendant's lack of sense, his lack of judgment, his failure to gasp his responsibilities of public service and his very raison d'être as a functionary is what in my view constitute the most impressive and distressing aspects of these disciplinary proceedings. The defendant is 50 years old and has spent 30 years in the Foreign Service. At this age and after so many years' service, he will not change his mentality or his behavior. . . . The defendant shows neither repentance nor the intention to mend his ways: merely bafflement and boasting." He "will continue to act as he has always acted and be what he has always been."

The case's referee, Paula Brito, analyzed the applicable penalties and, given the extenuating circumstances due to the "exceptional moral climate," recommended "suspension of duties and pay ranging from more than 30 to 180 days." However, the board ruled otherwise, in a slightly milder tone. On the one hand, Mendes was accused of disobedience, premeditation, and multiple offenses, and the extenuating circumstances were rejected. At the same time, the disciplinary board recommended that the punishment should be restricted to a demotion to the rank below that of consul.[22] Salazar, however, rejected the board's relatively mild findings, and on October 30, 1940, he ruled that Mendes should be dismissed from active service for one year, on half-pay, but afterwards be forced to retire. On June 19, 1941, Mendes's appeal was turned down, with the explanation that "a civil servant is not competent to question orders which he must obey."[23]

After his dismissal, Mendes reportedly told Rabbi Kruger (whom he met again in Lisbon): "If thousands of Jews can suffer because of one Catholic [i.e., Hitler], then surely it is permitted for one Catholic to suffer for so many Jews." He added: "I could not have acted otherwise, and I therefore accept all that has befallen me with love." Bereft of any income, and with a family of 12 children to feed, Mendes was forced to sell his estate in Cabanas de Viriato. The Jewish community in Lisbon granted Mendes a monthly allowance and let him eat at its soup kitchen with his children. When he died in 1954, he had been reduced to poverty. Two of his children were helped by the Jewish welfare organization HIAS to relocate to the United States. In 1966, Yad Vashem awarded Aristides de Sousa Mendes, posthumously, the title of Righteous Among the Nations.[24]

The first act of contrition and rehabilitation of Mendes by his own government took place on May 24, 1987, at the Portuguese embassy in Washington. On that occasion, Mário Soares, the country's president, posthumously decorated Mendes with the Order of Liberty. A

Cesar Mendes, son of Aristides de Sousa Mendes, viewing the tree in his father's name, in the Avenue of the Righteous, Yad Vashem, 1990.

year later, on March 13, 1988, the Lisbon parliament officially reha-bilitated Mendes, and his name was restored to the diplomatic corps. The vote was unanimous. The government thereafter ordered damages to be paid to his family. In Portugal there are now eight streets and a secondary school in a Lisbon suburb named after the brave consul. In May 1994, Bordeaux, the city where it all began, paid him tribute. President Soares unveiled a bust of Mendes on Esplanade Charles-de-Gaulle, and a plaque was unveiled on the wall of 14 Quai Louis-XVIII, the former Portuguese consulate office. In Cabanas de Viriato, next to the mausoleum where Mendes is buried, Dom António Monteiro, bishop of Viseu, publicly asked pardon in the name of the church hier-archy for turning down the pleas for help and support by Aristides de Sousa Mendes and his family.[25]

Adriano Moreira, who began his political career in 1946, and served as a minister in Salazar's government, underlined the significance of Mendes' action. "Aristides de Sousa Mendes's actions mark a turning point in the history of international law. From our Western perspective, the legitimacy of political power, which is based on the will of the people, is an original legitimacy; I have been elected democratically, therefore I am legitimate. That legitimacy is no longer adequate. We now need a legitimacy of practice: what have I done with that power? Aristides de Sousa Mendes attacked a principle which had hitherto been absolute: that the original legitimacy must be obeyed. The Nuremberg Tribunal established that people are also responsible to certain principles and that they cannot act against human values. The great quality of Sousa Mendes was that he obeyed the values of mankind."[26]

*   *   *

We end this chapter with the story of another Portuguese diplomat, José Augusto de Magalhães, who was his country's consul in Marseilles. Like Mendes, he felt he could not refuse transit visas to refugees, but instead of disobeying, as Mendes did, he asked to be replaced. In a letter of December 31, 1940, to his superior, Foreign Minister and Head of State António de Oliveira Salazar, Magalhães explained the reasons that led him to this decision—in words showing that his heart was filled with a humanitarian beat. "Our ancestors carved out our homeland on a strip of Europe facing the Atlantic, which today . . . is the only door left open to the rest of the world through which victims of political and religious persecution can escape. Can we, should we, betraying the mission entrusted to us by this position and by the providential government that has made Portugal happy at this difficult moment in history that humanity is now undergoing, obstruct the route and prevent the salvation of those needing to leave this Old World in turmoil?" As for his request to be replaced: "The negativist mission imposed by these latest [immigration] instructions is most unpleasant for me. I have always found it hard to say no—today more than ever. I would ask therefore to be replaced as soon as possible, preferably by a colleague who takes pleasure in pronouncing that word and in creating difficulties even for the most legitimate of requests.

Some creatures are born to do evil and others feel only pleasure from doing good: many consider the former to be strong and the latter weak. Out of a sense of loyalty I must declare that I belong to the latter group." It would be interesting to know what ensued for this man and his diplomatic career.[27]

Chapter 5

Denmark
An Unforeseen Miracle

Georg Ferdinand Duckwitz

Germany invaded Denmark and Norway without warning on April 9, 1940, and the occupation in both countries lasted until the end of the war—May 8, 1945. While in Norway the Germans installed a puppet government headed by Vidkun Quisling, who toed the Nazi line, Hitler surprisingly decided to treat Denmark with a velvet glove. The idea was to make it a "model" protectorate, very much different from the protectorate imposed on the dismembered Czech republic. The Danish government and king were left in power; the Danes and their parliament continued to govern themselves without German interference, and were allowed to retain their army and navy. The Germans recognized Denmark's sovereignty and even assigned a German ambassador to Copenhagen. All this was the result of a cool calculation based on several considerations. For outside consumption, it was meant to show the world that Germany knew how to be generous to a conquered country. There were, however, more realistic and immediate considerations. This approach, it was hoped, would prevent any disruption of the Danish supply of agricultural products to Germany in the quantities to feed the German population under wartime conditions. The price the Germans paid for this concession by agreeing to forgo antisemitic measures against the country's close to 8,000 Jews—a hard pill for the Germans to swallow.

There were, of course, high-level Nazis in Germany who bewailed this situation and asked for more drastic measures to be applied, including helping the very small Danish Nazi Party, headed by Frits Clausen, to gain control of the government, but these elements did not gain the upper hand. In the years following the German occupation, Hitler and his henchmen discussed various alternatives to strengthen Nazi control over a country whose people they considered an ethnic Germanic tribe. However, in the final account, cool considerations prevailed, and Clausen was told to wait for better days, and not do anything that might upset the tranquil situation and the business-like atmosphere in the country.

The German ambassador to Denmark, Cecil von Renthe-Fink, studiously avoided any interference in local politics and supported those who argued that in the interest of the feeding of the German people, it was in Germany's best interest not to drastically alter the tolerant policy. Danish Foreign Minister Eric Scavenius followed an accommodationist policy. In November 1941, after the German attack on the Soviet Union, he had Denmark join the anti-Comintern front of the Axis nations. Around the same time he had the police arrest and detain members of the Communist Party, and allowed a Danish legion to be organized under the aegis of the Waffen-SS to fight the Russians. In September 1942, Hitler again decided not to force the Jewish issue on the Danish government, in light of reports by German representatives in Copenhagen of Danish sensitivity about attempt to dictate their internal policies, including antisemitic measures.[1]

This policy was sustained in spite of efforts of some Germans to force the Jewish issue. The Danish government had told the Germans in no uncertain terms that it considered the Jewish issue a fundamental criterion of German non-interference in Danish affairs.[2]

There were approximately 7,700 Jews in the country, of whom 1,400 were refugees from Central Europe. Denmark had traditionally been good to the Jews, with no overt displays of antisemitism. As stated by David Melchior (son of the chief rabbi, Dr. Marcus Melchior) at the trial of SS chief Adolf Eichmann in Jerusalem, "We were equals among equals in our relations with the Gentile population, with con-

tacts in all walks of life." Insofar as the German occupation was concerned, everybody understood that there existed some kind of modus
vivendi between the Danish authorities and the Germans, under
which the latter would abstain from interfering in Denmark's internal
affairs, and consequently the status of the Jews would suffer no injury.[3]
Thus, while in other parts of Europe under German domination, the
Jewish population was being decimated, no harm befell the small
Jewish community in Denmark. On the local scene, the small and
insignificant Danish Nazi press tried to stir up trouble, and some
attempts were made to damage the Copenhagen synagogue. After
Denmark joined the anti-Comintern pact, an attempt was made to set
fire to the synagogue. The police caught the man; he was tried and sentenced to three years in prison.[4] In addition, a libel action brought
against a Nazi periodical in the Copenhagen District Court led to the
editor's being sentenced to a term in prison and a fine. In December
1941, when King Christian X learned of the first attempt to torch the
Copenhagen synagogue, he sent a warm message to Rabbi Melchior,
in which he expressed his "deep sorrow" at the incident, adding his
"happiness" that the damage was caused was light. He ended: "I wish
you and your community a happy new year. Yours, Christian."[5]

This tranquil state began to unravel in the summer of 1943, as the
Germans enacted a state of emergency in response to continuing acts
of sabotage by the Danish resistance. Convinced of the need to maintain a stricter hold on things, the Germans presented the Danish government with a whole list of demands, including the establishment of
military courts to punish political offenders. Refusing to submit to the
demands, the Danish government resigned, and the king declared
himself a prisoner-of-war. The Danish navy scuttled its ships in the
port of Copenhagen to prevent them from being seized. The Germans,
meanwhile, imposed military law and curfew hours, and declared that
offenders would be shot without warning.

Under the screen of the state of emergency, the Nazi leadership
decided that the time had come to deal with the country's Jews in one
giant swoop. The man responsible for this turn of events, and in
charge of the Nazi attempt to destroy the Jewish community in

Denmark, has been the subject of controversy ever since. SS General
Dr. Werner Best had been handpicked by SS head Heinrich Himmler,
in November 1942, to replace Ambassador Von Renthe-Fink, as
Germany's official representative. He bore the title of plenipotentiary
(*Reichsbevollmaechtigter*), and was, in fact, the top German official in
the country. Best had earlier served in France, where he had favored a
more lenient policy than his SS colleagues. Nominally, an emissary of
Nazi Foreign Minister Joachim von Ribbentrop, he was in fact subordinate to Himmler. His mission in Denmark was to keep the situation
calm at a time when German arms were no longer winning great vic-
tories on the battlefield and it was apparent that the war would drag
on longer than originally foreseen.

When he arrived on the scene in 1942, Werner Best saw no reason
to change the official "hands-off" policy of his predecessor insofar as
the Jewish issue was concerned. He adopted the tactics of attempting,
by moderate measures, to secure a degree of calm and, if possible,
cooperation in the occupied country. One ingredient in this policy, in
which he followed the lines of his predecessor, was an effort to postpone
and delay any proposal to formulate a "Jewish policy" for Denmark.
However, anti-German political manifestations steadily increased, and
in consequence, on August 29, 1943 a state of emergency was declared
and the small Danish army was disbanded. It appeared that the German
military commander, General Von Hanneken, was gaining the upper
hand at the expense of Best. Best was summoned to Hitler's headquarters to give an account of the worsening situation in Denmark, and
Hitler berated him for allowing things to get out of hand.

At this point, according to Georg Duckwitz, a maritime attaché in
the German embassy and Best's confidante to some extent, Best came
up with a way to redress the situation to his own advantage and regain
his former status. He would introduce a new factor that could be
played off against the military by suggesting to Hitler that the time was
ripe to round up and deport the Jews. Best's status in the eyes of the
Fuehrer would be reconfirmed.

Scholars still debate whether Best really wanted the anti-Jewish
operation to actually be carried out. The Danes were already upset

about the state of emergency, and had been promised that it was only a temporary measure. The proposed anti-Jewish action would consequently aggravate the already tenuous state of affairs. In Duckwitz's view, Best miscalculated. Given the lack of German military resources in Denmark, and the tense situation, he expected Hitler, as in the past, to postpone the anti-Jewish drive. The end result? The deportation plan would be foiled, the army would be shown not to be in full control, and Dr. Best would regain his former dominant status.

With this in mind, on September 8, 1943 Best dispatched a cable to Berlin, recommending that if the Jewish question was to be forced on Denmark, it would be best to do so while the state of emergency was still in force. He emphasized that a sizable German police unit would have to be transferred to Denmark. This all comes from Duckwitz's account.[6]

According to another source, on August 24, 1943, a ranting Hitler had reprimanded Best for his soft approach in Denmark and ordered him to take a tougher stand, including an ultimatum to the Danish government. Fearing he might lost his position, Best decided on a step that would restore him in the eyes of his master. Perhaps he felt that the plan to deport the Jews in a single swoop would be foiled by others in the Nazi establishment, for fear that it would further upset the Danish applecart. It was a gamble worth taking for a man apprehensive that his failure to maintain calm in Denmark would place a lid on his career in the SS. He proposed the deportation of the Jews but hoped that others would find ways way to scuttle the operation in order not to aggravate relations with the Danes and jeopardize the delivery of agricultural goods to Germany.[7] Acting on his own, Best dispatched a telegram (no. 1032) on September 8, 1943, asking for permission to carry out a large-scale action against the Jews of Denmark. At this point, Duckwitz entered the picture in a prominent way, first trying to scuttle a Nazi decision and then to derail the planned operation.

The scion of a commercial family in Bremen, Georg Ferdinand Duckwitz, from 1928 to 1933, had worked in Denmark as the director of a coffee firm. Captivated by the mesmerizing appeal of the

*George Ferdinand Duckwitz, the German maritime attaché
in Copenhagen, Denmark.*

Nazis, he joined the Nazi Party in 1932 at the instigation of Gregor
Strasser, and for a short while was employed in Alfred Rosenberg's
Foreign Department. However, he soon became disenchanted with
Nazism and turned into an opponent. In the years immediately preceding the war he worked for the Hamburg-America shipping line,
and this brought him back to Copenhagen in November 1939. His
extensive knowledge of Danish affairs, including the language, led to
his appointment as a shipping expert in the German embassy.

Duckwitz's job was to coordinate commercial shipping ties between
Denmark and Germany to the latter's advantage but without harming
the former's shipping interests. This served the purposes of the
German overlords after they occupied the country, in April 1940 in
that they were able to maintain a business-as-usual climate and thus
allow the Danes a semblance of sovereignty not permitted in other

occupied countries. Duckwitz stated after the war that, aware of the Nazi sensitivity on the Jewish issue, he persuaded his Danish colleagues (for example, in a conversation with Foreign Ministry Scavenius in August 1942) to make sure that the Jewish presence in the economy was not too obvious, without in any way detracting from the full civic rights enjoyed by Jews in the occupied country. He also supported the policy of keeping the Danish Nazi Party on a back burner, quenching their hope for an eventual takeover of the government, a step favored by some Nazis in the German Foreign Office.[8]

When Best appeared on the scene, Duckwitz became the confidant of the new plenipotentiary to the extent that he had any confidants at all. Duckwitz soon influenced him on many important issues. At first, Best was very much opposed to any action against the country's Jews. "In many conversations with him," Duckwitz noted, "he confirmed his position on this matter." Duckwitz added: "Therefore, I find it now, as I did then, humanly tragic that that it was precisely he who unintentionally provoked the action against the Danish Jews." What then took place is mainly culled from Duckwitz's postwar account of the train of events during the following critical days and weeks.[9]

On September 11, Best told Duckwitz about the telegram he had sent to Berlin three days earlier. This led to a serious verbal altercation between the two. That same evening, a worried Best asked Duckwitz to come see him. "I immediately noticed that he had only now realized the effect his unconsidered or too greatly considered step would have. He declared that his telegram was only of academic interest. No unwanted consequences would follow." For, Best told Duckwitz, the Jewish issue would once and for all be laid aside for good. Little did he realize, or at least admit, that he had set in motion a train of events which he could no longer control. At any rate, no longer sure of himself, he gave Duckwitz a free hand to do whatever was necessary to derail the planned deportation of the Jews by stopping the cable from reaching Hitler's desk at his forward military headquarters in East Prussia. Duckwitz decided to immediately fly to Berlin. On the way there, Duckwitz reflected on Best's naiveté. "He did not take into account the primitive reaction of a man like Hitler, who after receiv-

ing the infamous telegram number 1032, would see in it the opportune moment for the persecution of the Jews."[10]

Arriving in Berlin on September 13, Duckwitz soon learned that
Foreign Minister Ribbentrop had already forwarded Best's message to
Hitler's headquarters. Moreover, the Fuehrer had authorized the action.
"I had arrived too late." As Duckwitz pointed out, in the Third Reich,
a Fuehrer decision was like something out of the Gospels. "The highest authority had spoken. Its words were law." Duckwitz immediately
notified Best.[11] In addition, he decided to take matters in his own
hands, perhaps with Best's silent consent. On September 22, he flew to
Stockholm, and secretly met with President Per Albin Hannson, who
asked the Swedish ambassador in Berlin to ask the German Foreign
Ministry to verify Duckwitz's alarming account. The Foreign Ministry
denied that any deportation action was planned—clearly a lie. A similar disclaimer was forthcoming from the Danish Foreign Ministry,
which understandably was not privy to Hitler's decision. When he
returned to Copenhagen on September 25, Duckwitz learned that the
raid on the country's Jews was scheduled to start on the evening of
October 2. Duckwitz suspected that the Norwegian Nazi leader,
Terboven, who happened to have been at Hitler's headquarters at the
same time, had pressed for action against the Danish Jews similar to the
measures against the Norwegian Jews a year earlier.[12]

Duckwitz told Best that there was no way to prevent the action
from taking place, and thus there was only one way out of the impasse.
The German police force was so undermanned that it would be unable
to prevent the Jews from getting out of the country. "If only I could
build a bridge over the Oeresund [separating Denmark from Sweden]
so that all these people could save themselves in Sweden," said Best. To
which Duckwitz responded: "Be assured, the bridge will be built." Best
did not respond, but Duckwitz felt that he had been given the green
light to go ahead with whatever plan he had in mind. Presumably Best
felt that if the plan failed the blame would fall squarely on
Duckwitz.[13]

Earlier, during the tense period of August 1943, Duckwitz had
become acquainted with Eric Nils Ekblad, a counselor at the Swedish

embassy in Copenhagen. Eklad knew that Duckwitz was an opponent of Hitler and the Nazi movement, and passed on this impression to his circle of Danish friends (Hans Hedtoft-Hansen, Alsing Andersen, and H. C. Hansen), assuring them that they could rely on Duckwitz and work with him. However, "we were a bit uncertain," Ekblad later noted, "since it could have been a provocation," with Duckwitz playing the role of an anti-Nazi in order to trap the Danish underground. They felt he was trustworthy, however, and decided to go ahead and cooperate with him to rescue the Jews.[14]

During that same month of August, Ekblad was present at a secret meeting between Duckwitz and members of the Danish Social Democratic Party, such as Hans Hedtoft, Johannes Nordentoft, and Gyth. Duckwitz told them that the Germans planned to use the state of emergency to move against the country's Jews. Ekblad then asked Duckwitz to come to Sweden and meet the country's president, Per Albin Hansson. This indeed took place, on September 22, after Duckwitz's return from Berlin, with Duckwitz and Hansson meeting in Ekblad's home. The president agreed that if the Germans took steps against the Danish Jews, Sweden would in principle be ready to admit them and, as a sop to the Germans, would claim they were being interned. After this meeting, President Hansson asked Ekblad to return to Copenhagen to follow up on events. Ekblad's earlier visa to Denmark had by then expired, and in addition German intelligence suspected him of pro-Russian tendencies. To facilitate his entry to Danish territory, Duckwitz persuaded the German border authorities that the man was traveling incognito on an important diplomatic mission ("which of course was in full agreement with the truth," Duckwitz noted, having in mind something different than what the German border guards were led to believe). Then, on September 25, Duckwitz notified Ekblad that there was something serious in the air, and said he would let him know of further developments in a coded message.[15]

They met three days later, on September 28, together with some clandestine Danish associates (Vilhelm Buhl, Alsing Andersen, Hans Hedtoft-Hansen, and H. C. Hansen). Duckwitz told them that Best was very depressed and, short of disobeying the Fuehrer, was wavering between immediately carrying out Hitler's command (should Hitler not change his mind) and committing suicide. Duckwitz felt that the action would be launched on either Friday afternoon, October 1, or the evening of October 2—that is, within 72 hours. Additional security personnel had been sent from Germany to help with the operation.

It is unclear whether Duckwitz gave this warning with the explicit knowledge or tacit understanding of Dr. Best, but it was Duckwitz who was sticking his neck out. If the Gestapo discovered the leak, Dr. Best would be able to wash his hands of the whole affair, and Duckwitz would bear the brunt of the wrath of Hitler and his stalwarts for allowing the Jews to slip through their fingers. Best must have known that Duckwitz had developed secret contacts with the Danish underground. Duckwitz also passed on this alarming news to Svenningsen, a Danish Foreign Ministry official, who found it hard to believe, as his German counterparts had repeatedly assured him that no such drastic undertaking would take place. Of especial importance was Duckwitz's contact with Hans Hedtoft-Hansen, who during the war years was the main contact between the Social Democratic Party and the leaders of the resistance.[16]

As related by Hedtoft-Hansen after the war. "In the course of the autumn of 1943, rumor had been rampant repeatedly to the effect that the Germans intended now to carry out the deportation of the Danish Jews in the same manner as had happened in other countries. But just as often, the rumors had been denied. Through most of the occupation period I had contact with G. F. Duckwitz, who held the position of maritime expert at the German representation in Copenhagen. In our conversations, we had often been circling around this problem, and Duckwitz had explained that all the leading Germans here, with the possible exception of the Gestapo people, were, in their innermost hearts, against the Jew pogroms and exerting every effort to prevent a similar outrage from happening in Denmark. By the end of September 1943, when anxiety and nervousness was on the increase in all circles, Duckwitz pointed out to me that he was afraid that the game might be overturned now, and on September 28, he came to see me while I was at a meeting in the workers' old meeting place at 22 Romersgade.

'Now the disaster is about to occur,' he said. 'The whole thing is planned in full detail. Ships are going to anchor in the roadstead of Copenhagen; your poor Jewish fellow countrymen who are found by the Gestapo will be forcibly transported to the ships and deported to an unknown fate.' He was white with indignation and shame. I frankly admit that—although in those years, I was accustomed to get many surprising messages from this very man—I became speechless with rage and concern..... This was a bit too satanic. I just managed to say: 'Thank you for the news,' and Duckwitz disappeared. As far as he was concerned, he had done what was humanly possible in order to save the human lives which could be saved at all. My friends (Vilhelm Buhl, H. C. Hansen, and Herman Dedichen) and myself shared the tasks between us."[17]

Ekblad then rode with Duckwitz and the Danish group to look up the Swedish envoy, Gustav Von Dardel. In Ekblad's words, "I told him of the content of my talk with Duckwitz. At first, von Dardel was astonished, for the director of the Danish Foreign Ministry, Nils Svenningsen, had just told him that Dr. Best had a few days earlier assured him that the Germans had no intention of harming the Jews. Von Dardel decided to immediately communicate to his government the new German decision to go ahead with the planned action. On September 30, Von Dardel informed Ekblad that the Swedish ambassador in Berlin had told the German Foreign Ministry that if the action against the Jews took place, Sweden was prepared to admit the Jews to its territory and keep them interned until the end of the war.[18]

On Friday morning, October 1, Duckwitz notified Ekblad that the action would start that same evening; that about 9:00 P.M. Copenhagen would be closed off, and telephone service interrupted. The roundup of Jews would begin. Several boats were already docked in Copenhagen harbor to take the Jews to concentration camps. After passing the information to Von Dardel, Ekblad, with the help of Duckwitz, made his way back to Sweden to inform the Swedish government to be ready to admit the fleeing Jews.[19]

Duckwitz's last desperate hope was that the Wehrmacht (German army) would be unwilling to place all of its forces at the command of the Gestapo. He met secretly with Cammann, the commander of the German patrol vessels in Denmark and a former colleague at the Hamburg-America Line. Cammann promised not to have his boats seaworthy during the critical days of the Jews' escape to Sweden across the narrow channel separating Denmark from Sweden. Indeed, very few German naval patrols were at sea during the next few days. According to Duckwitz, Cammann was later reprimanded for his inaction by the German navy's regional commander.[20]

After the crucial meeting with Duckwitz on September 28, Hedtoft decided to alert the Jewish community. "I myself first went to the villa of the president of the Jewish community, barrister before the Supreme Court Carl Bernhard Henriques, at Charlottenlund. I shall never forget this meeting with the leader of the Danish Jews. . . . I asked to speak alone with Henriques, and when we were left alone I said in my upset, nervous, and unhappy state, 'Henriques, a great disaster is going to happen now. The feared action against the Jews in Denmark is about to come. It is going to happen in this way that, in the night between October 1, and 2, the Gestapo is going to look up all Jews in their homes, and then transport them to ships in the port. You must immediately do everything in order to warn every single Jew in the city. Obviously, we are ready to help you with everything.' Today, I may tell, that Henriques's reaction was different from what I had expected. What he did was to say just two words: 'You're lying,' and it took some considerable time, before I managed to persuade him that he must believe me. 'I do not understand how it can be true,' he kept repeating in despair. 'I have just been in the Foreign Ministry with Permanent Under Secretary Svenningsen, and he has assured me that it is his belief that nothing is going to happen.' I answered that Svenningsen's statements were made in good faith; he could only repeat what the Germans told him."[21]

Next morning, September 29, one day before the Jewish New Year festival, during the early service in the synagogue, Rabbi Marcus Melchior broke the news of the soon-to-be razzia to a startled congregation. Melchior stated that the Rosh Hashana services were hereby suspended, and the Jews were advised not to be in their homes during the next few days and to await further developments. In the meantime, thanks to Duckwitz's early information, three days had been gained which made it possible to make the final preparations for a counter-action by the underground.[22]

The Germans launched the action in the evening hours of October 1, 1943. Close to 500 Jews (many of them elderly) were caught and sent to Theresienstadt on boats docked in Copenhagen harbor. There they were visited by Danish and Swedish Red Cross representatives to make sure that their treatment was a bit better than that of the other unfortunate Jews in that camp, which the Nazis, to fool the world, termed a "model" camp; sort of a vacation retreat, with all sorts of amenities. What they did not disclose was that over 80,000 of the camp's internees were eventually dispatched to the gas chambers of Auschwitz. Of the Danish contingent, 20 died during the passage from Denmark to the camp, and 15 in the camp itself. The others were not sent to Auschwitz and survived. During their one and a half years internment, they regularly received the parcels sent to them through government agencies in Denmark. In 1944, a mission visited them on behalf of King Christian X, to see how they were faring.[23]

As for the overwhelming majority of Danish Jews, some 7,200 were secretly ferried by the Danish resistance across the Sound to Sweden during the months of October and November 1943. The Swedes freely admitted them, and they remained there until the war's end. Rabbi Marcus Melchior's family went into hiding on the island of Falster, arranged by the local bishop; then were ferried across to Sweden together with a group of 30 Jews.[24] On October 3, 1943, Dr. Best was able to proudly announce to Hitler: "My Fuehrer, Denmark is free of Jews (*judenfrei*)." Of course, this was not at all so, for most of the country's Jews were still on Danish soil, but in hiding, and awaiting their secret crossing into Sweden, which took place during that and the following month. But to outward appearances, no more Jews were to be seen in public—at least, until the war's end. As for Duckwitz's motivation in this large-scale rescue effort, he stated after the war, "Everyone is obliged to imagine himself in another person's position in a given situation. I do not think that my life is more important than

George Ferdinand Duckwitz lighting the Eternal Flame
in the Hall of Remembrance, Yad Vashem, 1971.

the lives of 7,000 Jews."[26] He certainly faced personal risks. Kannstein, the civilian director general at the German general head-quarters, cautioned Duckwitz that he had been singled out by the Gestapo, who were waiting for the opportune moment to move him out of Copenhagen. Duckwitz stated after the war that he told Kannstein he would continue to do whatever he could to prevent the implementation of the Fuehrer's order to deport the Jews. In the words of historian Leni Yahil, "There is no doubt of Duckwitz's major role in the Danish people's undertaking to save the Jews. His early warning on the deportation about to take place made it possible for Danes and Danish organizations to warn the Jews in time. We know of no other ranking German official who was involved in such a rescue mission, at a personal risk to himself."[27] After the war, Duckwitz returned to Copenhagen as a Foreign Ministry commercial attaché. His new diplomatic career took him to Helsinki, ambassador to Denmark, head of the East European Department in the Foreign Office, and ambassador to India. In 1971, Yad Vashem bestowed on Georg Ferdinand Duckwitz the prestigious honor of Righteous Among the Nations.[28]

Chapter 6

Warsaw, Genoa, and Rhodes
Yugoslav, Swedish, and Turkish Diplomats

The stories in this chapter take us to three different places, Warsaw, Genoa, and the Greek island of Rhodes, and to three diplomats representing three different countries, who stepped forward and intervened to save Jews from the Nazis. We begin with Warsaw.

Franjo Puncuch

Born in Slovenia, Franjo Puncuch studied in Warsaw and before the war served there as Yugoslavia's honorary consul, as well as commercial and economic attaché. In 1931 he married Janka Glocer, a Polish Jew. After the German conquest of Poland, he utilized his diplomatic privilege to extend help to Jews in Warsaw.[1] Among those he helped were Dr. Eva Lawendel and her daughter Wanda (born 1930), and other members of their family. He arranged their escape from the Warsaw ghetto in the summer of 1942 and found them a residence on the Aryan (i.e., non-Jewish) side, under assumed names, with a Polish family. In Wanda's words, "Mr. Puncuch found the false birth certificates for me, and he and my aunt supported me financially, as well as paid the family I lived with [name omitted]. He was the best father to me [her own father was with the Polish army in Russia]."

Puncuch also helped other Jews with safe places of residence, such as Bianka Kraszewski and her mother, to whom he gave money to defray expenses in their secluded hiding place. Once, when Bianka was between places, she stayed in Puncuch's apartment for a few days.

*Franjo Puncuch, the pre-war Yugoslav
consul-general in Warsaw, Poland.*

From there she was taken to a villa belonging to Puncuch in
Konstancin, where she remained hidden for a few weeks, until another hiding place was arranged for her. He also helped the family of Josef
Meshorer, whose mother was friendly with Mrs. Puncuch. The
Meshorers formally turned over their business to Franjo Puncuch, as
well as personal assets and valuables, to avoid confiscation by the
Germans. He in turn provided the Meshorer family with funds to ease
their existence inside the Warsaw ghetto, and later when they escaped
and lived on the Aryan side of the city.

Andrei, Franjo Puncuch's son, born in 1933, recalls that "from
1940/41, and until the Warsaw Ghetto uprising there were constant
visitors passing through our house, and hidden for a few days until safe
places could be found for them. I never knew their names or where
they were going. It was safer this way in case we were arrested. My
father had adequate funds from the company he was running to help

financially and to pay off the blackmailers." Puncuch had become the trustee of several Jewish businesses, to avoid their confiscation by the Germans, and this later proved of great financial help. Unfortunately, Puncuch was accidentally killed, on September 9, 1944, by a stray bullet during the Polish uprising in Warsaw during the summer and fall of that year. In 2004, he was awarded the Righteous title.[2]

Elow Kihlgren

In 1998, Max Stempel wrote to Yad Vashem of the help he had received from the Swedish consul in Genoa, Italy. Stempel fled from Belgium to France in November 1942. He was living in Nice when Italy surrendered to the Allies on September 8, 1943. Stempel and nine other Jews crossed into Italy from France in the mistaken belief that they would be safe there. However, arriving in Valdiere, they learned that the Germans had preceded them. A priest told them: "I know that you are Jewish refugees from France, and you cannot survive the hard winter in this mountainous region. We will help you. First, go to Genoa." And he gave them the name of Father Francesco Repetto. This kind cleric hid the group in a monastery, where they were told to remain silent, but this was difficult for the small children. After some 20 days, Repetto referred Stempel to Elow Kihlgren, a Swedish businessman and honorary consul-general. Kihlgren found an apartment for the nine of them and provided them with food. A week later, he came back with Gyda Boesgaard, the daughter of the Finnish consul, who arranged for Mrs. Mina Stempel and her two children (Clara, 4, and Jenny, 2) to stay with them in a villa outside the city, and far from the nightly air raids. It was thought that this place would be less stressful for the children, who would be able to play in the villa's garden. After three weeks, Mrs. Stempel rejoined the others in the Genoa apartment, evidently because the hosts feared keeping them for too long.

In April 1944, Kihlgren was brought in by the Gestapo for questioning on the charge of aiding Allied pilots whose planes had crashed. He was released upon the intervention of a Vatican representative, but was warned by his interrogator, "You certainly know the Jew Max

Stempel, from Belgium. Tell us, at least, where he can be found."
Kihlgren, naturally, denied any knowledge of Stempel. He decided,
however, that the Stempel group had to be moved out of the country
as quickly as possible, and he began making the necessary arrangements with border smugglers. However, they would not take the children along the dangerous route, so Clara and Jenny Stempel were
placed in a religious home. The adults (the Engelmans and their four
adult children, and Mina and Max Stempel) proceeded to the Swiss
border and crossed it safely, with the help of paid border smugglers.
Ten months later, the two Stempel children were also taken across the
border and reunited with their parents in Montreux. In September
1944, the Germans expelled Elow Kihlgren from Italy. After the war,
he returned to Genoa and to his position of honorary Swedish consul-
general. He died in 1974. In 2001, Yad Vashem conferred upon him
the title of Righteous Among the Nations.[3]

Selahattin Ülkümen

Moving eastwards, far removed from Europe's battlefields, we come
upon the tranquil Greek island of Rhodes off the coast of Turkey—a
popular summer resort in the Aegean Sea. A Jewish community existed in Rhodes since pre-Roman days, and the ancient Jewish historian
Flavius Josephus mentioned King Herod the Great's visit to the Jewish
community there in 40 B.C.E. The Jewish community of Rhodes had
its ups and downs under various rulers: Romans, Arabs, Crusaders,
and Ottoman Turks. Under Turkish rule, which began in the sixteenth
century, Jewish life prospered, and produced learned rabbis. In 1912,
the island came under Italian rule, which lasted until September 1943,
when Italy capitulated to the Allies, and the Germans took over. There
were then 1,700 Jews in Rhodes. Already losing the war, the Germans
decided not to miss out on this ancient Jewish community, and on July
24, 1944, they deported all of the island's Jews to Auschwitz. Only 160
survived the depredations of the camp.[4] A few dozen Jews escaped the
Nazi inferno, thanks to the intervention of the local Turkish consul-
general, Selahattin Ülkümen.

Our source is Mathilde Turiel, born in Izmir, Turkey, in 1910. She had moved to Rhodes in 1933, and in 1944 was a housewife with two children. She had kept her Turkish citizenship and had also automatically obtained Italian nationality upon her marriage to her husband; her two sons, consequently, had dual citizenship—Italian and Turkish. Life went on peacefully even after the war began. In Turiel's words, "The Jews of Rhodes were unaware of what was happening to the Jewish population of the rest of Europe and did not know what was going to happen to them. We had no news because all communications were cut off; radios had been confiscated." The war on the continent was far away, very far; North Africa had been liberated, and the Allies had landed in Italy. But this tranquil situation changed when the German occupation began. But here, too, nothing much occurred for months. Then, in July 1944, with their troops in full retreat on all fronts, the Germans decided to round up the island's Jews. On July 18, they ordered all the Jewish men to report to Gestapo headquarters n the following day; the next day, the womenfolk and children were also told to report. In Mrs. Turiel's words: "We were warned that if we did not do so, our husbands would be killed." As Mrs. Turiel was on her way with her two children and was about to enter the German headquarters, she met Ülkümen at the door. "This was the first time I had ever seen him. He told me who he was and that I should not enter. He instructed me to wait a few blocks away while he went in to attempt to release my husband and save us from imprisonment. The other women and children had already entered the headquarters. We were the last."

As later related by her husband who was inside the headquarters, Ülkümen told the Germans that he wanted the release of all the Turkish citizens and their husbands. Only about 15 men and women were Turkish, but Ülkümen included 25 to 30 others on his list even though he knew they were no longer Turkish citizens because they had allowed their citizenship to lapse. He was evidently trying to put some more names on his list. The Gestapo officers first objected, then bowed to Ülkümen's demand, and allowed the 40 to 45 Jews on his list (including Turiel's family) to head to the Turkish consulate in order to obtain documents certifying their Turkish nationality. However, documents could not be provided for everyone, so Ülkümen used another tactic, stating that under Turkish law, spouses of Turkish citizens were also under the jurisdiction of Turkey, irrespective of their own citizenship, and he insisted that all the non-Turkish spouses had to be set free. By then, the remaining 1,700 Jews were being boarded on ships on their way to the Greek mainland, from where they were scheduled to proceed by train to Auschwitz. The 40 to 50 Jews freed at Ülkümen's insistence were put under surveillance for a while. A few weeks later, as their front deteriorated, the German troops were withdrawn from Rhodes island, and Ülkümen's protected Jews breathed freely again. In January 1988, Mrs. Turiel, living in New York, learned Ülkümen's address and wrote to him to express her family's deep gratitude. She met him again that same year at an Anti-Defamation League dinner in Ülkümen's honor.

Emilia Tarika was another person saved by Selahattin Ülkümen. Born into the Mizrahi family in Turkey, she married a man of Italian nationality. She remembered the restrictions imposed by the Germans when they appeared on the island in September 1943, including the requisitioning of radios. When the Germans ordered all Jews to present themselves, "in total despair, I decided to consult the consul. He resided quite far away, and there was no transportation because of the gasoline shortage, so I went on foot. Suddenly a car stopped near me, and the man (it was the consul) asked me why I was so upset. I explained the situation, and he calmed me. I emphasized that there were others like me, married to foreigners. He told me that all of us should come at 11:00 A.M., outside the Albergo dell Termi Hotel, where he was scheduled to meet Nazi officials. Well, the person who told me all this was the man I was so desperately looking for in my despair, the Turkish consul, Mr. Ülkümen. I have always considered this incidental meeting to have been a miracle from heaven." After leaving the hotel, Ülkümen told the crowd of frightened people that he had managed to save the husbands. "Only someone who has trembled in the presence of the SS is capable of appreciating the courage of

*Selahattin Ülkümen, the Turkish
consul-general in Rhodes, Greece.*

Mr. Selahattin Ülkümen, who placed himself in front of the evil Nazi animals, and snatched Jews from their fangs." Some time later, the men were released. The number of people freed was now 45. In the meantime, the other Jews had been deported. In Mrs. Tarika's words, "We witnessed the exodus of all the Jews of Rhodes, on foot, old people, women and children with their luggage; some abandoned them."

Albert and Renata Amato also owed their life to Ülkümen. The Amatos too were Italian, but Albert's mother had kept her Turkish passport, and this fact miraculously saved their lives. By a lucky stroke, Mrs. Amato met the Turkish consul in the street and told him what was happening. She asked whether her husband's mother had to obey the German order to report. He categorically said no and stated that any Turkish subject, irrespective of religion, was under his protection. The Amatos were added to Ülkümen's saving list. Other persons saved by Ülkümen were Moise and Victoria Soriano, their two children, and Moise Soriano's parents (who were not Turkish citizens), Isy and Batami Alhadeff, Joseph and Sara Alhadeff, Maurice Amato, Albert

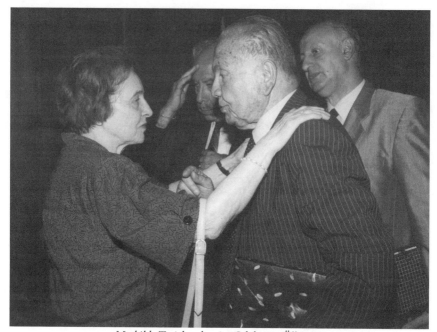

Mathilde Turiel embracing Selahattin Ülkümen,
the Turkish consul-general in Rhodes, Greece, who saved her life.

and Hartiye Franco, and Enrico Franco; Leon Rosa, Maurice and Vittoria Soriano as well as Elio and Rita Soriano.

On September 1, 1944, Turkey severed relations with Germany. According to one report, Ülkümen's residence was bombed by the Germans before he left the island, and his wife was severely wounded. The bombing has never been explained. At any rate, Ülkümen hurriedly left Rhodes on a Red Cross boat that took him and his wife to Athens, where he stayed in the Turkish embassy until February 1945. He then returned to Turkey. In 1989, Yad Vashem bestowed the Righteous title on Selahattin Ülkümen. On a visit to Israel in 1990, he planted a tree in the Avenue of the Righteous at Yad Vashem.[5]

Chapter 7

Budapest
The Apocalypse

Introduction

The tragedy that befell Hungarian Jewry in 1944 came when the tide of the war had turned definitely to Germany's disadvantage. It was merely a question of time before Nazi Germany would be vanquished by the Allies. Hitler, however, had a different agenda in mind. He was determined to go down fighting to the bitter end, taking with him all of Europe's remaining Jews. Hungary, with its large Jewish population of close to 800,000, loomed large in his demented mind. In order to properly appreciate the chaotic situation in Hungary when it was suddenly struck with the full fury of the Holocaust after the German invasion on March 19, 1944, one needs to trace the historical background of this troubled country. Under the Treaty of Trianon at the end of World War One, Hungary was forced to give up large chunks of its territory, mostly inhabited by ethnically non-Hungarian peoples, but resulting in the loss of two-thirds of its former size as part of the Austro-Hungarian Empire. This left the Jews as the only large visible minority in Hungary, with tragic consequences during the Nazi period. In 1920, Admiral Miklós Horthy assumed leadership of the country as regent after a brief spell of Communist rule under Béla Kun. With the appointment of Gyula Gömbös as prime minister in October 1932, Hungary began to align itself with Nazi Germany. Between 1938 and 1941, Hitler rewarded Hungary's alliance with him by enabling it to regain part of its lost territories—first a chunk of the dismembered Czechoslovakian state (the provinces of Kosice and Carpatho-Ruthenia), then lands from Romania (northern Transylvania) and Yugoslavia (the Novi Sad region). In 1941, enlarged Hungary had a population of 14.5 million, of whom 725,000 identified themselves as Jews (184,500 in Budapest alone). In addition there were approximately 100,000 Jewish converts to Christianity (62,350 in Budapest).[1]

The price to Hungary for aligning itself with Nazi Germany was the adoption of certain anti-Jewish measures. The first antisemitic law, on May 29, 1938, set a 20 percent ceiling on Jews in various professions in the economic field. This was reduced to 6 percent in the second antisemitic law, on May 4, 1939, which also introduced a racial definition of who was to be considered Jewish. Neither of these laws was fully satisfactory, so on August 2, 1941, with Hungary a military participant in Germany's war against the Soviet Union, a new law slavishly emulated Nazi Germany's 1935 Nuremberg Laws by prohibiting marriage and sexual relations between Jews and non-Jews. At the same time, however, Hungary consistently opposed German pressure to implement a Nazi-style Final Solution in its own territory and continued to protect its 825,000 Jews (which included the approximately 100,00 converts identified as Jews under the racial law of 1941), as well as provide a haven to thousands of refugees from Poland, Slovakia, and other areas.[2]

Before World War One, Jews were overwhelmingly represented in the professions of law and medicine, as well as in the press, publishing, film, and theater. This development had not always been viewed with alarm, for the Jews were assimilating into Hungarian life at an increasing rate.[3] As Hungary edged ever closer to an alliance with Nazi Germany, however, Jews began paying the price, especially after Hungary joined the war on the side of Germany. This alone led to more than 60,000 Jewish casualties, most of whom had been mobilized into so-called labor battalions. Even more harrowing was the fate of the 16,000 Jews in the annexed Carpatho-Ruthenia region, turned over to the Germans in August 1941 and subsequently massacred near Kamenets Podolsk, Ukraine, as well as the 700 Jews in and around the

Novi Sad region (of the former Yugoslavia) shot by Hungarian troops in January–February 1942. As for the labor battalions, with the retreat of the Hungarian army, tens of thousands of these men were turned over to the Germans, and hundreds were in turn killed. The surviving members of the labor battalions were herded to Germany, where most of them ended up in concentration camps. But the bulk of Hungarian Jewry remained safe from physical abuse, and the Germans were clearly unhappy about what they saw as Hungary's excessively mild anti-Jewish measures. Horthy met with Hitler at Schloss Klessheim in April 1943 and was sternly lectured to follow the example of Poland, where "the Jews who did not want to work were simply shot." Upon his return, Horthy told his cabinet how he had defended himself against Hitler's charge that the treatment of Jews in Hungary was "too mild" and he was not taking "far-reaching actions in the extermination of the Jews as Germany had done."[4]

The Hungarians anticipated the approaching Russian occupation with great anxiety and naively hoped that American and British troops would get there first. Secret contacts with the Allies were held in Istanbul and Stockholm, with negotiations continuing through 1943 and up to March 1944.[5] The Germans, however, took no chances. To prevent Hungary from stepping out of the Axis coalition and seeking a separate peace with the Allies, Hitler ordered the invasion of Hungary, which began on March 19, 1944, and virtually ended Hungary's existence as a sovereign state. With the invasion came 500 to 600 Gestapo and Security Service (SD) men and a Special Commando of 200–300 men under SS Colonel Adolf Eichmann, charged with implementing the Final Solution. Edmund Veesenmayer, Hitler's personal plenipotentiary, had greatly expanded powers (to keep close tabs on the new puppet Hungarian leadership), and SS General Otto Winkelmann was the representative of SS chief Heinrich Himmler, with jurisdiction over all the police and SS agencies, including Eichmann's special *Sonderkommando*. The Final Solution was about to descend on Hungarian Jewry with the full fury of an avalanche.[6]

The fact that Horthy had decided to stay on as head of state of the new puppet regime has given rise to the charge that he lent legitimacy to the placement of the Hungarian state apparatus at the service of the Germans. The free hand that Horthy gave to the new satellite government, headed by Döme Sztójay, who served concurrently as prime minister and minister of foreign affairs, proved disastrous for the Jews. The new government was filled with known antisemites, such as Andor Jaross, the minister of the interior, István Antal, minister of justice, and especially László Endre and László Baky, both of them state secretaries in the Interior Ministry, who were particularly zealous for the speedy liquidation of the country's Jews. As for the German overlords, equally intent on decimating this large Jewish stronghold, they wanted to move as quickly as possible in order to finish the job before the Red Army arrived. Hungarian Jewry was consequently subjected to the swiftest and most ruthless destruction process of the war, and with the notable exception of Budapest, the country was emptied of its large Jewish population in only a few months.[7]

Sadly, before the German invasion, the Jewish population had generally discounted the horror stories emanating from Nazi-occupied countries. What happened in Poland, they said, could not possibly happen in civilized Hungary. As for the Jewish leadership, it failed to take any precautionary contingency measures and neglected to inform the people about the Final Solution program being implemented in the other parts of Europe. More graphic information came from Rudolf Vrba (Walter Rosenberg) and Alfred Wetzler (Josef Lanik), who miraculously escaped from Auschwitz on April 7, 1944, and reached Slovakia on April 21, where they told their story to local Jewish leaders. The Vrba-Wetzler Report contained a detailed description of the camp facilities, processing of the incoming deportees, the selection, tattooing, and horrific gassing and cremation. Their report reached Budapest and was delivered to Ottó Komoly and Rabbi Fülöp Freudiger, of the Jewish community, as well as to top leaders of the Christian community, including Catholic Cardinal Jusztinián Serédi and Bishop László Ravasz, the head of the Reformed Church. It had previously been turned over to Giuseppe Burzio, the papal nuncio in Bratislava (who was expected to deliver it to the Vatican). The Jewish leaders in Hungary decided to keep the Vrba-Wetzler report confidential in order to prevent a panic. In the meantime, on June 19, 1944, Miklós (Moshe) Krausz, the Jewish Agency representative in Budapest, secretly forwarded an abbreviated version of the report to Switzerland, together with a memorandum on the ghettoization and deportation of the Jews in Hungary. The material was smuggled into Switzerland by Florian Manoliu, a member of the Romanian legation in Bern, who had close relations with George Mandel-Mantello, a Jewish businessman originally from Transylvania, who was then serving as the first secretary of the consulate-general of El Salvador in Geneva. Mantello made sure to give the report wide coverage in the Swiss press. This contributed to the intervention of world leaders, including President Roosevelt, the king of Sweden, and Pope Pius XII, all of whom urged Horthy to halt the deportation of Jews. By then, some 420,000 Hungarian Jews had already been deported to the death camps.[8]

Before this, and soon after the occupation began, the Germans methodically set in motion the machinery of destruction. They began with random arrests of up to 7,000 Jews, who were eventually sent to Auschwitz. A flood of anti-Jewish laws, spurred by the Germans and promulgated by the new Hungarian government, descended on the Jewish community. The new laws included prohibitions on ownership of telephones, radios, and automobiles, and on travel and changes of residence. The dismissal of Jewish civil servants and lawyers, and the exclusion of Jews from the press and theatrical establishments, was followed with the compulsory wearing of the Yellow Star. Jews were also barred from using public baths and swimming pools and could not frequent public restaurants, catering services, pastry and coffee shops. They were ordered to declare their property ownership, including a listing of all jewelry and gold, securities, and savings and checking accounts, and their safe-deposit boxes in the banks were blocked. Jewish commercial and industrial establishments were ordered closed, and later reopened under Christian managers assigned by the Hungarian government.[9]

As for the deportation process, the advance of the Red Army made it necessary for the Germans and their Hungarian collaborators to act quickly. On April 7, 1944, Interior Ministry State Secretary László Baky ordered mayoral, police, and gendarmerie organs to prepare for the roundup, concentration, and deportation of all Jews, without regard to sex, age, or illness. The master plan called for Jews to be concentrated in temporary ghetto-like stations in places totally isolated from the other parts of the city, and in centers with adequate rail facilities to facilitate swift entrainment and deportation, with the Hungarian gendarmerie and police officials forcing the Jews to surrender their valuables. As the Eichmann SS team was relatively small, the massive arrest and deportation of the Jews was to be carried out by thousands of Hungarian gendarmes under the command of Lieutenant Colonel László Ferenczy.[10]

On April 26, the Hungarian government approved this criminal act, under the blatant lie that the deportees were being loaned to Germany for the performance of labor duties, adding that the "workers" were to be accompanied by their families. At a conference on May 8–9 attended by State Secretary László Endre and top administration, police, and gendarmerie officers from around the country, and chaired by László Ferenczy, it was decided that the Jews of Carpatho-Ruthenia, northeastern Hungary, and Northern Transylvania were to be deported first, between May 15 and June 11. Alternative deportation routes were discussed at a later meeting, with the decision that four trains a day were to be routed to Auschwitz through eastern Slovakia.[11] These plans went hand in hand with the calming of Jewish fears, and lulling the Jewish leadership to inaction with false promises. On the day of the German invasion, March 19, SS officers Krumey and Wisliceny assured Jewish leaders that there would be no arrest, no violation of personal and property rights, and no deportation simply because someone was Jewish. Continuing to lull the Jewish community into inaction, on March 31, 1944 Eichmann assured a Jewish delegation that the short-term anti-Jewish measures would only last until the war's end, after which Jews would be free to do whatever they wanted.

The Jewish leaders deluded themselves with the thought that the fast approach of the Russian army, coupled with the precarious military situation of the Germans, would enable the Jews to somehow ride out the storm.[12]

The deportations proceeded with swift precision, beginning on April 16 with the arrest of 14,000 Jews in Munkács and thousands of others in the surrounding region. People were awakened by Hungarian gendarmes at the crack of dawn, given only a few minutes to pack essential clothes and any food they happened to have in the house, and taken to the local synagogues, where they were robbed of their money, jewelry, and valuables. Then, after a few days, they were marched to the nearest concentration centers, normally brickyards and lumberyards. The overcrowding was terrible, what with the lack of sanitary facilities. In some places, many were kept for several weeks under the open skies. The Hungarian government, which was informed of the "success" of this initial operation, gave its approval. This was followed on May 3 with the roundup of close to 160,000 Jews in Northern Transylvania, with temporary ghettos set up in brickyards, a glass factory, stables, farms, and pigsties. The deportations began on schedule on May 15, with each train carrying 3,000 Jews crammed 70 to 90 in each padlocked freight car. During the first 24 days, 289,357 Jews had been deported in 92 trains—a daily average of 12,056 people deported. On the whole, from May 15 to July 8, between 434,00 and 437,000 were deported, mostly to Auschwitz, where most were gassed upon arrival. The whole countryside had been cleared of Jews. The stage was set for the more than 200,000 Jews in Budapest.[13]

Following the storm raised by the publication in Switzerland and elsewhere of the Auschwitz Report, and the protests from foreign leaders, Horthy decided, on July 7, to suspend the deportations scheduled for the capital's Jews. The Jews in Budapest had been spared. Eichmann and his men were told to leave the country. Before they left they rounded up 1,220 imprisoned Jews in Kistarca camp, outside Budapest, and an additional 1,500 internees in Sárvár, and sent them to Auschwitz.[14]

In Budapest itself, the Jews had in the meantime been restricted to 2,681 so-called Jewish houses marked with the Yellow Star sign. The number of such houses was subsequently reduced to 800. The relocation decree was issued on June 16, over the signature of the mayor, and the relocation was ordered completed within eight days. After that deadline, no Jew was to be found anywhere except in a Yellow Star house. Movement outside these crowded houses was restricted to the hours between 2:00 and 5:00 P.M. As for the thousands of converts in Budapest, they were assigned separate houses marked with a Yellow Star and a Cross. On August 5, 1944, rumors about the impending renewal of deportations were rampant, but this was rescheduled for August 25. In the meantime, on August 21, the diplomatic representatives of the neutral countries and the Vatican delivered a blunt note warning that the resumption of deportations would "deal a death blow to the reputation" of Hungary. The deportations scheduled for August 25 did not take place, the primary reason being Romania's abandonment of the Axis two days earlier, and soon thereafter its declaration of war on both Germany and Hungary, its former allies. Horthy followed this up, on August 29, by replacing Döme Sztójay with General Géza Lakatos as prime minister as part of a renewed effort to extricate Hungary from the losing war. The situation for the remaining Jews had improved, and Horthy still hoped that the Russians could be prevented from entering Hungary by the declaration of a unilateral cease-fire.[15]

On October 15, 1944, with the Russians already on Hungarian soil, Horthy decided to act, suddenly declaring Hungary's exit from the war. However, the Germans had prepared themselves for this, and that same day allowed the pro-Nazi Arrow Cross (Nyilas) party to stage a coup d'état and remove Horthy from power. He was replaced by the leader of the Arrow Cross, Ferenc Szálasi. Frenzied gangs of Arrow Cross youth immediately took to the streets and began an anarchic spree of murder and looting, killing several hundred Jews on the first night of the coup, dragging them to the banks of the Danube and dumping them into the river. The Arrow Cross terror continued unabated in the following weeks, and on December 28, they attacked the Jewish Hospital on Bethlen Square, capturing 28 able-bodied Jews whom they massacred two days later. On January 11, 1945, they robbed, tortured, and massacred 92 patients, doctors, and nurses at the Maros Street Hospital in Buda. An estimated 17,000 Jewish lives were lost to these marauding bands. Some of the most horrible atrocities were committed by a gang led by Father András Kun, a vitriolically antisemitic Catholic priest, who was executed as a war criminal after the liberation.[16]

SS Colonel Eichmann wasted no time and returned to Budapest on October 17. The next day he reached an agreement with the new regime for the transfer of 50,000 Jews for work in German plants. They were to be rounded up by Hungarian gendarmes. In addition, 35,000 Jews, including 10,000 women, were organized into labor companies and deployed to dig trenches and construct defensive fortifications along the southern and southeastern perimeters of the capital. Some died on the way to their work assignments; others were tortured to death; still others died of exhaustion and starvation, with many more quartered under the open sky. The survivors were destined to join a death march to Hegyeshalom, where they were handed over to the Germans for forced labor assignments in Vienna and vicinity. These marches officially began on November 8, in inclement weather, and many fell by the wayside. Those left behind in Budapest were moved out of the Jewish houses. Some 63,000 (eventually rising to 70,000) were herded into 162 buildings in a designated ghetto. The only exceptions, numbering about 15,000 (the figure eventually rose to 25,000), were the "protected" Jews—that is, Jews who had "protective passes" issued by the diplomats of the neutral countries (more fully described later in this chapter)—who were moved into an International Ghetto. Of these, 7,800 were under the protection of Switzerland, 4,500 of Sweden, 2,500 of the Vatican, 698 of Portugal, and several hundred of Spain. Here, too, conditions were far from ideal, since the Arrow Cross was on a rampage, plundering and killing Jews even in the government-sanctioned "protected" houses. In the meantime the city came under siege from the advancing Red Army, which began an intermittent bombardment that added to the havoc, confusion, and mayhem. Conditions in the ghetto were horrendous, with patients dying for lack of medical care, and bodies began to be stacked up. When the ghetto on the Pest side of the city was liberated on January 17, 1945 by the Red Army, approximately 3,000 bodies were still awaiting burial.[17]

The losses sustained by Hungarian Jewry were stupendous, considering the swiftness (relative to other countries) of the German and Hungarian actions against them. Prior to the German occupation of Mach 19, 1944, the Jewish community suffered approximately 63,000 casualties during the war (42,000 in the labor battalions, 20,000 deported as aliens, with many massacred near Kamenets-Podolsk, and close to 1,000 in the Bácska region). During the German occupation, the toll of Jewish victims was 501,507 casualties—of which close to 440,00 were deported to Auschwitz between May 15 and July 8. Overall losses thus amounted to 564,507. In Budapest, 119,000 Jews survived: about 69,000 in the ghetto, 25,000 in the protected houses of the International Ghetto, and an estimated 25,000 in hiding. An additional 25,000 luckily survived the depredations of the concentration camps and labor battalions.[18]

Of significance in this tragic story is the effort by a team of diplomats to stem the avalanche of terror. Budapest is where many diplomats in 1944 joined hands to ward off and disrupt the German-Hungarian plan to deport the city's Jews. They were largely successful in this endeavor. Thanks to their superhuman efforts in a setting of apocalyptic dimensions, tens of thousands of Jewish lives were spared. The Budapest rescue saga is proof of the great achievement made possible by a coalition of diplomats intent on going the extra mile in the cause of fundamental human values.

The Swiss Team

Carl Lutz

The Swiss representatives in Budapest were among the first foreign diplomats to help Jews during this tumultuous and tragic period. This is especially true for Carl Lutz, the Swiss diplomatic official charged with representing the interests of countries that did not have diplomatic ties with Hungary or were at war with it. Historians agree that in many respects Lutz led the way and his diplomatic colleagues followed. The idea of how to help may have come to Lutz in his capacity as representing British interests, which included responsibility for matters pertaining to emigration to Palestine, then ruled by Britain. For this purpose he allowed Miklós (Moshe) Krausz, a Hungarian Jew who headed the Budapest branch of the Palestine Jewish Agency, to open an office dealing with emigration matters in the Glass House, a building at 29 Vadasz Street purchased by the Swiss legation as an adjunct office for its emigration and foreign interests section, and therefore enjoying extraterritorial status.[19]

After the war, Lutz stated that when the Germans invaded Hungary, on March 19, 1944, "For me as a Christian, the care for Jews was a moral command, and I sought to assist the thousands who were condemned to death." On the day following the German invasion, "thousands of frightened people lined up who sought protection," for they knew that Switzerland, as a neutral country, represented a host of foreign nations, and therefore was in a better position than other neutral legations to issue visas. As a first priority, Lutz went to see the all-powerful German ambassador, Veesenmayer, as well as the Hungarian foreign minister, to get their approval for allowing a contingent of several thousand Jews to leave for Palestine. His proposal was sent to Berlin. While awaiting a response, Lutz tried another scheme. On June 26, 1944, when the Hungarian government approved his request for the emigration of the 7,000 Jews named by Lutz and some 800 more requested by representatives of other neutral states, Lutz immediately exploited this venue to interpret the 7,000 to mean family heads, which in effect meant emigration possibilities for many more; in fact, for about 40,000 people. Within a short while, a Swiss collective passport with 2,200 names was completed and supplied with a Hungarian exit visa and a Romanian transit visa. The fate of this undertaking—the departure of so large a group—was now in the hands of the Germans, Hungary's overlords, and the matter was referred to Hitler himself. After six tense weeks, Lutz was told that Hitler was willing to consent to the plan, but on the condition that a much larger group of about 100,000 Jews was to be "lent" for "labor" in Germany. In other words the Germans demanded the resumption of the deportations that had been stopped in early July 1944. Lutz repeated his request several times, but it was formally rejected by the Germans on August 14. Romania's extrication from the Axis alliance nine days later rendered the whole issue impracticable.[20]

Who was this man who, as a career diplomat, went out of his way to try to save as many Jews as possible, even inviting the representative of a Zionist organization to work out of a Swiss-owned building in order to assist in the rescue of Jews? Born in Walzenhausen (Appenzell canton), Switzerland, in 1895, Carl Lutz stated that his mother taught him that "one must in every situation be ready to be of help to fellow men, without any personal consideration." He went to the United States to further his studies. In 1920, after a stint at Wesleyan College, in Warrenton, Missouri, he joined the Swiss embassy in Washington, D.C. Several years later, he was posted as secretary at the Philadelphia consulate; then in St. Louis, Missouri. In 1935, he was sent to Palestine, to head the Swiss consulate in Jaffa. There, at the outbreak of the war in September 1939, he interceded on behalf of the 2,500 German settlers in Palestine who were being deported as enemy aliens by the British. The Germans did not forget this kindly act by Lutz, and years later it stood him in good stead with the German authorities in Hungary. In 1941, he was sent to Berlin, and in January 1942 he arrived in Budapest as vice-consul to represent the interests of the United States, Britain, and other countries (eventually including Canada, Belgium, Argentina, El Salvador, and Paraguay) that had severed relations with Hungary because of its alliance with Nazi Germany. Already in the fall of 1942, well before the German occupation began,

Lutz, as the representative of British interests, together with Miklos Krausz, distributed certificates of immigration to Palestine to nearly 200 children and their adult chaperones, who were all able to leave the country before the Germans stormed in.[21]

After the German invasion on March 19, 1944, Lutz and Krausz continued to explore various schemes for emigration out of the country, working at first from Lutz's office and then from the Glass House. They may been inspired by the example of George Mantello, the vice-consul in Geneva for El Salvador (a country whose interests Lutz represented in Budapest). With the consent of Consul-General Castellanos, Mantello was issuing certificates that identified the bearers as Salvadoran nationals and distributing them to Jews in need in various places under German occupation. At any rate, when Lutz came up with the scheme of turning the 7,800 authorized names into a list four times larger because it included whole families instead of individuals, he and Krausz assembled 50 Jews in the Glass House to carry out the tedious administrative task of collecting photos from about 4,000 persons, whose names Lutz then entered on four collective passports of 1,000 names each. He then issued a "protective letter" (*Schutzbrief*) to each of the 4,000 people to protect them until the group's eventual departure for Palestine. Eventually he issued protective letters to as many as 50,000 Jews.

When Raoul Wallenberg appeared on the scene on July 9, 1944, Lutz instructed him on the best uses of these protective passes, and gave him the names of government officials who were receptive to appeals for assistance and were prepared to negotiate on this issue. Lutz's protective letters served as a model for similar documents issued by other neutral countries, as well as by the International Red Cross representative in Budapest, Friedrich Born. During the Arrow Cross reign of terror, starting mid-October 1944, the Zionist youth underground manufactured and distributed false Swiss documents in a desperate attempt to save Jews from the marauding Arrow Cross gangs. Lutz as well as other neutral diplomats, including the papal nuncio Angelo Rotta and Raoul Wallenberg, interceded with the new Hungarian government to recognize the protective documents, hold-

Carl Lutz, the Swiss diplomat in Budapest, Hungary.

ing up as bait the possibility that their governments would recognize the new regime. When the Arrow Cross decided to establish an International Ghetto for holders of protective passes, Lutz procured 25 high-rise buildings in which to concentrate his wards.

Lutz's rescue work was a bit complicated by his government's refusal to recognize the new Arrow Cross regime. "I then suggested [to the Arrow Cross government] that the protection afforded to those holding protective letters would be interpreted by the Swiss government as a positive gesture; at the same time, I promised to plead for the recognition of the new government." This tactic worked, and the government assured him that the Swiss-protected houses would not be harmed. But this was not a blanket guarantee. As Lutz recalled, "During this period, the Arrow Cross government threatened to cancel our extraterritorial privilege when such recognition did not arrive.

I tried to gain time, stating that one must wait a little while longer for the decision, since our foreign minister was bedridden. Later, I argued that the emissary carrying the recognition note was probably held up in Vienna. . . . My nerves were then already stretched thin, as there was hardly any time for even eating and sleeping."

On the eve of the infamous death march to the Austrian border on November 10–22, 1944, Lutz stood for hours in the freezing snow in the Obuda brickyard, where he tried to save people by distributing protective letters. "Heart-rending scenes took place. Some 15,000 of these unfortunate persons stood in line, freezing, trembling, hungry, with wretched-looking packages, and holding out their documents. I shall never forget those anguished faces. Again and again, the police had to intervene, for the people came near to me, ripping off my clothes as they gave voice to their pleas. It was the last glitter of the will to life before submitting to the state of resignation that so often led to death. How often I followed the marching column of brickyard people in my car, in order to persuade them that not everything was lost, until the heavily armed guards blocked the road for me." Nearly 40,000 Jews were then forcibly marched to the Austrian border under horrific conditions. Lutz made use of certificates still in his possession, following the deportees, and freeing those whose names he was able to fill in on the documents. Those so saved were allowed to return to Budapest, already under siege by the Red Army.

With the tightening of the Soviet military grip on Budapest in December 1944, all foreign representatives were ordered to leave the beleaguered capital. The Swiss ambassador, Maximilian Jaeger, had already departed on November 10. But Lutz, unwilling to abandon the thousands of Jews who had found a refuge in the International Ghetto, decided to remain behind. "I refused," Lutz stated, adding that in so doing he risked losing his diplomatic privileges. However, "my main concern was the people under my protection. A German diplomat told me that the Arrow Cross had ordered not to harm the protected houses as long as I was in Budapest." This was the result of a German intervention, as a token of thanks to Lutz for his concern about German interests in Palestine at the start of the war. "My staying in Budapest

People lining up outside the Glass House, Budapest, for the opportunity of earning a Protective Letter or a visa by the Swiss diplomat Carl Lutz.

then became a moral question." For over two winter months, Lutz and his wife, Gertrud, lived in the former British embassy building "in a wet, unheated cellar, often lacking candles and water," and bombarded by the Soviet Army. Even there Lutz found room to take in Jews and hide them. On January 30, 1945, the building caught fire as a result of the Russian bombardment. It burned for three days. At the time, Lutz was hiding in the cellar with 25 Jews; they were trapped, but somehow managed to survive. When the Russians stormed the building, Lutz jumped through a window and managed to reach the Swiss legation in Buda, the section of the city occupied only a month later, in February 1945. While he was there, the building underwent incessant bombings and received four direct hits.

Swiss diplomat Carl Lutz (right) with Israel President and Mrs. Yitzhak Ben-Zvi.

In a 1961 interview, Lutz stated that what concerned him most was
how he could help the persecuted Jews without, being declared per-
sona non grata by the Hungarian government, which would have
entailed his expulsion from the country and the collapse of his rescue
undertaking. "I didn't have the time to dedicate myself fully to my
basically humanitarian duty, because my official function of representing the interests of enemy nationals in Hungary demanded more
attention as the war situation became more critical."

A year after the war's end, on March 28, 1946, Carl Lutz received
an official letter of thanks and appreciation from the Jewish Agency
Executive in Jerusalem (the forerunner of the Israel government). It
read in part: "From the many reports that reached us last year and continue to arrive every day, everyone praises the immense assistance you
gave the Jews in Hungary during your service there as a Swiss consul.
All of our friends concur that a great many Jews, reaching into the

| SVÁJCI KÖVETSÉG
IDEGEN ÉRDEKEK KÉPVISELETE

KIVÁNDORLÁSI OSZTÁLY
V., VADÁSZ-UTCA 29.

2085/GE
1944 | | SCHWEIZERISCHE GESANDTSCHAFT
ABTEILUNG FÜR FREMDE INTERESSEN

ABTEILUNG AUSWANDERUNG
V., VADÁSZ-UTCA 29. |

Die Schweizerische Gesandtschaft, Abteilung fremde Inte-
ressen, bescheinigt hiermit,
dass

    B A N D S I M O N und
        F R A U

im schweizerischen Kollektiv-
pass zur Auswanderung einge-
tragen ist, daher ist der (die)
Betreffende als Besitzer eines
gültigen Reisepasses zu be-
trachten.

Budapest, 23. Oktober 1944.

A Svájci Követség, Idegen
Érdekek Képviselete, ezennel
igazolja, hogy

    B A N D S I M O N és
        neje

a svájci csoportos (collectiv)
utlevélben szerepel és ezért
nevezett érvényes utlevél bir-
tokában levő személynek tekin-
tendő.

Budapest, 1944. október 23.

A Swiss Collective Visa issued by Carl Lutz
to a Hungarian Jewish couple.

thousands, owe their lives to your noble intervention before the authorities and your constant readiness to help wherever possible. . . . The Jewish Agency, which represents the Jewish people throughout the world, wishes to tell you that your name will be forever etched in the history of our people, as one of the few upright and courageous persons who dared to stand up and confront the persecutors of our lives."

Upon his return to Switzerland, Lutz was reprimanded by the Foreign Ministry for having issued so many Swiss certificates to Jews who later, armed with these documents, sought entry into Switzerland. Swallowing his pride, Lutz remained in his country's diplomatic service and served in various posts. When he retired in June 1961, he was consul-general in Bregenz, Austria. In 1964, Yad Vashem awarded Carl Lutz the honorific title of Righteous Among the Nations. He died in 1975.[22]

Harald Feller

Several other Swiss diplomats were equally helpful to Jews. One of them was Harald Feller. Born in 1913, he was sent to Hungary in 1943 as first secretary and juridical counselor of the Swiss legation, under Ambassador Maximilian Jaeger. His work consisted mainly in sorting out conflicts between Swiss and Hungarian laws when they affected Swiss nationals in the country. In his youth Feller had dreamed of an acting career in the theater and took some lessons, but his father made him study law. He was later sometimes able to use his acting experience to impress and confuse opponents.

Among others, Harald Feller saved Eva Koralnik-Rottenberg (born 1936), together with mother, Berta Rottenberg-Passweg, and her sister Veronica (born 1944). First, in the late summer of 1944, he arranged a place in one of the Swiss-protected houses for Eva and Berta, and two other women. All four women had lost their Swiss nationality because of marriage, either their own or of one of their parents, to a Hungarian citizen, but Feller, overlooking this formal handicap, provided them with the necessary documents, so that they could stay for several weeks in the Swiss house. Eva related that Feller had told her parents to remove the Yellow Star, especially since her mother was pregnant with Eva's sister. Eva was told to say that her father was a Hungarian soldier at the front. "In the meantime, I will try to arrange for you to go to Switzerland," he told the frightened women. Mrs. Rottenberg gave birth to Veronica on August 15, 1944, and was registered as of the Protestant faith. Then, on October 4,1944, Feller came and personally led the women to the station to board a train for Vienna accompanied by a man from the Swiss legation. He told them that a trustworthy person would meet them in Vienna. Arriving there, a city that was part of Nazi Germany, the women were met by a stranger who took them to stay for the night in, of all places, the Metropol Hotel, which also served as the Gestapo headquarters. The following morning they went by train ride to Feldkirchen, and that night they slept on benches in the station. Next day, the party proceeded to St. Gallen, Switzerland. All arrangements had been made beforehand by Feller.

This was not the only rescue operation undertaken by Harald Feller. When the Swiss ambassador Jaeger left the country in protest at the coup d'etat by the Arrow Cross on October 15, 1944, the 31-year-old Feller became the Swiss legation's chargé d'affaires; in other words, his country's official representative in Budapest. In this capacity he provided Vice Consul Carl Lutz with the indispensable diplomatic protection and backing necessary for his vast action to save Jews. Moreover, from late October 1944 until the city's occupation by the Soviet Army in early 1945, Feller himself hid at least a dozen Jewish refugees in his private apartment in the Buda section of the city, thus saving their lives. Among them were the writer Gábor Devecseri, together with his wife Klara and their two sons, as well as Klara's parents, Mr. and Mrs. Huszar; Gyula Molnár, Aurel Erdély, Mr. Hecht and son (brought by Feller from the Kistarca camp), Gerda Lenz and Judith Sussmann, Renate Dery, son Hans, his wife and daughter; Ella Neumann-Denneberg, Berta Rottenberg-Passweg and two daughters; Viola Monar-Goldberger, Else Matray, Mrs. Kodaly and Mrs. Magdolna Pallo. As for Professor K. Kerényi, Feller had him falsely listed as his private secretary under a different name while his family was sheltered in Feller's home. With the exception of Mrs. Molnár, Feller paid for the expenses of all the others. "I did not take the slightest payment from any of these wards of mine," Feller stated. Mrs. Mólnar, before leaving for Switzerland, left two gold cuff-links in Feller's coat pocket without his knowledge. "I discovered this after the departure of the women. I left the cuff-links in the alms box of the church on Klebelsberg Street, which the Swiss people usually attended. Of all the Jews I helped, I allowed myself not the slightest payment or gift."

One of the persons helped by Feller, Gábor Devecseri, was the author who translated into Hungarian some of the classic works of the Swiss writers Spitteler, Keller, and Albert Steffen, an undertaking that he continued while hiding with Feller. On December 28, 1944, Feller and his Hungarian fiancée, Valeria Perényi (whom he later married), at great risk to themselves, went to a Jewish-marked house to find Mrs. Devecseri's mother and husband, the Hussars, and brought them to Feller's private quarters. "I shall never forget the reunion between parents and daughter." In the case of Gyula Mólnar, he approached Feller in October 1944 and pleaded for help save his wife, a former Swiss national. She was one of the four women that Feller sent to Switzerland via Vienna. As for Gyula himself, "I had promised Mrs. Mólnar to do my best to help her husband, who was unable to leave Hungary. I felt ashamed not to honor such a promise. I took him to the quarters of my house *garçon* [steward], on whose silence I could fully rely."

When Feller declined to leave the Hungarian capital in the footsteps of the Hungarian government, which had relocated in Sopron to avoid capture by the advancing Red Army, the remaining Hungarian authorities called off the police protection formerly given Feller and his Swiss staff. Feller persuaded several policemen, who did not wish to leave the city, to stay with him on condition that they would protect him and wards, even by force of arms, in the event of a raid by the Arrow Cross militia. In a city under severe turmoil, with law and order broken down, Feller was always in danger of physical harm to himself when out in the street. Indeed, on December 28, 1944, he and his Hungarian fiancée, Valeria Perényi, were arrested and taken to Arrow Cross headquarters at 42 Andrássy Boulevard, where for six long hours they were brutally interrogated by Father András Kun, a viciously anti-semitic Arrow Cross cleric. After his release, Feller told the Swedish consul Per Anger that he had been beaten so brutally that he lost consciousness. When he recovered, he had heard the Arrow Cross men say that he was going to be taken to the "cold room," a very sophisticated torture chamber from which few came out alive. Then, somehow, Feller hit upon a gambit, stating, "Of course you can take my life, but then I guarantee that your 'minister' in Bern will be swinging on the gallows tomorrow." Feller was released at once.[23]

Several days before this incident, on December 24, Christmas Eve, Feller gave refuge to the Swedish ambassador, Ivar Danielsson, together with Raoul Wallenberg and others, after Arrow Cross bands attacked and sacked the Swedish legation. Feller secretly hid them in the chancellery of the Swiss legation. Four other Swedish legation staff members had also been kidnapped: Consuls Lars Berg, Asta

Nilsson, who headed the Swedish Children's Fund, and her secretary, Margarete Bauer. Feller and his fiancée, together with Friedrich Born of the International Red Cross committee, immediately went out in search of them. They found them and managed to obtain their release, and hurriedly took them for shelter in the Swiss chancellery. Wallenberg left Feller's hideout two days later, but Danielsson and the others remained under Feller's protection until the fall of the Buda section of the city to the Red Army in February 1945. Several days later, Feller was kidnapped by Soviet secret agents (NKVD) and taken to Lubyanka prison in Moscow, where he was ceaselessly questioned for months. No reasons were given, but it is well to remember that at the time Switzerland had no diplomatic relations with the Soviet Union, and this may have roused Soviet suspicions of a Swiss-German plot to thwart the Soviet advance into Eastern Europe. After one year's imprisonment, the Swiss government succeeded in having him released.

Returning to Switzerland in 1946, Feller decided to leave the diplomatic service. His illegal one-year imprisonment in Moscow had a traumatic effect on him. "I was no longer the same person." While in Moscow, "I had much time to think things over." When he returned home, he decided that a diplomatic career "was no longer part of my life." For a time, he worked as a state attorney in Bern canton. Upon his retirement, he returned to his youthful passion—the theater. For 18 years he worked, without pay, as stage manager of a theater group in Thorberg prison. "I often went behind the scenes and gave advice. Over time, the inmates realized that I knew something about the theater. And so they asked me whether I would like to become their stage manager, although as a state attorney I belonged to the other side and put people behind bars. . . . In spite of this, many inmates were able express themselves through theater plays." As for his help to Jews in Budapest during the war years, "When I committed myself to help Jews whose lives were in danger, I did it out of humanitarian motivations, not really as part of my official function." In 1999, at the age of 85, Yad Vashem awarded Harald Feller the title of Righteous Among the Nations.[24]

Peter Zürcher and Ernst Vonrufs

In late 1944, Peter Zürcher (born 1914), originally a businessman, agreed to serve as a secretary in the Swiss legation in Budapest. This happened when Carl Lutz moved his activities across the Danube River to the hilly Buda section of the city, and there was a need for someone to represent Swiss interests in the larger and more exposed Pest section, which was expected to fall first into Soviet hands. As for Ernst Vonrufs, in 1935 he came to Budapest to head a Swiss textile firm. During the tumultuous period following the German invasion, Vonrufs sent his family (wife and two children) back to Switzerland. "I had resolved to leave within a few weeks or months, as soon as I had turned over the management of the firm to reliable hands. However, things turned out differently." At this critical juncture, Vonrufs was asked to help Zürcher to represent Swiss interests in the beleaguered Pest section, where officially some 10,000 Jews (but unofficially, as many as 17,000) were sheltered in Swiss-protected houses. Vonrufs served as secretary to Zürcher in their combined effort to continue protecting the Jews under the responsibility of the Swiss legation, and the Swiss Ministry of Foreign Affairs gave both of them diplomatic status even though they were not professional diplomats. In Zürcher's words, "We started our work toward the end of 1944. It would take too long to list all our responsibilities with respect to the legation's work." Both worked energetically to save Jews under Swiss protection in the city, and in that capacity, they put themselves in considerable danger.

On January 1, 1945, Zürcher met with Ernö Vajna, who was responsible for the defense of Budapest on behalf of the Arrow Cross regime, which had by then relocated westward to Sopron. As shells fell outside, Zürcher asked Vajna to stop the murderous Arrow Cross rampages against residents of the Swiss-protected houses. Another meeting with Vajna took place in Sopron, also attended by Vonrufs, to again plead for the welfare of the Jews in the protected houses and not to allow the destruction of the ghetto as was then rumored. The two men also asked for special protection for a group of 25 American citizens. Vajna agreed to let the Americans be moved to the Swedish houses in the International Ghetto. As for the thousands in the Swiss-protected houses, Vajna agreed to hold off the Arrow Cross raids, but with one proviso: the people in the houses would be checked to verify that they were bona fide holders of Swiss protective letters, and the houses would be searched to make sure that no weapons were stored there. If any weapons were discovered, all the residents would be held responsible and face the consequences. When the two Swiss officials protested, Vajna relented, and agreed that only the manager of the individual house (*hausmeister*) and the residents of the apartment where weapons were found would be held responsible. Zürcher and Vonrufs pointed out that Arrow Cross militiamen sometimes purposely destroyed the Swiss certificates held by people they questioned, thus leaving them exposed to harm without any protective documents. The two Swiss officials suggested that a new list be drawn up of people entitled to protection. Vajna agreed, but on condition that the people on the new list were indeed in possession of legitimate Swiss protective letters. The new list was to be turned over to Vajna by 8:00 A.M. on January 10, 1945. Vajna assured the two Swiss diplomats that he would give the necessary instructions to the police in Budapest.

Notwithstanding Vajna's promise, the Arrow Cross reign of terror continued unabated. When Zürcher's secretary, Maria Kormos, was abducted, he sent four men, dressed in Arrow Cross uniforms probably obtained from the Zionist underground, to supposedly bring her in for questioning. The trick worked and she was released. Zürcher hid her in his flat until he could obtain fake documents and arrange a place where she could stay until the liberation. Zürcher also related a particularly gruesome incident. One morning, coming to work, he saw two Jewish men hanging from a tree, with a note addressed to him attached to their bodies as a warning. Another near-catastrophic incident was when Zürcher and Vonrufs were told to remove all Jews from the Swiss-protected houses and relocate them into the Jewish ghetto, where conditions were far worse. In Zürcher's words: "I then, out of some inspiration . . . I responded that in that case, measures would immediately be taken against Hungarian nationals in America. . . . An empty threat, actually a bluff. But a bluff that worked. The protected persons in the Swiss houses remained there until Budapest's liberation."

On January 16, 1944, Pest fell to the Russians. Several days of pandemonium and civil unrest followed. Finally, on January 31, Zürcher and Vonrufs succeeded in establishing contact with the Russian city commander, General Tschernischov, who promised that no harm would befall them. Both men fared better than their compatriot Harald Feller, and were not imprisoned by the country's new masters. On instructions from the Swiss government, Zürcher and Vonrufs stayed on in Budapest for a while, before returning home to Switzerland.

Two years after the war's end, Dr. Wilhelm Karoly, who had been sheltered by Zürcher, wrote him a letter of thanks and appreciation in which he mentioned how Zürcher ran to and fro every day, "with determination, death risks, diplomatic tact," in the effort to save thousands of people. "You and Vonrufs headed these activities from the Swiss legation during the months of the Szálasi regime. You saved the lives of many thousands of Jews." Peter Zürcher and Ernst Vonrufs were awarded the Righteous title by Yad Vashem in 1998 and 2000, respectively.[25]

Friedrich Born

Until the middle of July 1944, the International Red Cross (IRC) was not particularly concerned with the protection of the rights and interests of Jews per se. It scrupulously adhered to the German interpretation that the Jews were not "internees" but "detainees," a penal rather than civil category, and rejected demands by major Jewish organizations that it confer the status of "civilian internees" upon the Jews held in the ghettos and the labor and concentration camps. Friedrich Born, who replaced Jean de Bavier as the IRC representative in Budapest in May 1944, began to play a more active role early in July, gradually taking an interest in the Swiss- and Swedish-initiated emigration schemes, and the protection of Jewish children. After Tangier, then under Spanish jurisdiction, expressed its readiness to admit 500 children, the IRC bowed to Jewish demands to take these "foreign-protected" children under its aegis, but sadly nothing came of it. By far Born's most important contribution was the sheltering of

*International Red Cross Protective Letter, issued by
the office of Friedrich Born, Budapest, Hungary.*

children in Budapest itself and the safeguarding and supplying of
Jewish institutions, including the Jewish ghetto, especially during the
Arrow Cross era. For this purpose, Born created a special division
known as Section A within the Budapest IRC and as its head appoint-
ed Ottó Komoly of the Jewish council (who worked closely with Carl
Lutz and Raoul Wallenberg). In addition, he entrusted Section B to
Reverend Gábor Sztehló of the Good Shepherd Mission, a Protestant
organization. Soon after this he arranged for many of the city's hospi-
tals, soup kitchens, homes for the handicapped and the aged, research
and scientific institutes, and shops to be provided with signs in
Hungarian, German, French, and Russian stating: "Under the
Protection of the International Committee of the Red Cross." At one

*Friedrich Born's children planting a tree
during a ceremony at Yad Vashem.*

time, Section A was in charge of 35 buildings, had 550 employees, and offered protection to nearly 6,000 children. Its facilities were used, as well, to house 1,000 Jewish refugees.

Born was also responsible for the establishment of Section T (Transportation Unit), manned by 25 to 35 recruits from Labor Service Company No. 101/359, the so-called Clothes-Collecting Labor Company. Section T engaged in relief, rescue, and resistance operations, rescued thousands of Jews from the death marches to Hegyeshalom in late 1944, and supplied the children's houses and the ghetto with food and fuel. Early in December 1944, Hans Weyermann arrived from Geneva to assist Born. Although the relationship between the two IRC representatives was not the most harmonious, they managed to divide their responsibilities during the critical weeks before the capital's liberation. During the Soviet siege of Budapest, Weyermann remained in the Pest part of the capital, whereas Born continued to represent IRC interests in the Buda section. On December 3, Arrow Cross gangs invaded the IRC special camp on Columbus Street and killed several of the residents, including the chief physician. Born frequently appealed to government officials to ease the plight of the Jews, especially Baron Gábor Kemény, the foreign minister.[26]

Several members of the former Jewish underground testified to Born's active help in his capacity as IRC representative in Budapest. Peretz Ravasz related that Section A was originally created to deal with the transfer of 500 children to Tangier, then under Spanish control. When this plan failed, Section A concentrated on helping Jewish children in Budapest, under the sponsorship of the IRC. It eventually rescued thousands of children and their adult teachers. "As one of the heads of the [Zionist] Pioneers Underground, I was personally involved in these rescue efforts. . . . I have no doubt that Mr. Born knew what was taking place in the section for which he was responsible to the Hungarian authorities, as well as to his organization in Switzerland, and it is doubtful that they would have consented to illegal activities on their behalf. I personally met Mr. Born several times. With his knowledge and signature, I obtained a certificate under a false name, as a Christian working for the IRC, together with a certificate of the Hungarian Foreign Ministry confirming my job as an emissary. Other very active personnel received similar documents."

Hansi Brand, who headed one of the IRC offices in Budapest, confirmed that "thanks to Mr. Born and his efforts, we were able to use the IRC as a cover for our work to rescue Hungarian Jews, and Mr. Born gave us his full support and assistance, thereby jeopardizing his post and even his life." Raphael Benshalom, writing after the war, related that as a Jewish underground operative, he was inducted into the work of the IRC, where, with Born's silent acquiescence, he engaged in clandestine work. "It is clear to me today, as it was then, that Dr. Born was well aware of our underground activities in the [IRC] office, and gave us his full support." Finally, Yosi Shefer was active in moving Jewish children into houses under the protection of the IRC. Shefer was responsible for the administrative work, including the falsification of records, whenever necessary to protect the children admitted. "I received a certificate, written in four languages, testifying to my work as an IRC secretary, and signed by Born. This document was then considered as equivalent to a diplomatic certificate, and was distributed only to department heads who needed to circulate freely in the streets."

Born is credited with the rescue of 6,000 Jewish children, sheltered in houses under the protection of the IRC. An untold number of other people were saved and sheltered in various welfare institutions under the protection of the IRC, including hospitals, soup kitchens, and homes for the aged and handicapped. In a ceremony at Yad Vashem in 1987, when the late Friedrich Born was declared a Righteous Among the Nations, Jacques Moreillon, the head of the International Red Cross, declared: "At the beginning there is a man; the man has an ideal; the ideal becomes an organization . . . and the organization kills the ideal." In Friedrich Born's case, the various organizations he created in Budapest did not kill, but saved the lives of thousands, and thereby upheld the principle of the sanctity of human life.[27]

The Swedish Team

Raoul Wallenberg

Any discussion of large-scale rescue in Hungary by foreign diplomats must put Raoul Wallenberg at the top of the list. Not only because of the mystery of his disappearance at war's end, but principally because of the man himself, and his superhuman efforts to save the Jewish community in Hungary—efforts that may well have contributed to his tragic fate. Wallenberg's arrival in Budapest on July 9, 1944 was the result of a decision by the United States government earlier that same year. On January 22, 1944, President Roosevelt, bowing to pressure from many organizations, ordered the establishment of the War Refugee Board (WRB), headed by John W. Pehle of the Treasury Department, for the purpose of rescuing the Jewish victims in imminent danger of death. Facing its first major test with the Nazi conquest of Hungary on March 19, 1944, the WRB saw an opportunity to act through the Swedish government. This occurred in June 1944, when Carl Ivar Danielsson, the Swedish minister in Budapest, asked for a special diplomat to be dispatched to Budapest to deal with the many requests for emigration to Sweden. At about the same time, U.S. Secretary of State Cordell Hull asked Sweden to persuade the Hungarians to desist from further acts of "barbarism" against the Jews. The request was forwarded via Herschel Johnson, the American ambassador to Stockholm, and Ivar C. Olsen, the WRB representative in Sweden. Pressure to do something about the tragic situation of the Jews in Hungary also came from Swedish Chief Rabbi Marcus (Mordechai) Ehrenpreis and Norbert Masur of the World Jewish Congress. The Swedish Foreign Ministry then decided to send Raoul Wallenberg to Budapest on a special relief and rescue mission.[28]

Raoul Wallenberg was born in 1912 into one of Sweden's most prominent aristocratic and banking families. Sadly, his father Oscar died three months after Raoul's birth. Raised by his mother and his paternal grandfather Gustav Wallenberg (his mother, Maj Wising, remarried in 1918 to Fredrik von Dardel), Raoul studied architecture at the University of Michigan in Ann Arbor, then joined his family's banking business and worked for some time in a branch of a Dutch bank in Haifa, Palestine, where he first came into contact with Jewish refugees from Nazi Germany, an experience which stirred him deeply. Returning to Sweden, he entered into a partnership with a Hungarian Jew, Koloman Lauer, who operated a Swedish-based import and export firm. Wallenberg used this occasion to travel widely in Nazi-occupied Europe, including three trips, in 1941, 1942, and 1943, to the as yet non-occupied Hungary, though an ally of Nazi Germany. In 1944, he learned that the Swedish government was looking for someone to work in its legation in Budapest as a cover for the WRB for the purpose of saving the remnants of Hungarian Jewry, originally over 750,000 strong, but being decimated by the Germans and their Hungarian collaborators.[29]

Swedish diplomat Raoul Wallenberg.

Following the German occupation of Hungary, Lauer and other Jews of Hungarian origin who were anxious to save their relatives in Hungary, hit upon the idea of sending Wallenberg to Budapest for that purpose. This coincided with appeals from the Swedish diplomats in Budapest for an additional person to help with the overcharged work at the Swedish legation. First Secretary Per Anger reported that the entire staff of the legation was working night and day to handle the many requests for visas, which in many cases had to be denied, following instructions from Stockholm. Because of this workload, Ambassador Danielsson asked the Foreign Office to send a special emissary to Budapest whose principal task would be to take care of passports. Ivar Olsen of the WRB, U.S. Ambassador Herschel V. Johnson, and Rabbi Ehrenpreis joined in proposing Raoul Wallenberg for the post of special envoy.[30]

Before agreeing to this dangerous mission, Wallenberg posted a series of conditions that were rather severe and inordinate for a diplomatic envoy. He asked for a free hand in everything involving rescue efforts, including permission to provide asylum in the Swedish legation building, to use bribery, and to employ Allied intelligence agents, whose names he received from the British and American embassies, to contact trusted people with links to the Hungarian government and the Germans. He also asked for authority to meet with Hungarian Prime Minister Sztójay and Admiral Horthy, to keep in direct contact with the Foreign Office in Stockholm without having to go through channels in the legation in Budapest, and for his mission to be financed with American money (principally from the JDC-Joint Distribution Committee). Finally, he asked for his official rank to be secretary of the legation. On June 23, 1944 the Swedish government agreed to these conditions, and Wallenberg left for Hungary. He arrived in Budapest on July 9, 1944, one day after the official halt of the deportations went into effect, carrying two rucksacks, a sleeping bag, a windbreaker, a revolver, and a list of 630 Hungarian Jewish applicants for Swedish visas, including 300 or 400 already approved by the Swedish legation in Budapest.[31]

Friends, relatives, or business associates in Sweden had sponsored the people on his list, and the Swedish government had issued the necessary visas. When he arrived in Budapest, he learned that the Hungarian government, bowing to international pressure, had just ordered a halt to the deportation of Jews. However, fear remained that the Germans would force Hungary to renew the deportations in order to do away with the last major Jewish community in the country—the more than 200,000 still alive in Budapest. After taking over Section C in the Swedish legation, and anxious not to waste time, Wallenberg went to see Swiss diplomat Carl Lutz, from whom he learned about the use of protective passes (*Schutzbrief*) to grant numerous Jews diplomatic protection on various dubious claims. Wallenberg decided to exploit this method, issuing thousands of such documents, which at the time were honored by the Hungarian government. Many of the beneficiaries were housed in buildings purchased by Wallenberg that flew the Swedish flag and were treated as extraterritorial.

The Swedes now had three types of passports: the regular Swedish passport issued to citizens of the country, a temporary passport given to those who had family or business connections with citizens of Sweden, such as the 600 on Wallenberg's list, and the protective passports, also known as letters of protection. Wallenberg designed an impressive new document, printed on blue and yellow paper, decorated with the Swedish national coat of arms, and written in German and Hungarian. The text was specially designed to make the documents more forceful: "The Royal Swedish legation in Budapest confirms that the aforementioned will travel to Sweden in accordance with the scheme of repatriation as authorized by the Royal Swedish Foreign Office. The aforementioned is also included in a collective passport. Until his repatriation the holder and his domicile are under the protection of the Royal Swedish legation. Validity: Expires 14 days after entry into Sweden."

Holders of these passports were exempted from the obligation to wear the Yellow Star sign and were permitted to go outside during the curfew hours imposed on Jews. Many of them were also released from forced labor. In the summer months, about 4,500 people had these passports. Of course these protective passports had no formal standing under international law, but they commanded respect and, not least, gave their holders a sense of security. At first Wallenberg only had permission to issue 1,500 protective passports. But he persuaded the Hungarian authorities to allow him to issue another 1,000, which he eventually raised to 4,500. In reality, Wallenberg issued many more than this number. In addition, with the assistance of a large dedicated staff in Section C (eventually reaching 400), most of whom were Jews hired to help with rescue operations, Wallenberg set up an extensive network of hospitals, a day-care center, and soup kitchens for Jews under the protection of the Swedish government.[32]

In the meantime, in July 1944, with the Russians already in Romania, Horthy replaced Sztójay with General Lakatos, and pro-Nazi ministers were dismissed. Adolf Eichmann was also sent packing. At the same time, all attempts to allow people possessing Swedish protective letters to emigrate to Sweden through Germany ran aground. In the Swedish houses the number of people rose to more than twice authorized by the government, in 31 buildings hoisting the Swedish flag.

Wallenberg utilized secret and devious methods to manage the finances for this huge undertaking, including bribery of certain officials. Some of the money sent by Olsen in Stockholm (originally from the JDC in the United States) was transferred to a special account in Wallenberg's name in a Swiss bank in Zürich, which transferred it to other Swiss banks. To achieve his humanitarian goals, Wallenberg used everything from bribery to threats of blackmail. As reported by Swedish diplomat Per Anger, Wallenberg was a clever negotiator and organizer, unconventional, extraordinarily inventive and cool-headed, and something of a go-getter. Besides this, he was very good at languages and well grounded in Hungarian affairs. "At heart he was a great idealist and a warm human being."[33]

Elizabeth Kasser, who served as a personal interpreter for Raoul Wallenberg, and accompanied him to his many meetings and confrontations with Fascist officials, described his unique personality in a 1981 newspaper interview. "I have never met such a devoted human being. He never cared about what might happen to him. Probably, he felt invulnerable. Entering a room with 15 men, Raoul Wallenberg would always be the center-figure in the room. This 33-year-old had a particular charisma. . . . He was usually taciturn. He had difficulty tolerating chatty, talkative people. He was indifferent to what he ate. He never had time to eat. Probably also never got a night's uninterrupted sleep. At dawn you would see him on his bicycle bringing food baskets to his wards."[34] No wonder that Wallenberg more or less shocked the other diplomats at the Swedish legation with his unconventional methods. In early October 1944, Wallenberg planned to return to Sweden, because it seemed as if he had completed his assignment, but events suddenly overtook him. The situation of the Jews in Budapest suddenly was transformed into a nightmare, and this forced Wallenberg to stay on.

On October 15, 1944, with the Red Army closing in on Hungary, Horthy announced a unilateral ceasefire. It seemed as if the worst was over for Budapest Jewry, but just at that moment Horthy's government was overthrown with Nazi aid and replaced by an even more stridently pro-Nazi and antisemitic regime headed by the Arrow Cross and its leader, Ferenc Szálasi. An unprecedented reign of terror descended on the city, as Arrow Cross gangs launched a killing spree of Jews in the streets, with some being drowned in the freezing waters of the Danube River.

This is when Wallenberg turned into a legendary figure. At this crucial stage, he again went into action, pleading with the new regime to recognize the protective passes and houses of the Swedish government and the other neutral states, and using as a ploy the hope that the Swedish government would recognize the Arrow Cross regime. It was a risky gamble, for Sweden had already declined recognition on various excuses. The Hungarian authorities announced that the passport holders would be allowed to leave the country on November 15 if the Swedish government recognized the Szálasi regime. Playing for time, Wallenberg kept the Hungarian regime hoping for recognition by his government. In the meantime, the number of Jews holding genuine as well as forged Swedish protective passes increased tremendously after the Arrow Cross coup of October 15. The number rose to over 7,000, and counting those with forged ones, to well over 10,000. Many of them were housed in the 32 buildings protected by the Swedes. Wallenberg's staff included 355 employees, 40 physicians, two hospitals, and a soup kitchen. Most of the staff were Jews or converts who had obtained immunity for themselves and their families.[35]

SS Colonel Adolf Eichmann returned to town on October 17, eager to complete the liquidation of Hungarian Jewry. With transportation to Auschwitz no longer practicable because of the Russian advance, he ordered what turned into a death march toward Austria for tens of thousands of Jews. Wallenberg followed the straggling marchers in his car, many of whom were felled by Hungarian gendarmes for not keeping up with the rest, and succeeding getting hundreds of them released

Protective Letter, probably issued by Raoul Wallenberg,
and signed by Swedish ambassador Danielsson.

on the spurious claim that they had, or were on the process of obtaining, Swedish nationality. Per Anger, his colleague at the Swedish legation, saw Wallenberg pulling Jews without passports off the trains, using other kinds of official documents, such as driver's licenses, vaccination records, or tax receipts, to fool the German guards, who could not read Hungarian.

It was an unforgettable sight. On a cold November 1944 day, not far from the Hungarian-Austrian border, in the words of eyewitness Sandor Ardai, a young-looking stranger, who someone whispered was a Swedish diplomat named Wallenberg, walked past the SS officer supervising the deportation train, climbed onto its roof, and began

KÖNIGLICH
SCHWEDISCHE GESANDTSCHAFT

```
L a d á n y  Pál  kmsz.
   Csepel-Királymajor.
 /: Bpest,VI.Liszt Ferenc tér 6. :/


                           A Sved kir. Követség igazolja, hogy  L a d á n y
Pál /: 1890-ben született, anyja Vörösvári Ilona :/  részére 39/60.
sz. alatt svéd védőutlevelet állitott ki.-
                      A H.M. Ur 152.730 /Eln/42. sz. rendelete értel-
mében az idegen állampolgárok az Idegen Állampolgárokat Gyüjtő szá-
hoz /Budapest Aréna ut 55./ vezényeltettek.-
                           Ezen levelet a felettes parancsnokságainál való
felhasználás végett Önnek a mai napon kiadtuk.-

Budapest, 1944. október 29.
```

Svéd kir. követségi titkár.

Swedish Protective Letter issued and signed in Budapest,
Hungary, by Swedish diplomat Raoul Wallenberg.

handing safe-conduct passes through the doors, which had not yet been locked. In the words of one witness, Wallenberg "paid no attention when the Germans ordered him to get down, or when the Arrow Cross men began firing their guns and shouting at him to go away. Ignoring them, he calmly continued giving passes to the outstretched hands. . . . After Wallenberg had distributed the last of the passes, he told everyone who had one to get off the train and walk over to a caravan of cars parked nearby. . . . The Germans and the Arrow Cross were so dumbfounded that they let him get away with it," wondering who was this brazenly courageous diplomat who openly defied the Nazis in order to save as many Jews as possible.

Miriam Herzog also related how she came across Wallenberg. "The conditions were frightful. We walked 30 to 40 kilometers a day in freezing rain, driven on all the time by the Hungarian gendarmes. We were all women and girls and I was 17 at the time. The gendarmes were brutal, beating those who could not keep up, leaving others to die in the ditches. It was terrible for the older women. . . . I didn't have a Swedish passport, but I thought it was worth a try and I had this tremendous will to survive, even though I was so weak from dysentery and wretched from the dirt and lice that infested me, that all I could do was find a space on the floor and lie down. Suddenly I heard a great commotion among the women. 'It's Wallenberg,' they said. I didn't think he could really help me, and anyway I was too weak now to move, so I lay there on the floor as dozens of women clustered around him, crying 'Save us, save us.' I remember being struck by how handsome he looked— and how clean—in his leather coat and fur hat, just like a being from another world, and I thought, 'Why does he bother with such wretched creatures as we?' As the women clustered around him, he said to them, 'Please, you must forgive me but I cannot help all of you. I can only provide certificates for a hundred of you.' Then he said something which really surprised me. He said. 'I feel I have a mission to save the Jewish nation, and so I must rescue the young ones first.' I had never heard of the idea of a Jewish nation before. Jewish people, of course, but not a Jewish nation. He looked around the room and began putting names down on a list, and when he saw me lying on the floor he came over to me. He asked my name and added it to the list. After a day or two, the hundred of us whose names had been taken were moved out and put into a cattle car on a train bound for Budapest. There were a lot more danger and hardships for us, but we were alive—and it was thanks entirely to Wallenberg."[36]

In collaboration with the International Red Cross, truck convoys were organized to distribute food to the deported. Further, at Wallenberg's initiative, checkpoints were set up on the roads leaving Budapest and at the border station to hinder the deportation of Jews holding protective passports. In this way, an estimated 1,500 Jews were saved and returned to Budapest. As reported by Per Anger, "I witnessed Wallenberg stopping the deportation of a total of several thousand Jews at train stations, from the Swedish houses, and during the death march to the Austrian border." Those released were sent back to

Budapest, to the International Ghetto set up by Wallenberg and other diplomats, including 31 Swedish houses, and where some 20,000 (some estimates place the number as high as 30,000) Jews were sheltered, in a city under siege by the Soviet army. At this point, Wallenberg began to issue protective passports without distinction, even to people who had already been arrested and were being assembled for deportation.[37]

The future Israeli journalist and politician Joseph (Tommy) Lapid related: "One morning, a group of these Hungarian Fascists came into the Swedish-protected house and said all the able-bodied women must go with them. We knew what this meant. My mother kissed me and I cried and she cried. We knew we were parting forever and she left me there, an orphan to all intents and purposes. Then, two or three hours later, to my amazement, my mother returned with the other women. It seemed like a mirage, a miracle. My mother was there—she was alive and she was hugging and kissing me, and she said one word: 'Wallenberg'." In the meantime, on November 18, Szálasi ordered the establishment of two ghettos. The 31 buildings already in Swedish possession, housing thousands of people, were allocated to the International Ghetto. All told approximately 30,000 were housed in the International Ghetto.[38]

Jenö Lévai, historian of the Holocaust in Hungary, stated that "it is of the utmost importance that the Nazis and the Arrow Cross militiamen were not able to ravage unhindered. They were compelled to see that every step they took was being watched and followed by the young Swedish diplomat. From Wallenberg they could keep no secrets. . . . Wallenberg was the 'world's observing eye,' the one who continually called the criminals to account." As the Soviets tightened their ring around Budapest, while at the same time Arrow Cross pursued its relentless killing sprees, Wallenberg found his task staggering. In addition to saving Jews from the hands of the Arrow Cross, he struggled to obtain food for the tens of thousands of Jews in the ghetto and in the protected buildings. When the Swedes turned down Szálasi's demand to vacate their legation in the embattled city (the Soviet army was about to close its ring around Budapest) and move to western

Hungary, on December 10, Arrow Cross militiamen attacked and vandalized the Swedish legation. Wallenberg once sent Jews dressed in Arrow Cross uniforms to free a large number of Jews on the way to deportation.[39] Annoyed by all this, SS Colonel Adolf Eichmann, meeting with Wallenberg, hinted that his safety would be in jeopardy if he did not stop meddling and interfering. On December 16, Eichmann reportedly threatened that he would "shoot that Jew dog Wallenberg." The German legation in Budapest complained about the Jewish office in the Swedish legation as headed by Wallenberg. To offset these threats while continuing his rescue operation, Wallenberg was forced to go underground, and he took care to sleep each night in a different location.[40]

The Swedish Foreign Office in Stockholm, it must be confessed, had some reservations with regard to Wallenberg's methods. On November 13, Ambassador Danielsson was asked in a telegram, "Would it not be preferable that he leave before the arrival of the Russians?" Apparently Danielsson thought otherwise. At the same time, the Swedish legation was also concerned about Wallenberg's methods. In the words of Per Anger, "We were worried that the Wallenberg operation would expand to such a scope that it would swamp us and precipitate Nazi countermoves that would endanger the legation's continued operation." In the final account, it came down to the question of "how far Wallenberg and we dared to bend the bow when we had no support from home. True, it was bent to the breaking point, and probably all of us were aware that, in the worst event, it could end up costing all of us our lives. Good triumphed, however, and the work was able to continue right up to the end with utterly heroic contributions, especially by Wallenberg. Our greatest worry was Wallenberg's safety. The Arrow Cross men hated him open and intensely." Wallenberg learned several times that they intended to murder him. Disregarding these threats to himself, toward the end of 1944 Wallenberg moved his operations across the Danube from Buda to Pest because that was where the ghettos were located, whereas the Swedish legation was in Buda. He also increased the size of his staff in Section C to 600.[41]

A final threat loomed on the horizon as Budapest was on the verge of falling to the Russians. In January 1945, Wallenberg learned that the Germans were tinkering with the idea of blowing up the ghetto with its 70,000 residents before withdrawing from Pest. He personally threatened the German commander and Ernö Vajna, the Arrow Cross leader in charge of the defense of Budapest, with dire retribution by the Allies if they carried out this plan. According to one account, Wallenberg warned the German commander that he would be tried for war crimes after the war if he went through with this criminal act. The German general relented and the ghetto was spared. This saved the lives of the 70,000 residents of the ghetto.[42]

In his final report to the Swedish government on December 7, 1944, Wallenberg noted that the situation for Hungarian Jews in Budapest had further deteriorated. He indicated that probably about 40,000 Jews, including 15,000 men from the labor service and some 25,000 captured in their houses or on the street, had been forced to march to Austria on foot, a distance of 240 kilometers. Due to inclement weather and the harsh marching conditions, many had died on the way. Others were shot for simply not being able to keep up. At the border, they were taken over by Eichmann's SS Special Commando with violent blows and were put to hard labor on border fortifications. As for Jews in the ghettos, there were probably more than 69,000 in the Central Ghetto, and 33,000 in the International Ghetto. Of these 7,000 were in Swedish houses, 2,000 in Red Cross houses, and 23,000 in Swiss houses. In the 31 Swedish houses on Pozsonyi Street and vicinity, conditions were anything but satisfactory, as four to twelve persons shared a room. In addition, some 335 employees as well as 40 doctors and house wardens lived on the premises. Two hospitals had been set up, with a total of 150 beds. A soup kitchen was also in operation. A doctor had been assigned to every house, but the number of patients suffering from contagious diseases was rising every day. An epidemic of dysentery, not yet large, had broken out. Health conditions in the Swedish houses were still relatively good, and only five infected persons had died so far. There was, however, the danger of an epidemic, and what was required was a hospital with at least 200 beds. Freedom of movement of legation personnel and clients was sharply curtailed. While on business in the city they were often taken into protective detention, making it necessary for the legation to get involved in freeing them. In spite of these hardships, Wallenberg wrote that he was determined to go on with his rescue efforts. On January 10, 1945, a week before the Russian occupation of Pest, Raoul Wallenberg told Per Anger, "For me there's no choice. I've taken on this assignment and I'd never be able to go back to Stockholm without knowing inside myself I'd done all a man could do to save as many Jews as possible."[43]

Tragedy struck the young Raoul Wallenberg, but from an unexpected side—the liberating Russians. On January 17, 1945, as soon as the Russians won control of Pest, Wallenberg was apprehended on orders from Moscow and held in confinement, probably on the suspicion that he was a spy for the Western Allies. As he was led into a Russian military jeep, his parting words were, "I don't know whether I am being taken as a guest of the Soviets or as a prisoner." When last seen in Budapest, he was only 32 years of age. The Soviet government, in time to come, concocted various explanations to explain the mystery of his disappearance, and to this day the full picture is still missing. At the same time, from various sources, it is possible to cautiously reconstruct the following course of events. A day after the Pest section of Budapest was invested by Soviet troops on January 15, 1945, Soviet Deputy Foreign Minister Vladimir Dekanazov informed the Swedish ambassador in Moscow, Staffan Söderblom, that Wallenberg had been located and steps had been taken by Soviet military authorities to protect him and his belongings. The other Swedish diplomatic personnel were being moved to Bucharest, Romania.[44]

However, soon thereafter, the Soviets changed position and denied any knowledge of Wallenberg's whereabouts. They repeated this disclaimer in the following years, such as to Gunnar Hägglöf, the Swedish ambassador, in January 1946. On August 18, 1947, Deputy Foreign Minister Andrei Vyshinsky wrote to Rolf Sohlman, Hägglöf's successor, that Wallenberg was not in the Soviet Union and "he is unknown to us." He added: "Wallenberg might have left the Soviet troop area on his own initiative, enemy air attacks might have occurred, Wallenberg might have succumbed to enemy gunfire, etc. . . . It only remains to be assumed that during the battles in the city of Budapest, Wallenberg succumbed to or was imprisoned by Szálasi's supporters."

The Swedish government did not buy this, and after a lapse of several years, in 1952, it wrote twice to the Soviet ambassador in Stockholm, K.K. Rodionov, that "there can be no doubt whatever that he was taken into custody by Soviet authorities." As to allegations that Wallenberg issued false passports or other identity documents to persons close to the pro-Nazi Hungarian regime and was conducting illegal intelligence activities, "the Swedish government wishes most emphatically to state that such suspicions against Wallenberg must be regarded as entirely unjustified. If passports and other identification documents have been found in the wrong hands in some cases, this cannot be blamed on Wallenberg. . . . Wallenberg's desire was to assist the Jewish population, and to help other politically persecuted people." On August 5, 1953, in response to a further inquiry by Sweden, the Soviet ambassador to Sweden repeated the standard claim that "one can only assume that he either happened to be killed at the time of the street fighting or fell into the hands of Szálasi's supporters."[45]

Then, suddenly, bowing to pressure by Sweden, on February 6, 1957, Deputy Foreign Minister Andrei Gromyko announced that the Soviet authorities had discovered a document signed by the head of the infirmary at Lubyanka prison, A.L. Smoltsov, stating that Wallenberg had died on July 17, 1947, and that this information had been reported to the head of the Soviet security service, Viktor Abakumov. The Smoltsov statement read as follows: "I report that the prisoner Wallenberg, who is known to you, died suddenly last night in his cell, probably as a result of a myocardial infarction. In keeping with the instructions you have given that I should care personally for Wallenberg, I request instructions as to who is to be assigned to carry out an autopsy to determine the cause of death. July 17, 1947. Head of the Prison Medical Department, Colonel in the Medical Service— Smoltsov." The report contained the following notation in Smoltsov's handwriting: "Have personally informed the minister. Order was given to cremate the body without autopsy. July 17, Smoltsov."

The new Soviet version placed the blame squarely on the shoulders of the late Abakumov, who was charged with having given the Soviet Foreign Ministry incorrect information about Wallenberg for several years, and this supposedly explained the previous Soviet disclaimers that Wallenberg was in the Soviet Union. Since Smoltsov died in May 1953, and Abakumov was executed in 1953 in connection with the purge of the Soviet security service after Stalin's death, it was impossible to confirm this new revelation. The Swedish government's response, on February 7, 1957, stated that it "strongly regretted" this meager information, and that "nothing is said about the motives for Wallenberg's imprisonment nor about his fate during subsequent years. . . . For Raoul Wallenberg's mother and relatives, who had to live in terrible uncertainty for so many years, the Russian statement must signify yet another severe blow." The Swedish government also found it hard to believe that all other documentation about Wallenberg's Soviet imprisonment except for the report mentioned in the Soviet reply had been obliterated.[46]

In the following years, the Soviets adamantly stuck to this version, although eyewitnesses claimed to have seen Wallenberg at a later date in Lubyanka, Vladimir, and Lefortovo prisons, as well as other places (labor camps and mental institutions) in the Soviet Union. Many years passed without progress. In October 1989, during Gorbachev's tenure of power, Wallenberg's diplomatic passport, cigarette case, motor registration certificate, prison register card, foreign currency, and diary came to light in the basement of the KGB headquarters at Lubyanka prison and were given members of his family.[47] The pressure on the Russian government did not abate, and after the dissolution of the Soviet Union, the Russian government agreed to form a Russian-Swedish working group to investigate and report on what had befallen Wallenberg. This team published its findings in 2000. It reconfirmed the Soviet spy suspicion, as well as the likelihood that Wallenberg was either shot in 1947, on orders of the Kremlin, or died as a result of the lack of proper medical treatment and the harsh conditions at

Lubyanka, coupled with the cruel interrogations he underwent at the hands of the Soviet intelligence officers. In addition, the Swedish-Russian investigative team found that Wallenberg's fate was discussed and decided at the highest levels of the Soviet government, including Stalin, Molotov, and Beria. However, to this day, the full Soviet record of his arrest and incarceration are missing, and the details of his fate remain an unsolved mystery. As reported by the investigative team, "Unfortunately, we still do not have a complete, legally tenable account of Raoul Wallenberg's fate or the reason for his arrest, despite the tremendous efforts of everyone involved. Documents appear to have been destroyed; key persons have died or are either unable or unwilling to remember. It is not therefore possible to close the Raoul Wallenberg file."[48]

The working group noted that a warrant for Wallenberg's arrest, signed by Bulganin, the deputy defense minister, on January 17, 1945, had been sent to General Malinovsky, the Russian commander in Hungary, with a copy to Abakumov. Bulganin had ordered Wallenberg sent to Moscow, probably with Stalin's consent. No reason for the arrest was given. Wallenberg arrived in Moscow on January 25, and the Lubyanka records show his arrival at the prison on February 6, together with his driver Vilmos Langfelder. Swiss diplomat Harald Feller was also arrested and arrived in Moscow on March 4. Wallenberg underwent several interrogations at Lubyanka and then was moved to Lefortovo on May 29, where he and Langfelder remained throughout 1946. In March 1947, Wallenberg was moved back to Lubyanka. The last recorded interrogation of Wallenberg took place on March 11, 1947. Much earlier, in February 1945, Wallenberg reportedly protested against his treatment and detention, and asked to be put in touch with the Swedish mission in Moscow. He wrote again in 1946, this time to Stalin. In the estimation of the working group, the Soviets may have considered the best proof of his guilt the fact that neither the Swedish mission in Moscow nor the Swedish government had done much on his behalf.[49]

The working group further disclosed that in April 1945, the United States envoy in Moscow, Averell Harriman, suggested a joint US-

Swedish demarche on Wallenberg, but Swedish Ambassador Söderblom showed no interest, claiming that Wallenberg had probably died in a car accident or been murdered while still on Hungarian soil. Söderblom repeated this assertion in meetings with high Soviet officials, and added in a conversation with Abramov, "It would be splendid if the [Swedish] mission were to be given a reply in this spirit, that is to say, that Wallenberg is dead. It is necessary first and foremost because of Wallenberg's mother, who is still hoping her son is alive. She is wasting her strength and health on a fruitless search." On June 15, 1946, Stalin received Söderblom, in the presence of Deputy Foreign Minister Lozovsky (later executed on Stalin's orders). According to Söderblom's report, Stalin made a note of Wallenberg's name and pointed out that the Soviet side had given orders to protect the Swede. Söderblom surprisingly to Stalin once again stated that Wallenberg had certainly fallen victim to an accident or been kidnapped. In the words of the Swedish working group, "The passivity with which Staffan Söderblom dealt with the Wallenberg case was remarkable," raising questions about his judgment. Officially, the Soviets still claimed that they had no knowledge of Wallenberg's whereabouts. So, on August 18, 1947, Deputy Foreign Minister Vyshinsky, basing himself on disclaimers by his own intelligence sources, sent a personal note to the new Swedish ambassador, Rolf Sohlman, stating that "Wallenberg is not in the Soviet Union and is unknown to us." Nor had he been found in a camp for prisoners-of-war and internees. "This only leaves the assumption that Wallenberg died during the fighting in the city of Budapest, or that he was captured by members of the Arrow Cross."[50]

What, in truth, was the nature of the Soviet suspicions against Wallenberg? Evidently the Russian military command in Hungary was very irritated by continually encountering people he had furnished with foreign documents. The situation was not made any better by the fact that a substantial number of falsified protective passports, both Swiss and Swedish, were in circulation. Quite a few of these had ended up in the hands of Arrow Cross members and others of the Nazi persuasion, who sought protection from trial and retribution by the new

Communist masters of the country. Wallenberg was already compromised, in their eyes, by having accepted American money for the aid operation. The Russians probably also learned that Wallenberg's immediate contact in Sweden was Ivar Olsen, who, on top of being the WRB representative there, was also the chief American intelligence officer for the Baltic region under the OSS (Office of Strategic Services, the forerunner of the CIA), and was responsible for agents in Norway, the Baltic states, and the Balkans. It cannot also be ruled out that some OSS agents perceived Raoul Wallenberg as an agent. When the Russians later learned that Wallenberg had been the prime mover in the rescue of the Jews and, besides that, he planned to remain in Hungary after the war to support the cause of the Jews, their mistrust of him increased. Probably Wallenberg's touted reconstruction plan for Hungary was, to the Russians, nothing more than an attempt at continued covert espionage.

Briefly, as far as can be cautiously judged, the Russians were convinced in 1945 that Wallenberg had undercover assignments in collusion with American intelligence, and the Jewish rescue action was only a cover for espionage. In addition, the Russians may have discovered that Wallenberg received funds from the Joint Distribution Committee, an organization they regarded as a Zionist world power hatching anti-Soviet plots. Finally, Raoul Wallenberg represented the Wallenberg family, the wealthiest and most powerful family of financiers in Sweden. While the Wallenberg-owned SKF concern supplied ball bearings to the Soviet aircraft industry, the Wallenbergs were also suspected of having transmitted feelers from members of the German anti-Communist movement seeking to negotiate a separate peace with the Western Allies. Therefore, Wallenberg's contacts with high-level Nazis in Budapest as part of his rescue operation may have been perceived by the Soviets as part of an attempt to arrive at a separate peace at the expense of the Soviet Union.[51] The main purpose of his arrest, therefore, may have been to use him in an exchange deal. As stated by Lars Berg, secretary at the Swedish legation in Budapest: "For the Russians, with their understanding, or, more accurately, their lack of understanding for human problems, it was completely inconceivable that Wallenberg, the Swede, had come down to Budapest to try to rescue Hungarian Jews."[52]

Sweden too shares a bit of the blame in the protracted but half-hearted effort to resolve the Wallenberg mystery. In the estimation of Per Anger, who served as a secretary in the Swedish legation in Budapest during the war years, it seems as if the Swedish government soon came to feel that the Wallenberg matter was an unpleasant irritating factor in its relations with the Soviet Union. Anger adds that the lack of energy and the timidity which characterized the Swedish government during the years after the war could hardly have helped but affect the Russian attitude. "There is every reason to believe that more forceful action from the beginning by Sweden would have led to Wallenberg's release, especially if an exchange had been proposed for some Soviet spy caught in Sweden. . . . One gets the feeling, reading between the lines, that even the Russians expected a proposal of this kind from Sweden. These are the lost years in the Wallenberg case." The United States, through its embassy in Moscow, showed great interest in the Wallenberg case as early as 1945. But the Swedes failed to follow up on this, and no cooperative effort on this matter was ever established between the American and Swedish missions in Moscow. "Still another example of the paralysis that characterized Swedish behavior during the years just after the war!" Anger adds, "One asks whether a real will existed behind all the inquiries and appeals that have been made? Has it not been merely a game of make-believe in which the government, for the benefit of domestic Swedish opinion, made a show of sparing no effort in a case that they neither believed in nor wanted to believe in, because it was more comfortable that way?" In the words of one observer: "Had the Swedish government pounded on the table earlier, you would have had Wallenberg in Stockholm long ago!"[53]

In summary, the working group suggested the following possible explanations for the death of Wallenberg in July 1947: he succumbed to hardship and inhuman treatment, mental and physical strain; he was shot on orders from Molotov and Abakumov, with or without Stalin's knowledge; a heart attack was induced by various forms of mental torture (including sound and light), medical experiment, and perhaps poison; he was liquidated for refusing to cooperate. Finally, it may be that Beria ordered his execution in 1947. Beria was trying to foment the myth of a Jewish conspiracy, and for this he needed Wallenberg in order to fabricate a conspiracy case that he could later present to the paranoiac Stalin. However, the interrogation reports shown Stalin were false. But it would have been embarrassing, even dangerous, to suddenly inform Sweden that Wallenberg had been in a Soviet prison in Moscow all along. What satisfactory explanation could one possibly give? His story would have created a scandal. It became essential, therefore, to remove the problem. Putting Wallenberg in another prison or camp was virtually the same as revealing his existence sooner or later. Anything Raoul Wallenberg himself might say upon release would have been extremely embarrassing to the Soviets. Therefore the likelihood of a decision to be rid of him.[54]

On November 26, 1963, the year that Yad Vashem's Commission for the Righteous started its work, it awarded Raoul Wallenberg the title of Righteous Among the Nations. The commission's head, Supreme Court Justice Moshe Landau, noted the importance of respecting the wishes of Wallenberg's mother not to give up hope for the recovery of her son. However, Mrs. Maj Von Dardel was not satisfied with this statement, and refused to accept the honors in her son's name, instead asking that efforts be redoubled to find and free him. Until her own death she remained adamant in her belief that he was still alive. After her passing in 1979, a tree-planting ceremony took place at Yad Vashem, in the presence of her two children, Guy Von Dardel and Nina Lagergren. In the following years, Yad Vashem continued its efforts to resolve the riddle of Wallenberg's disappearance. Among other things, it asked the Russian Orthodox Church representative in Jerusalem to intercede on Wallenberg's behalf. In January 1986, the State of Israel awarded its first honorary citizenship to Raoul Wallenberg. The ceremony in the office of President Haim Herzog was attended by the Swedish ambassador to Israel. Wallenberg also received honorary citizenship in the United States, Israel, and Canada. The Wallenberg family and all people of good will still wait for a full explanation of the fate of this heroic and tragic figure, who, by his benevolent acts in Budapest, exemplified the best and the most elevated form of humanitarian behavior.[55]

Per Anger

Raoul Wallenberg's principal aide in Budapest, Per Anger, was posted to Berlin as a Swedish diplomat before arriving in Budapest, where he served as secretary until 1945. Immediately after the German occupation in March 1944, and before Wallenberg's arrival, the Swedish legation was besieged by Jews pleading for help. As Anger recalls, supplicants jammed the reception room, and the queue snaked a long way down the street. In a rather short time, the legation issued no less than 700 provisional passports and certificates. The wording of the documents was approximately as follows: "It is hereby certified that the Swedish relatives, domiciled in Sweden, of John Doe, have on his behalf applied to the appropriate authorities for Swedish citizenship, upon which a decision may shortly be expected. For this reason, the legation calls upon all authorities, both civil and military, in an action concerning John Doe, to take due consideration of the matter cited above."

By early July the legation had already issued 450 passports (termed temporary passports) signed by Ambassador Danielsson and stamped with all the seals. This was the first example of what was later named *Schutzpass,* or protective passport, which Wallenberg later issued by the thousands. This undertaking followed upon Horthy's offer to allow the few hundred bearers of Swedish passports and some 7,000 bearers of immigration certificates issued by the Swiss consulate, as representative of Britain, to leave the country. This plan did not materialize since, as related earlier, Hitler had conditioned his approval on Horthy's allowing Hungarian Jews, mainly those still in Budapest, to be deported.[56]

Lars Ernster, professor of biochemistry at the University of Stockholm, related in a postwar letter his father-in-law's rescue by Per Anger. Lars Ernster, a labor service worker for a German antiaircraft battery outside Budapest, had the job of carrying ammunition to the antiaircraft guns during the continuous American air raids. His father-in-law Hugo Wohl, the managing director of a Hungarian radio facto-

*Yad Vashem Council Chairman Gideon Hausner presenting a Certificate of Honor to
Swedish diplomat Per Anger, during a ceremony at Yad Vashem, 1983. Looking on,
Dr. Mordecai Paldiel, director of the Righteous Among the Nations Department.*

ry with close connections to Sweden, was informed by Per Anger that
he was authorized to issue him and his family "emergency passports;"
a promise carried out on June 10, 1944. In Ernster's words: "With this
document in my hand, I was released from the *Arbeitsdienst* [forced
labor] and placed in a special Swedish company—symbolic service
with light labor and the possibility of spending the nights at home,"
thus escaping further jeopardy to his life. With the Arrow Cross coup
d'état, on October 15, 1944, Anger arranged for Ernster and family to
be moved to one of the Swedish houses. "I spent the last months of the
war in one of the office buildings belonging to the Swedish legation in
Budapest and every day witnessed the heroic efforts of Swedish diplomats—in particular Per Anger and Raoul Wallenberg —to save Jewish
lives from the Nazi terror."[57]

On one occasion, the legation received an appeal for help from a
Swedish woman, in Stockholm, who had formerly been married to a

Hungarian Jew and wanted to rescue their ten-year-old son, Ragnar. The boy was living with his paternal grandparents in Pécs in southern Hungary, because his father had been drafted into a Hungarian forced labor battalion for Jews. Per Anger was assigned to see what could be done, and early one morning he drove out to Pécs, about 120 miles from Budapest. The deportations had not yet taken place there. Ragnar's old grandmother refused to let him be taken away. In Per Anger's words, "I explained that his father should be allowed to decide the question, and so we all went out to the internment camp on the outskirts where he was working. He realized that this was a chance of rescue for his son and immediately gave his permission. Then, with great emotion, he parted from his son. I put the boy in the legation car, took the Yellow Star from his chest, and returned with him to Budapest. Ragnar lived with us for a while and then was sent by plane to Stockholm, where he was happily reunited with his mother. Later I learned that the day after my visit, all the Jews in Pécs had been shut up in a ghetto and were shortly thereafter deported to Poland."[58]

With the Arrow Cross takeover, the persecution of the Jews reached a Dante-like pitch that defied description. In Per Anger's words, "At night, we could hear the shots of the Arrow Cross militiamen's submachine guns when Jews, after being robbed of everything including their clothes, were shot down and thrown into the Danube." Armed Arrow Cross members often broke into places under the Swedish legation's protection, plundering food and trying to carry off the personnel. "We—Wallenberg, Ekmark, [Lars] Berg, Mezey, Carlsson, and I [all of the Swedish legation]—remained on full alert day and night, often having to rush out en masse to try and avert an attack by the Arrow Cross. Bluff and threats were good ways of driving them off."[59] One day, Per Anger rushed out to a station from where a trainload of Jews was about to depart. "I explained that a terrible mistake had been made, since apparently they were about to deport Jews who had Swedish protective passports. If they were not released immediately, I would make sure that [German ambassador] Veesenmayer was informed." The trick worked. "I went into the cars to call the roll, but found only two Jews with protective passports. However, with the help of the Hungarian police officer there, Batizfalvy (who secretly cooperated with Raoul Wallenberg and me), I succeeded, despite the SS commandant's orders, in freeing 150 Jews from the station even though 148 had no protective passports."[60]

Relations with the Hungarian government became increasingly strained, especially after the legation's refusal to move out of Budapest to western Hungary, a decision regarded as an "unfriendly act," which in diplomatic language meant a hostile act toward the regime. The situation was exacerbated by the fact that the Swedish government had expelled the diplomatic representative of the Arrow Cross government in Stockholm. Switzerland, by contrast, had allowed the Arrow Cross representative, a consul, to remain in Bern for the time being. It was this card that the Swiss Harald Feller took advantage of in maintaining the appearance of good relations between the Arrow Cross regime and the Swiss government. Per Anger felt that his government could have allowed the Arrow Cross man to stay on for a few more weeks, in order to guarantee the rescue operation of the Swedish legation in Budapest. To expel another country's chargé d'affaires is a pretty clear message that you don't want any diplomatic relations with that country. This brusque move "pulled the juridical rug out from under" the Swedish rescue efforts. In Anger's estimation, "If the Russians had not arrived at just that time, the consequences for the Jews in the Swedish houses would have been terrible. In all probability, the Arrow Cross men, having discovered that recognition by the Swedish government was not in the offing, would have carried out their threats and blown the Swedish houses and their residents to kingdom come, or liquidated them in some other way. All the Swedish efforts would have been in vain."[61]

As the Russian armies closed in on Budapest, Ambassador Danielsson decided to keep the legation in Budapest. The acting Hungarian foreign minister responded that his government would no longer be responsible for the safety of the Swedish team. "To my question of whether by that he meant violence against the mission," Per Anger asked, "I received only evasive replies. I then returned at once to the legation to warn the others. They should not remain at the lega-

Swedish diplomat Per Anger standing between Gideon Hausner (left)
and the Swedish ambassador to Israel (right) during a ceremony
in the Hall of Remembrance, Yad Vashem, 1983.

tion during the next 24 hours and should preferably not spend the
night in their usual lodgings." True enough, at 5:00 A.M. on the morning of December 24, a group of about 50 Arrow Cross men, armed
with submachine guns, forced their way into the Swedish legation. "It
was clear that they intended to carry off the staff forcibly," which they
proceeded to do. Anger sought out the German military commander,
who refused to intervene. He continued to the Swiss chargé d'affaires,
Feller, who promised all his support and at once put his staff to work
to find out what had happened to the Swedes. Wallenberg had succeeded in escaping at the last minute. Later that day, Danielsson
turned up at the Swiss legation.[62]

Anger then moved to an affiliate of the Swedish legation on the
Buda side of the city, across the Danube, in a small two-story apartment house known only to the members of the legation and intended
for use in an emergency. "We barricaded the door and sat down to
wait," as Christmas settled in. "That was one Christmas Eve I will
never forget. . . . When there was a knock on the door, we cocked our

pistols and thought that the Arrow Cross men had now found our hiding place. It was instead some members of the legation staff. . . . Later Wallenberg, too, came to my apartment. He had remained on the Pest side during the critical hours and in that way had escaped the Arrow Cross." Meanwhile, the Arrow Cross militia proceeded to vandalize the Swedish legation building.[63]

Returning to Sweden after the war, Per Anger worked in the Foreign Ministry and in 1946 was posted to the Swedish legation in Cairo. He then filled various posts in Austria, Canada, and Australia, until his retirement. In 1980, Yad Vashem awarded Per Anger the title of Righteous Among the Nations.[64]

Carl Ivar Danielsson and Lars Berg

Carl Ivar Danielsson, the Swedish ambassador in Budapest, supported the rescue operations conducted by Per Anger and Raoul Wallenberg. Soon after Hungary's occupation by the Germans in April 1944, Danielsson proposed granting temporary passports to people who had connections with Sweden. At first the Swedish government refused, but given the increasing gravity of the situation, in April it allowed Danielsson to stamp Swedish visas on passports, thus guaranteeing Swedish protection to their holders, but this was done only in a few cases. Danielsson informed his superiors that most of those who came to him had no passport whatsoever or any other document in which he could stamp a visa, so he again proposed issuing temporary passports to people who had some connection with Sweden. Danielsson followed this up on June 20 with a request for King Gustav V to intervene "but immediately, before it is too late." Four days later he sent a full report describing the deportations with authentic statistics, and warning that the Germans intended to deport the Jews of Budapest before July 15. On June 30, 1944, King Gustav V sent a telegram to the regent of Hungary, Horthy, with a request to halt the deportations. As already told, Horthy bowed to outside pressure and ordered the deportations stopped on July 7, 1944.[65]

Danielsson did not stop at that. On August 21, he and the Vatican nuncio, Angelo Rotta, presented a joint protest to the Hungarian government, a memorandum also signed by the representatives of Switzerland, Portugal, and Spain. The document explicitly condemned the intention of the government to renew the deportation of Jews; this time those of Budapest: "We also know, and from an absolutely reliable source [the "Auschwitz Report"] what deportation means in most cases, even if it is masked as labor service abroad. . . . It is absolutely impermissible that people should be persecuted and sent to their death simply for their racial deportation."

Surprisingly, the rescheduled deportation was cancelled by another source, SS head Heinrich Himmler, on August 24, one day before the *Aktion* was supposed to begin, for reasons having to do with his secret efforts to explore the possibility of a separate peace with the Western Allies.[66] As already mentioned, when the Hungarian government asked the diplomatic corps to move out of Budapest, Danielsson refused, justifying it by his commitment to guarantee the safety of the Jews in the Swedish houses. Fearing Arrow Cross retribution, Danielsson urged his government to grant a temporary recognition of the regime in the interest of the sheltered Jews. In Per Anger's words: "In telegram after telegram during the fall of 1944, Danielsson pointed out the importance of extending some kind of recognition to the Szálasi government to make continued rescue work possible. Besides Switzerland—we pointed out—Turkey and Spain, too, had accepted Szálasi's representatives in their countries, whereby their missions in Budapest could go on working undisturbed. But the answer from Sweden was a categorical no."[67]

Lars Berg was sent to Budapest in August 1944 to help Per Anger with the issuing of Swedish passports. He worked side by side with him in the common rescue efforts. Both Carl Ivar Danielsson and Lars Berg were awarded the Righteous title by Yad Vashem in 1982.[68]

Valdemar Langlet

We now come to Valdemar Langlet, the representative of the Swedish Red Cross in Budapest. Langlet was a lecturer in Swedish language at the University of Budapest, but in June 1944 he was asked to assume the leadership of the Swedish Red Cross (henceforth SRC) in

*Valdemar Langlet, the Swedish Red Cross
representative in Budapest, Hungary.*

the city, with diplomatic status as a member of the Swedish legation. Born in 1872, he was fluent in several languages, including Esperanto. After the death of his first wife, Signe, he remarried to the 29-year-old Russian-born Nina in 1929. The two arrived in Budapest in 1931 and stayed there until 1945. In 1938 Langlet became an unpaid cultural attaché at the Swedish legation. When the SRC post in Budapest opened, it was at first felt that Count Folke Bernadotte, head of the SRC in Sweden, would himself take it, but this did not materialize for reasons not fully known. Ambassador Danielsson recommended Langlet on June 19, 1944. In light of the critical situation for the Jews in Budapest, Langlet began functioning as the SRC representative even before official authorization was received from Bernadotte.[69] Formal confirmation came through on June 21. The official appointment, sent on August 17, 1944, stipulated that Langlet was to be subordinate

to the Swedish legation in Budapest, "and every important action by
the delegate requires the approval of minister beforehand." This resulted in some friction, as Sweden simultaneously also appointed Mrs.
Asta Nilsson as the SRC's official representative within the legation.
According to Per Anger, Nilsson's task was restricted to help for children, nothing else, and for this purpose she was not under Langlet's
authority. Differences of opinion and sometimes mistrust often arose
between Langlet and Nilsson because of the failure of the SRC in
Sweden to clearly define their respective spheres.[70]

Langlet reportedly issued and signed as many as 2,000 protective
letters bearing the SRC emblem. These documents had no legal basis
under international law, but were honored by the Hungarians for their
own political reasons. Most of these letters, it should be emphasized,
were issued without the knowledge of Ambassador Danielsson.[71] In
addition, under Langlet and his private secretary Alexander Kasser, the
SRC distributed medical assistance to 16 Hungarian hospitals, as well
as provisions to 14 homes for the elderly and public canteens. Also of
importance, Langlet worked on a voluntary unpaid basis, and was
financially supported by private donors, mostly Jews, who placed
houses and their contents at his disposal to assist him in his work on
behalf of Jews.[72]

Because of the unclear formal nature of Langlet's work, tension and
uncertainty persisted between him and his immediate superiors at the
Swedish legation. In a letter to the Foreign Ministry on September 9,
1944, Danielsson complained about Langlet's issuing letters of protection in the name of SRC and presenting them to the legation as a *fait
accompli,* asking whether he had to tolerate this. Danielsson added that
the Hungarian authorities honored such documents, and this fact
might be reason enough to allow Langlet to continue. However, on
September 20, 1944, Prince Carl, the SRC head in Sweden, wrote that
"this should not happen. In fact, according to instructions transmitted
by the Red Cross, he is forbidden to take such measures without the
minister's approbation, and eventually of ours." Evidently, a question
had arisen about how much confidence the SRC had in Langlet, who
disregarded the prohibition and continued to issue such documents.[73]

Carte d'identité hongroise avec traduction allemande.

Carte d'identité hongroise. La traduction du texte de protection
signé par Valdemar Langlet apparaît en page suivante.

A Protective Letter issued by Valdemar Langlet,
the Swedish Red Cross representative in Budapest, Hungary.

Dr. Gedeon P. Dienes, who in 1944 was Langlet's private driver and
emissary on many missions, stated that he knew Langlet from his studies of Swedish at the university. In 1944, he placed himself at Langlet's
disposal on behalf of a clandestine group of concerned individuals. "He
asked us to help him distribute *Schutzbriefe* [protective letters] to needy
people. He gave us a typewriter and a stencil. We distributed these documents as well as other materials. . . .The SRC had four or five cars,
which were used for moving people to secure places. Many came to his
office or to my apartment on Krisztina Street to get letters of protection. There were probably thousands of such documents. I remember
that on one occasion I handed out about a hundred such documents to
people in the forced labor service. These documents, of course, had no
international legal force, but an ordinary policeman or soldier had no
knowledge of their legitimacy. . . . The important thing was to save
human lives. This was the primary thing." Langlet also placed people in

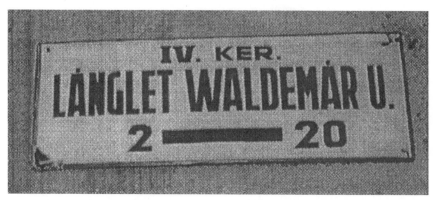

A street in Budapest, Hungary, named after Valdemar Langlet.

convents and hospitals under the protection of the Red Cross—in all about a dozen such places. In Langlet's words: "People jokingly began to call us the city's biggest landlord." In early December, Arrow Cross militiamen broke into the offices of the Swedish Red Cross, arrested the staff, and prohibited any further activity.[74]

Much of our information about Langlet's work comes from Jewish underground operatives. Peretz-Ladislav Revesz was a member of a Zionist underground cell. In a 1964 statement, he related that Herman Adler sent him to Langlet's home to pick up false credentials for needy persons. At a later date, Adler himself sought refuge in Langlet's home, and was then helped to secretly flee to Romania. In November 1944, when Jews were forced to move into a ghetto, Langlet provided some with protective letters. "I received from him some protective letters which I distributed to several families. Myself, I received from Mrs. Langlet a document stating that I was free to circulate at all times. She knew by then that I was a Jew and a fugitive." In a 1945 letter to Valdemar Langlet, Ladislaus and Mrs. Bartha, two others he had aided, thanked him "for saving our lives; only Almighty God is able to reward you in the way you deserve."

After their departure from Hungary in April 1945, the Langlets received a letter signed by 14 former residents of protective houses profusely thanking them for working "day and night" to help persecuted Jews; residents of protected houses, children, the sick, the hungry, and the aged. "We part from Professor Langlet and his wife with a heavy heart, for he is leaving Budapest. Your departure is an irreplaceable loss." Francois Pollak, in a 1946 letter, thanked Langlet for saving his sister, Edita Loewensteioiva, and her children, from deportation, as well as other families. "Blessed is the Swedish people to be rewarded with having persons like the Langlet family counted among its citizens."[75]

Valdemar and Nina Langlet left Hungary on May 26, 1945. Back in Sweden, and with very limited means, the Langlets first settled on a small farm. Valdemar went back to writing, while Nina gave piano lessons. He wrote a book on his experiences in Hungary. On January 2, 1945, Langlet was honored by the SRC with a medal, and on June 4, 1949, with the Swedish Royal Order of the Northern Star. For their help in saving so many Jews under the most difficult circumstances. Yad Vashem in 1965 conferred upon Valdemar and Nina Langlet the title of Righteous Among the Nations.[76]

Romanian, Spanish, and Italian Diplomats

Florian Manoliu

The following story began in Switzerland but is inextricably linked to the work of the Swiss diplomat Carl Lutz in Budapest. Florian Manoliu was a Romanian diplomat posted as a commercial attaché at the Romanian consulate in Bern. He was allied with Romanian political elements opposed to Romania's alliance with Nazi Germany, such as Grigore Gafencu, a former foreign minister, who had fled to Switzerland after Ion Antonescu's assumption of dictatorial power, and Iuliu Maniu, a former prime minister, who had remained in Romania. During his travels back and forth between Switzerland and Romania, Manoliu often carried secret messages for Gafenco and Maniu. While in Bucharest, Manoliu became acquainted with Georg Mandel. Mandel's financial dealings eventually landed him in Geneva, where he happened to encounter some politicians and diplomats from El Salvador who were making an exploratory tour. Impressed by his personality and his manifold contacts, they invited him to assume con-

sular responsibility as an honorary Salvadoran consul, with special
attention to Hungary and Yugoslavia, countries with which El
Salvador had no diplomatic ties. The small Latin American country
was evidently anxious to find new outlets for its main product, coffee.
Although Mandel had never been to Central America and did not
know Spanish, he accepted the offer. To make his name more palat-
able to listeners, Mandel added "Mantello" to his family name, which
to European ears sounded a bit more Latin. The Salvadoran consul-
general, José Arturo Castellanos, appointed him as the Geneva consulate's general secretary, and soon agreed to Mantello's request to
issue a certain number of certificates testifying the holders were
Salvadoran citizens. Mantello issued hundreds of such documents and
distributed them to Jews in France, Belgium, and the Netherlands, for
free. The text stated that the holder was a citizen of the Republic of El
Salvador, which requested all governments to render all possible help
to their compatriot. At the bottom Mantello signed in his capacity as
the general secretary of the general consulate. It appears, in retrospect,
that the president of El Salvador, Castenadu Castro, implicitly agreed
to this.[77]

When Mantello learned that Jews were being deported from the
Transylvania region of Hungary, where his family lived, he asked
Manoliu, on his next trip to Romania, to take some Salvadoran cer-
tificates to his relatives in Bistrica. He also asked Manoliu to deliver
1.000 signed blank Salvadoran certificates to Consul Carl Lutz in
Budapest on his return journey. Lutz and his staff would fill in the
names and use the documents in addition to their own *Schutzbriefe*, as
they saw fit. At the time, El Salvador was negotiating to get
Switzerland—in other words, Carl Lutz—to represent its interests in
Hungary.

Manoliu set out on his journey on May 22, 1944. The Gestapo,
probably tipped off by its secret agents in Bern, arrested him during
his stopover in Vienna and held him for an entire week, in spite of
rules governing the immunity of diplomats. The Germans apparently
suspected that Manoliu was carrying secret Romanian peace feelers,
now that the Red Army was fast approaching the country's eastern bor-

ders. Fortunately, Manoliu had arranged for the Romanian consul in Vienna to meet him at the train station and take his diplomatic pouch, which contained the Salvadoran certificates, for safekeeping. Manoliu was taken to Berlin and interrogated about the purpose of his trip. "Aren't we allies?" Manoliu replied. "Why are you questioning me?" After holding him for eight days, the Germans allowed Manoliu to return to Vienna, but then only upon his written assurance that he would go straight to Bucharest and not stop off in Budapest.

Before leaving Vienna, Manoliu retrieved back his diplomatic pouch from the Romanian consulate. On or about June 3, he left for Bucharest to deliver a message from Gafencu to Maniu, and remained there until June 10. Then, instead of returning to Switzerland as his German-authorized transit visa dictated, he traveled to Bistrice in search of Mantello's family. He found neither the Mandel family nor any other Jews. All of the city's Jews had been deported to the death camps. For several days, Manoliu traveled to various towns in Transylvania, such as Koloszvár, Satu-Mare, and Des—all emptied of Jews. Disobeying earlier German instructions, Manoliu arrived in Budapest on June 17 or 18, where he planned to hand over the 1,000 Salvadoran certificates to Carl Lutz and also to meet with Miklós Krausz, who represented the Palestine Jewish Agency and worked hand in hand with Lutz. Manoliu carried with him a letter in Hebrew from Dr. Chaim Posner, who represented the Jewish Agency in Geneva, stating that he was completely trustworthy. Manoliu went to the Swiss compound in the building that had formerly housed the American embassy and there met with Carl Lutz, to whom he turned over most of the Salvadoran papers. Lutz took Manoliu to Krausz's hideout. At first Krausz was afraid that Manoliu was part of a Gestapo trap, but he was reassured when Manoliu handed him Posner's Hebrew letter. The two met again secretly in the offices of the Romanian legation and in the private home of that country's consul, Joachim Daianu.[78]

Manoliu agreed to take back to Switzerland a report by Krausz on the situation of Jews in Hungary as a result of the deportations, together with a short version of the Auschwitz Report, written by two Jewish escapees from that notorious camp. We have already mentioned the unprecedented escape from Auschwitz of Rudolf Vrba (alias Walter Rosenberg) and Alfred Wetzler (Josef Lanik), two Slovakian Jewish prisoners. They made their escape on April 7, 1944, and arriving in Zilina, Slovakia, they a prepared a detailed report on the mass extermination under way in Auschwitz. In a report of about 30 pages, they described the unbelievable barbarism at this camp, the infrastructure with its gas chambers, the security installations, and the barracks, as well as the selection methods and the number of people killed country by country. They also reported on preparations made to receive Hungarian Jews. On May 27, 1944, two other escapees arrived, Arnold Rosin and Czeslaw Mordovicz, who had already witnessed the arrival of 12,000 Hungarian Jews. This terrible account known as the Auschwitz Report, the first live testimony to emanate from Auschwitz, found its way to Budapest and into the hands of Miklós Krausz. Aided by Manoliu, Krausz prepared a short summary of the Auschwitz Report and added a detailed description on the ghettoization and deportations taking place in Hungary.[79]

The Krausz report, addressed to Dr. Posner on June 19, 1944, was a five-page abridgement of the original 33-page Auschwitz Report, which stated that 1,765,000 Jews had been murdered. The other document was the Hungarian Report, which detailed the ghettoization and deportation of Hungarian Jews, town by town; by June 7, some 335,000 Jews had already been deported, with Budapest next in line, and with the active, if not enthusiastic support of the Hungarian government. "The whole Jewish race in Hungary is condemned to death," Krausz stated. "There are no exceptions, there is no escape. . . . There are only two possibilities left to us: suicide or the acceptance of our fate. . . . I do not know whether I will have another opportunity to write to you. It would, however, be a satisfaction to me if you could publish this letter and the enclosed reports either now or at a later date, so that the world may learn of the cruelties committed in the twentieth century in so-called civilized countries." As for "Herr Konsul Lutz," Krausz continued, he was a wonderful person, who spared no effort in favor of Jewish interests. Manoliu hand-carried both reports to Switzerland, hoping not to be apprehended and frisked while passing through German territory. Arriving safely in Geneva on June 20, he delivered the report to Posner, but not before making a copy which he turned over to Mantello. The alarming content of the report was referred to R. McClelland of the War Refugee Board, who thought it sufficient to merely send a cable to WRB headquarters in Washington. The full text did not reach Washington until October 1944.[80]

Copies of the Auschwitz Report had already been filtered into Switzerland by various routes, but it had not been made public. Lutz and his superior, Ambassador Jaeger, had informed the Swiss Foreign Ministry under Marcel Pilet-Golaz by diplomatic courier, but Bern kept silent. The document went from secret bearer to secret bearer, from diplomat to official and back. Lutz cautioned Manoliu not to reveal that he had received the Auschwitz Report through his mediation. He feared that the Germans might pressure the Foreign Ministry to recall him and scuttle his rescue operation. Mantello, however, decided to break the silence on the Auschwitz Report by informing the Swiss public at large. He quickly edited the long text to manageable proportions, retaining all the essential elements, and sent this shortened version to the churches, members of parliament, opinion makers, and the public at large. The Auschwitz Report had a tremendous echo. World leaders, including the pope, intervened, warning Hungary of the consequences if the deportations did not stop. Jewish leaders asked the Allies to bomb the railroad line linking Kosice-Kassa in Slovakia to Auschwitz-Birkenau. As already mentioned, on July 7, Horthy bowed to world pressure and stopped the deportations. The Jews in Budapest breathed a momentary sigh of relief.[81]

As for the Salvadoran citizenship documents, thousands were distributed through Lutz's office, who by then also represented El Salvador. Ironically, not one Jew in Hungary was really a Salvador citizen, but many received such certificates. In a letter to Mantello on September 25, 1944, Lutz confirmed that thousands of Salvadoran documents had been distributed through his office, and that the Hungarian authorities had decided to honor these documents. Lutz also informed Mantello, in a later communication, that he had extricated persons holding Salvadoran certificates from the November 1944 death march. He assured Mantello that he would remain at his post to represent the interests of El Salvador up to the end. Lutz reportedly himself filled in names on the blank Salvadoran forms Manoliu had brought to him.

As for Manoliu, things turned sour for him, as his country came under a Communist dictatorship enforced by Soviet arms. He left for Switzerland, arriving in September 1947, and sought a six-month extension of his stay. He had fled from his homeland, he stated, fearing arrest because of his close connections with the anti-Communist political leader Maniu. He had been fired from his job without any severance pay. He eventually left with his wife and daughter for Argentina, where he lived until his death in 1994. In 2001, Yad Vashem bestowed the title of Righteous Among the Nations on Florian Manoliu.[82]

Angel Sanz-Briz

Spain's interests in Budapest were represented by Angel Sanz-Briz. When the Arrow Cross assumed power, Ambassador Sanz-Briz was asked by his government, the Fascist regime headed by Francisco Franco, to suggest ways to save Jews who claimed Spanish ancestry. Sanz-Briz requested permission to provide such persons with Spanish documents, based on a 1924 law, promulgated by the then dictator Don Miguel Primo de Rivera, which cleared the way for Jews of Spanish ancestry living abroad to claim Spanish citizenship. The Hungarian government acceded to Sanz-Briz's request to afford the protection of the Spanish legation to a group of 200 Jews who in truth really had little or no Spanish ancestry. Following the example of Carl Lutz, Sanz-Briz increased the 200 individuals to 200 families, and of course made sure that the Spanish documents were not numbered higher than the 200 mark. All of these people were saved from deportation to the camps. As reported by Sanz-Briz to his government, close to 250 of them were given Spanish passports, while some 1,900 others received Spanish protective letters. Sanz-Briz attached a list of names to his report.

*Angel Sanz Briz, the Spanish minister in
Budapest, Hungary.*

In a postwar account of his rescue work, Sanz-Briz noted that the Hungarian government made its consent to the 200 figure conditional on Spain's agreeing to admit them to Spain and pay their traveling expenses. "I agreed to these conditions. I changed the figure of 200 individuals to 200 families. I increased the 200 families indefinitely. But I took care that no document or passport held by Jews carried a number above 200." Many of these people were sheltered in houses flying the Spanish flag.

Sanz-Briz was an astute diplomat, as demonstrated by the following incident. When he learned that the Arrow Cross regime had named a new governor for the Budapest region, Sanz-Briz decided to show his respect by paying him a private visit. He was received coldly by the governor, who excused himself by saying: "All the foreign diplomats who have come to visit me only did so to protest the treatment of Jews. None of them care about the suffering of the Hungarians in

Spanish Protective Letter, issued by Angel Sanz Briz,
the Spanish minister in Budapest, Hungary.

Transylvania and Bessarabia, now under Soviet occupation. They have been robbed of their property and reduced to a life of misery." When Sanz-Briz returned to his office, he sent the governor a warm letter, and enclosed a significant sum of money with a request to use it for the good of the Hungarian refugees. "From this moment, I could count on him and on his full cooperation. He immediately ordered his men to honor all buildings posting a sign that read: "Extraterritorial Building—Owned by the Spanish Legation." With the help of local Jews, Sanz-Briz was able to rent several buildings as residences for Jews with Spanish credentials. "Whenever I learned that someone in one of these buildings had been arrested by the police, I managed with a simple phone call to the governor to gain the person's freedom and have him returned to the Spanish protected building, where we sheltered thousands of persecuted Jews."

It goes without saying that the Germans were not too happy about Sanz-Briz, who represented a country that was a silent ally of Nazi Germany, and a dictator whom Germany had helped win the Spanish Civil War. Von Thadden, at the Foreign Ministry in Berlin, instructed the German embassy in Budapest to carefully observe the rescue activities of the Spanish legation. The results of the surveillance were reported to Berlin by an SS officer in an October 24, 1944 dispatch, and by the German envoy in Hungary, Edmund Veesenmayer, in his dispatch of November 13, 1944.[83] The German embassy in Madrid asked for clarifications from the Spanish Foreign Ministry, and was falsely assured, on December 7, 1944, that "these were more in the nature of formal steps than having a practical character."

With the Red Army approaching Budapest, Sanz-Briz was instructed to leave the city and go to Switzerland to prevent his falling into Soviet hands, a country with which Spain did not have diplomatic relations (in fact, Spain had sent a legion of volunteers to fight alongside the Germans on the Russian front). "I left Budapest in mid-December for Vienna without informing the authorities, so that they would believe I was still in the Hungarian capital." His place at the Spanish legation was taken over by Jorge-Giorgio Perlasca, whose story appears next. After the war, Sanz-Briz served as consul-general in New York and represented Spain at the United Nations. In 1965, Yad Vashem declared Angel Sanz-Briz a Righteous Among the Nations.[84]

Giorgio Perlasca

When Angel Sanz-Briz left Budapest secretly in December, his place was taken by an unassuming Italian posing as a Spanish diplomat: Giorgio Perlasca. His is a fascinating story of a man beholden to the Italian brand of Fascism who quite by coincidence happened to be in Budapest and there found himself under the diplomatic mantle of another Fascist government (Franco's Spain), and in that capacity saved hundreds, if not several thousands, of Jews from the pro-Nazi Arrow Cross regime. Very little was known of him and his background

The Italian-Spanish diplomat
Giorgio Perlasca.

in the years immediately after the war, although his name appeared in several studies on the Holocaust in Hungary. He was in fact forgotten until accidentally rediscovered. It happened in 1987. In a letter to Yad Vashem that year, Prof. Eveline Blitstein-Willinger (an immunologist in Berlin) revealed that "six months ago I found out about the existence of Mr. Giorgio Perlasca, an Italian citizen 79 years old, a man who lived in Budapest, Hungary, during the Nazi regime. After the inauguration of Szálasi and the return of Sanz-Briz and his colleagues, he was the leader of the Spanish legation. Together with his friends and co-workers, Perlasca accorded protection (about 3,000 passports) to Hungarian Jews, risking his own life, and tried to help as much as he could. . . . To my astonishment, nobody knows his name, nobody thanks him for what he did. He was really sincere, he didn't do anything for personal advantage, he never tried to make a profit. . . . We are asking you to honor this great man with a noble soul before it is too late."

Twenty years earlier, Dr. Blitstein-Willinger had left Transylvania for Berlin, where she worked as a researcher at the university and organized a group of people of Hungarian origin, who met once a month to talk about their past lives, of books read, and of their work. In 1983, the subject turned to events in Budapest during the war years, and especially to Raoul Wallenberg. It was getting late at one of these sessions when Mrs. Irene von Borosceny, a Hungarian countess, told about her work for the International Red Cross in Budapest. She said she had also known another extraordinary man, an Italian named Giorgio Perlasca, and had documents that she would show at the next meeting. "One week later we met again at the home of Dr. Vera Braun. There were just six of us, all women, and Irene von Borosceny talked for over two hours. . . . As Irene spoke, I began to tremble. I remember that it was very hard for me to fall asleep that night. I kept asking myself, how is it possible that a man like that is living somewhere in Italy and nobody has ever even heard his name? What is it that the people he saved haven't told the world about him? Why haven't the newspapers written articles about him? Why hasn't the Italian government honored him as an exceptional person? So I decided to take the initiative and organize a group to help Perlasca. My sister, Dr. Maria Vera Willinger, became the first member, and then we were joined by Dr. Maria Hedig, Professor Diamanstein, Dr. Ruth Gross, Attorney Heribert Hanish, and Mrs. Anne Marie Brunner. We found out his address and decided to send him a monthly financial contribution." This started the ball rolling, insofar as Yad Vashem was concerned.[85]

Born in 1910, Perlasca served as an army private during Italy's invasion of Ethiopia in 1935. For the next two and a half years, his artillery unit fought as part of the Italian contingent supporting Franco in the Spanish Civil War. Once demobilized, he married and joined SAIB, the initials in Italian for "Livestock Import Company" (*Società Anonima Importazione Bovini*), an Italian firm importing agricultural products, such as livestock and frozen meat, in exchange for clothes, hats, or socks. Sent to Yugoslavia with his wife Nerina, he witnessed the German invasion there in April 1941, and the roundup of Jews immediately thereafter. In his words, "I was there when the Jews were being deported from Belgrade... One morning, a line of carriages, escorted by the SS and crammed full of Jewish women from the city, passed right under our window. They were singing a religious hymn. I can still hear the sound of their voices. I remember those women very well; they were fully aware that they were going toward a dark destiny, but they were also very proud. The hymn they were singing was not a song of desperation. And yet they knew full well that they were being taken away."

By end of 1942, Perlasca was in Hungary. In September 1943, when the Germans installed the recently deposed dictator Mussolini as head of the German-puppet Fascist state known as the Saló republic in northern Italy, the regime asked Italian residents in Budapest to return home. Perlasca refused to comply; as a man proud of his Italian heritage, he viewed with great disfavor the sycophantic new Italian regime acting under German dictates. So when the Germans entered Hungary in March 1944, he feared arrest. Thinking how best to save himself, he remembered that he had a certificate he had been given in Barcelona by the Franco regime before returning home from the Spanish Civil War. It read: "Dear Brother-in-Arms, no matter where you are in the world, you can turn to Spain."

Deciding to utilize this ploy, Perlasca called at the Spanish embassy, headed by Angel Sanz Briz, and asked for help. Sanz-Briz put him up in a villa enjoying extraterritorial status, where he stayed for 10 days. Then he decided to turn himself in, and was sent to an internment camp in Kékes, from where he was moved, in the fall of 1944, to another internment camp. On October 13, on the strength of a permit from the Ministry of Internal Affairs granting him a 15-day stay in Budapest for medical examination, Perlasca left in a car belonging to the Swedish diplomatic delegation and arrived in Budapest two days before the Arrow Cross takeover. Not knowing where to go, he returned to Sanz Briz and again asked for help. Sanz Briz hesitated for a moment, then gave him a Spanish passport and a letter addressed to the Hungarian Ministry of Internal Affairs, stating that on October 13, 1944, Spain had acceded to Perlasca's request, of two years earlier, to grant him Spanish citizenship. For that purpose, his first name had been changed from Giorgio to the Spanish-sounding Jorge.

Sanz Briz then invited Perlasca to join the small staff of workers at the Spanish legation and help with the legation's work on behalf of Jews, especially those residing in the Spanish-protected houses. "I was happy about it. I was glad to be able to do something useful." When Jews benefiting from international protection were moved to the so-called International Ghetto in mid-November, Perlasca was constantly on the lookout for the safety of his then hundreds of residents. This included the risky job of visiting police headquarters to protest an Arrow Cross break-in at one of the houses. In one such incident, Perlasca requested an appointment with the Arrow Cross strongman József Gera. The meeting soon turned tumultuous. "Gera went into a real hysterical fit. He started running back and forth across the room, yelling that the Jews were all the same, that they had thrown a bomb into the theater where he was giving a speech, that it was time they should all be exterminated." When Perlasca explained that the Jews were under the protection of a friendly government, Gera shot back: "But why isn't Franco fighting against the Jews?" Perlasca explained that Spain was protecting the Jews because of the need to maintain a balanced foreign policy. When the war was over, he said, it would be a time for showing appreciation to other people. Sensing a hidden message meant for himself, Gera changed his attitude. "He let me know how fond he was of Spain and assured me that our wards would be treated with all due respect. In the end, he shook my hand. I remember how uncomfortable I felt during that handshake. I was shaking hands with a man who could sign a death sentence as easily as a greeting card."[86]

On November 29, Sanz Briz informed Perlasca that he was leaving the following morning—but not for Sopron, the new seat of the Hungarian government, as demanded by the Hungarian authorities. Sanz-Briz told Perlasca of the regime's pressure for Spain to grant *de jure* recognition of the Szálasi government. "And I can't do that." Sanz-Briz continued. "I've been able to keep them hanging for a month and a half, but now the moment of truth has arrived. They won't accept just words anymore, they'll want something in writing, something official. I've got to leave under cover." It is not known whether Sanz-Briz also told the startled Perlasca that he had been ordered by his government to leave the country to avoid falling into Russian hands. Then, looking Perlasca in the eyes, the Spanish ambassador said: "Listen to me, Perlasca. You have been invaluable, and I appreciate everything you've done. I've been able to get you a German visa. You can leave too. I'm going to Bern, and I can assure you that from there, I'll make sure you receive a visa. . . . Wait here for a few days and then come to Bern. Believe me, unfortunately, there's nothing more we can do here."

"Don't do anything special," Sanz Briz counseled. "Wait for the right moment and then come away." The next morning Perlasca went to the Ministry of Foreign Affairs to present his credentials. That afternoon, Hungarian radio announced that Sanz Briz had left Hungary for a brief period and that, until his return, Spain's affairs would be handled by the embassy secretary. Luckily for Perlasca, his name was not specifically mentioned, for someone might have identified him as the former representative of an Italian meat business.[87] From December 1, 1944, to January 16, 1945, Perlasca was the official representative of the Spanish government in Budapest, although Madrid knew nothing about it. Perlasca felt it was a risk worth taking in light of the increasing chaos in Budapest; a city about to undergo a siege by the approaching Red Army, with communication to the outside world reduced to a minimum and finally stopped altogether.

"At first, I didn't know what to do, but then I began to feel like a fish in water; I continued giving out protective passes and looked after the Jews in the safe houses flying the Spanish flag. As the proverb says, 'Opportunity makes the thief.' " As the representative of fascist Spain, Perlasca had access to the highest Hungarian authorities, and in the desperate situation facing their country, they were anxious for Spanish support. Perlasca and his staff issued several thousand protective passes, many of whose recipients were moved into the eleven Spanish houses in the International Ghetto after November 15. On one occasion Perlasca had a confrontation with some police officers who tried to force the people out of one of the houses. Perlasca warned them of the diplomatic repercussions. One of the officers replied that since Sanz-Briz had left the country, diplomatic relations with Spain had ended. Perlasca responded by fabricating the canard that Sanz-Briz had only gone to Switzerland for a diplomatic conference. "The flag is still flying. I am in charge. I am the legal representative of Spain." Seeing a group of Jews being marched away from another Spanish-protected home, Perlasca insisted that they be returned. The Hungarians backed down.

According to Edith Weiss, one of the residents of the Spanish house at 44 Pannonia Street: "It happened often in those days that the Hungarian Nazis would come and march Jews down to the Danube and kill them there and throw their bodies into the river. One day they came and took us downstairs and were going to march us to the river. But Perlasca arrived. He was mesmerizing. In that forceful, powerful way of his, he told them to go away and leave us alone. The leader of the Nazis—there were eight of them—was so stunned he couldn't even talk. Perlasca had such authority, he was so strong, that there was no way anyone could contradict him. They simply went away. In another confrontation with an Arrow Cross member, when told that Sanz Briz's departure meant that relations between Spain and Hungary had been ruptured, Perlasca blurted out: "Hold everything! You're making a mistake. Sanz Briz has not fled, he has simply gone to Bern in order to communicate more easily with Madrid, seeing as it's no longer possible to communicate from there. . . . Go ask at the Ministry of Foreign Affairs! Sanz Briz informed two officials there of his departure. His trip involves a very important diplomatic mission!" He then threateningly added, "You are speaking with the official representative of Spain!" The gambit worked.[88]

Avraham Ronai, born in Budapest in 1932, related how Perlasca saved him. His father had been in the business of importing cork from Spain. A Seville firm he had dealt with sent the family a letter asking whether it could be of any help. Avraham took the Seville letter to the Spanish embassy and showed it to one of the secretaries. A man came out of an adjoining room and read the letter over the secretary's shoulder. He then nodded to her and went back to his room. A short while later, he returned and handed Ronai a *Schutzpass* (protective letter) made out to all four of Ronai's family. The man was Perlasca. "I personally saw Perlasca come to our house almost every day, bringing powdered milk and food." One day, while Perlasca was on the scene, some Arrow Cross men tried to take away the inhabitants of one of the Spanish protective houses. Perlasca walked up to them and peremptorily said: "How dare you behave like this on the property of a friendly country? I insist that you release these people, otherwise you will have problems with your superiors. If I have to cable Madrid about this violation of Spanish interests, there will be grave consequences." The Arrow Cross men withdrew. The protective passes stated that the bearers had applied for Spanish citizenship and the embassy was entitled to issue entry permits to them. All competent authorities were asked to keep this fact in mind, "in connection with any possible measures," and to grant the bearers favorable consideration and exempt them from labor service. Perlasca habitually pre-dated the passes to November 4, so they would correspond to the period when Sanz-Briz was still in Budapest.

The following is taken from Perlasca's diary entry for December 2: "New raids this morning. They rounded up everybody who didn't have a Spanish safe-conduct letter. I succeeded, though, in getting them all into our houses on the promise that I issued each of them one of our letters of protection by the end of the day."

December 3: "Total success! At noon I was received by the vice foreign minister. I was a little nervous because I was afraid I might see someone who had known me from before I began passing as Spanish. Luckily, all of those staff people are in hiding, either in Sopron or in the various embassies." The vice minister accused Spain of not regularizing its relations with the government. "Don't be surprised, then, if the Hungarians take retaliatory measures." Perlasca: "I reminded him that there are thousands of Hungarian citizens living peacefully in Spain, but if, for any reason whatsoever, the Spanish embassy and the Hungarian government were to fail to reach a satisfactory solution concerning conditions for the Jews under Spanish protection, the Spanish government, albeit with great regret, would have to put its relations with Hungary under review. The vice minister asked me if he was to consider this a threat. Yes, I answered." The vice minister left, then came back with greetings from [Foreign] Minister Gábor Kemény, "and assured me that, as far as they were concerned, a way to an agreement would surely be found. I thanked him and repeated our requests. We thus reached an understanding that was also put in writing. It contains the declaration that the Hungarians are satisfied with the explanation given for Sanz Briz's departure, and obligates all Hungarian military units to respect the letters of protection issued by the Spanish embassy."

December 17: "Today in Gera's office I met the minister of internal affairs, Ernö Vajna. Until now I've always avoided him because I prefer to deal with the Foreign Ministry. I seem to remember, in fact, that Vajna came to Kékes when I was interned there, and I'm afraid he might recognize me. But luckily that didn't happen."

December 18: "Today I went to the Foreign Ministry to [falsely!] communicate that the Spanish government had sent a telegram reiterating its positive view of the Hungarian request, but, given the delicacy of the international situation, that it was forced to ask the Hungarians for patience. I assured him, however, that the Spanish government will certainly be in a position to respond favorably by December 31. . . . What will become of my organization if the Russians don't get here before the winter's out? I hope I'll be able to keep faking it."

December 25: Perlasca to the residents of all his houses: "A month ago I asked you to put away your arms. Now I am asking you to keep them ready. In case of attack, defend yourselves!"

December 27: "The food is running out. I have an agreement with a baker to bring us bread every day. I bought some ham from the Red Cross, and we have purchased dried fruit, sugar, honey, lard, and anything else we could find.

On January 6, 1945, with Russian shells falling everywhere, and rumors rampant in the beleaguered city that the Hungarians intended to torch the Jewish ghetto with its 70,000 inhabitants, Perlasca went to see Interior Minister Vajna. He warned him that the world would never forgive so evil a deed. Vajna answered: "You know the wicked-

ness of the Jews." Perlasca: "Signor Vajna, in my last letter I stated
clearly that the Spanish government will be forced to take retaliatory
measures if our protectees should become victims of your cruel treatment. If, by January 10, the Spanish government has not received a
reassuring communication from me, the retaliation will begin. You
should know that there are 3,000 Hungarian citizens living in Spain,
and the government has decided to intern them and confiscate their
property if its protectees here in Budapest are mistreated." Vajna
responded that Perlasca was speaking in a way unbecoming a diplomat. Perlasca: "The situation demands it." Vajna asked for guarantees
that the Hungarians in Spain would not be harmed. Perlasca: "Senor
Vajna, the Latin people have never persecuted foreigners without reason."[90] In Perlasca's view, the leaders of the Arrow Cross secretly
hoped that in the event of a total collapse, they would be granted asylum in Spain.

After the war Perlasca often mentioned the following incident, as
here recounted to journalist Michael Ryan in 1990: "I went down to
the train station in Budapest . . . to the loading docks. There were hundreds of people collected there, and when the trains came, the Nazis
would put them into cattle cars to deport them to Germany. These
were more or less the same kinds of cars I had used to transport animals in my business. . . . I saw two children about 12 years old in the
long line of people. They looked exactly the same, like twins. I took an
instant liking to them. I thought, 'I can't let them go.' So I said to
them, 'You see that big black car over there? Go to that car, open the
door, and get in. The driver knows what to do.' They ran and got in.
Then an officer of the SS, a major, went to the car and started to bring
them back. I planted myself in front of him and said: 'No! This car is
extraterritorial. It has diplomatic immunity. Look at the diplomatic
license plates! Look at the Spanish flag!' But he insisted. He wanted
those kids. He pulled out his pistol and began to threaten me. Raoul
Wallenberg came over and said to him, 'Hey, watch what you're doing.
This man is the representative of the Spanish government. This is a
diplomatic car.' The SS major said, 'You're interfering with my job.'
The Nazi got more and more angry. . . . And we were all shouting and

screaming. Then an SS colonel came up and said, 'What's going on?' The major explained, and finally the colonel just said, 'Let them go. Their time will come.' The Nazis went away, and I got the kids. Then I turned to Wallenberg and said, 'Who was that man?' Wallenberg looked at me, surprised, and said, 'You don't know? That was Adolf Eichmann." When the two boys arrived at the Spanish legation and took their coats off, one was a boy; the other a girl. They were brother and sister. Perlasca kept them with him for a few days, then turned them over to the Red Cross. "I always remember how I saw them walking forward together in that line. I think I remember them rather than so many others because they were so strikingly alike, because they were alone and because they were so beautiful."[91]

Perlasca participated with the other diplomats stationed in Budapest in a joint effort to stop the deportation of Jews by appealing to the conscience of the Hungarian regime. On November 17, 1944, Perlasca, Carl Ivar Danielsson (Sweden), Harald Feller (Switzerland), Count Pongracz (Portugal), and Angelo Rotta (The Vatican) sent a memorandum to the Hungarian government asking for the immediate cessation of all deportations of Jews, as well as humane treatment for those already in concentration camps doing forced labor. They also asked the government to honor the protective letters issued by the neutral powers. They returned with another memorandum on December 24, 1944, protesting the "cruel" measures against harmless people, including children. "Why is it necessary to force these children to live in a place that resembles a prison, where they will see nothing but the misery and suffering of women and old men, persecuted solely on the basis of their racial origin. Every civilized people respects children, and the entire world would be shocked if it were to learn that Hungary, a country with a noble and Christian tradition, has taken action against minors." Perlasca later related that after signing the memorandum, he asked for a private audience with the Vatican nuncio, Angelo Rotta. "I told him the whole truth [about myself]. At the beginning he refused to believe it, but then he enjoyed hearing how I had succeeded in tricking the Germans. He was happy to hear that I was a Lombard like him. He told me that in the interest of the common good, my deceit could be forgiven. . . . If they should find out, I could always ask for refuge from the papal nuncio or the Swiss legation."[92]

When the Russian troops invested Budapest on January 16, 1945, they arrested Perlasca and briefly put him to work cleaning the streets of rubble and corpses. He managed to escape and took shelter with friends in the capital. "I had a total of 3,700 pengö with me, a leather bag, a kilo of spaghetti, a few walnuts, and two packs of cigarettes. Everything I owed had been stolen from me by the Russians at the legation or had been destroyed in the fire at Villa Szécheny. The adventure had come to an end, but another one was beginning; the adventure of hunger."

Before making his way back to Italy, Perlasca was given several letters of thanks and appreciation by his former wards. The one from the residents of the Spanish house at 35 Szent Istvan Street, dated April 18, 1945, reads: "We have regrettably learned that you are leaving Hungary in order to return to your homeland, Italy. On this occasion, we wish to express the affection, recognition, and high regard of thousands of Jews, persecuted by the German Nazis and Hungarian Fascists, who found themselves under the protection of the Spanish legation. We shall, never, never, forget that you not only worked incessantly, day and night, for our shelter and nourishment, but that you also looked after those who needed to be fed, the elderly and sick— with a kindness that we find hard to express in words. . . . Your name will never, never, be missing from our prayers, as we pray to God to bless you, for only He can properly reward you."

Somewhat earlier, on January 16, 1945, Perlasca was given a letter signed by 21 of his wards, reading: "Today, the 16th of January 1945, as the Soviet troops are entering our neighborhood and we finally feel liberated from Nazi tyranny, we feel obliged to thank you for everything you have done for us, saving us from certain death. We have never doubted your courage, your self-sacrifice, and the risks you have incurred for us on every occasion. We solemnly wish to make this declaration . . . in eternal recognition of your efforts on our behalf."[93]

On his return to Italy, Perlasca's former employer refused to give him any back pay, and as a result he was forced to eke out a living with

Dr. Mordecai Paldiel inviting Italian diplomat Giorgio Perlasca (third from left) to plant a tree in his name in the Avenue of the Righteous, Yad Vashem, 1989.

great difficulty. In 1988, Yad Vashem awarded Giorgio Perlasca the title of Righteous Among the Nations. A year later, on September 25, 1989, Perlasca visited Israel and planted a tree in his name in the Avenue of the Righteous at Yad Vashem. In 1991 the Spanish government awarded him one of its oldest and highest decorations for outstanding services to the nation: the title of Knight Commander of the Order of Isabella (*Encomienda de Isabel la Catolica*), and the Hungarian parliament awarded him the Order of the Gold Star. In Italy, the president of the republic, Francesco Cossiga, named him *Commendatore Grand'Ufficiale,* and the government decided to grant him a lifetime annuity. He died in August 1992 at the age of 82.

Asked whether he had been religiously or politically motivated, Perlasca replied: "Neither. I found myself in a given situation and I reacted to it. I couldn't ignore it. There's an Italian saying, 'It's the opportunity that makes a thief.' I had the opportunity, and I took it." In a more serious vein, Perlasca explained "I couldn't stand the sight of people being branded like animals. Because I couldn't stand seeing children being killed. That's what I think it was; I don't think I was a hero. . . . All of a sudden I found that I had become a diplomat, with a lot of people depending on me. What do you think I should have done? As it turned out, I think being a fake diplomat was a big help, because I could do things that a real diplomat couldn't do. I mean . . . diplomats are a strange breed. They're not exactly free to do what they want to do. There's etiquette, there are formalities, hierarchies, people to answer to, your career. A lot of things, a lot of constraints that I didn't have." Then, innocently turning to the questioner, "Anyone in my place would have done what I did." And then, what finally convinced him to stay in Budapest, and not leave for safety in Switzerland, was the promise he had made to his wards not to abandon them. "Yes, because I had solemnly sworn that I would stay. And at that point, you understand, I couldn't do anything but stay." Eva Lang, one of Perlasca's beneficiaries, dedicated a poem in his honor:

Our bodies bore the burden of a star,
But that man, who saved thousands, made our burden lighter,
Turned the yellow star of shame into a decoration.
That man, who saved thousands, still lives, but he is silent.
I must shout for him.[94]

The Vatican's Ambassador

Angelo Rotta

The final story in this chapter concerns the papal nuncio (ambassador) and doyen of the diplomatic corps in Budapest, Angelo Rotta. Together with colleagues like the Swedish diplomats Carl Ivar Danielsson and Raoul Wallenberg, the Swiss Carl Lutz, and the Spanish-Italian Giorgio Perlasca, Monsignor Rotta was active in the effort to stem the Hungarian government's zeal to rid the country of its Jews. Soon after the German occupation of the country on March 19, 1944, he appealed to the heads of the Catholic Church and the regime then headed by Admiral Horthy to end the persecution, emphasizing that the real meaning of the deportations was no longer a secret. They were not, as officially touted, for work purposes, but in fact ended up with death in a concentration camp, principally Auschwitz which was not too far away. While he claimed that he was representing the Holy See, Rotta went much further and did not always seek the approval of his superiors in his confrontational meetings with Hungarian officials on the Jewish issue. True enough, he was mostly concerned at first with the plight of the many baptized Jews, but with the passing months and the intensification of the persecutions by the Szálasi regime, which took power with Nazi help on October 15, 1944, Rotta's concern extended to all the Jews in the country. As early as July 6, 1944, during a discussion with Hungarian officials, he gave vent to his outrage when he described the handling of the Jewish question as "abominable" and "dishonorable" for Hungary.[95]

On May 15, when he first learned of the plans to deport the country's Jews, Rotta addressed a stiff note to the head of state, Horthy. "The simple fact that people are persecuted simply because of their racial origin is a violation of their natural rights. If the good Lord gave them life, no one in the world has the right to remove it from them or deny them the means by which they can maintain it, as long as they do not commit any crimes. . . . As part of my duty, I have informed the Holy See of what is happening in Hungary, and I would have also to inform it of the deportations now being planned and which sadly have already begun . . . [and I hope that the pope] would feel obliged raise his voice in protest." A similar strongly worded letter went out to the minister of foreign affairs. "The whole world knows what the deportations mean in reality. . . . For all this, the apostolic nunciature finds it necessary . . . to appeal to the Royal Hungarian government, in its campaign against the Jews, not to overstep the limits that natural divine law prescribes, and to avoid any action that the Holy See could not but strongly protest." Rotta spelled out two conditions: that the rights of the baptized Jews were to be respected, and that the measures against all Jews should be within the framework of "fundamental respect for the human person."[96]

Rotta then took it a step further by liberally distributing Vatican protective letters to hundreds and perhaps thousands of Jews threatened with deportation regardless of their religious views. Many of them were sheltered in houses flying the Vatican flag. A witness living in Israel testified to having received a protective letter with Rotta's signature, confirming that all 220 men in his labor battalion were under the nunciature's protection on the spurious excuse that 24 of them had shown an interest (real or not) in the Catholic faith. That sufficed for Rotta to extend his protective umbrella to all the Jewish men in this battalion. To Nina Langlet, who, together with her husband Valdemar, represented the Swedish Red Cross, Rotta disclosed that he had received permission from the authorities to issue no more than 2,500 protective letters but in fact had issued over 19,000 such documents. Many holders of these documents were sheltered in buildings flying the Vatican flag.[97]

When Prime Minister Sztójay assured Rotta that the deportations of Jews, stopped in early July, would not be resumed, Rotta countered, on July 28, by expressing gratitude for the relaxation of the "really draconian regulations applying to Jews," but adding, "Yet when we look at the wishes of the nunciature in this question, it immediately becomes obvious that the concessions are far from satisfactory." Following rumors that the deportations were about to resume, Rotta, as the doyen of the diplomatic corps, and Danielsson, the Swedish ambassador, called on Reményi-Schneller, the deputy prime minister, on August 21, and handed him a note expressing their concern. "We are also aware—and from a completely reliable source—what deportation means in most cases, even it if is cloaked under the description 'work abroad.' " The note went on to denounce the "inhuman" treatment of Jews, since "it is quite inadmissible to persecute people and drive them to death simply because of their ancestry." In addition to Angelo Rotta, as the apostolic nuncio, and Carl Danielsson, the Swedish minister, the note also carried the signatures of Carlos de Liz-Texeira Branquino and Antoine J. Kilchmann, respectively the Portuguese and Swiss chargé d'affaires.[98]

Much earlier, on June 8, 1944, while the deportation of Jews was at a fever pitch, Rotta went to see Cardinal Jusztinián Serédi, the primate of the Catholic Church, and reproached him for not opposing the government's anti-Jewish measures energetically enough. Serédi defensively replied that he had done everything conceivable and a pastoral letter read from the pulpit would not help, but "would only do greater harm to the Church and the faithful." The primate added that the fact that the Holy See maintained diplomatic relations with Germany, which was guilty of so many barbarous acts, was wrongly interpreted by the people as reflecting the attitude of the Holy See toward the persecution of Jews.[99]

After the pro-Nazi Arrow Cross coup of October 15, 1944, and the institution of a reign of terror against the country's remaining Jews, concentrated in Budapest, Monsignor Rotta implored the new foreign minister, Baron Gábor Kemény, to use moderation. On October 21, he had a long exchange of views with the head of state, Szálasi, who promised not to resume the deportations. In a subsequent letter, Rotta asked that forced labor be done under humane conditions, and that the rights of those holding protective letters be honored. The nunciature thereupon took under its protection 25 religious institutions and houses in which several thousand Jews were sheltered. Several thousands more were given protective letters.[100]

Instigated by SS Colonel Adolf Eichmann, the new government launched a death march of tens of thousands of Jews toward the Austrian border in inclement weather. Learning of this, the nuncio invited his diplomatic colleagues to a meeting that resulted in a new memorandum, handed to Szálasi by the nuncio and the Swedish ambassador, on November 17. In it, they restated their complaint that in spite of promises to the contrary, the deportations have resumed and the operation "is being carried out with such brutal severity that the whole world condemns the inhumanity of the process." Also, everyone by now knows what lies in store for the deportees, not work, but a "cruel reality." As even small children, old men, and invalids are being deported, it is quite clear that work is not the intent. "On the contrary, the brutality with which the removal is being carried out makes it possible to foresee what the end of this tragic journey will be." Rotta and Danielsson, on behalf of the neutral powers, asked the government to "revoke the decision to deport the Jews and halt the measures already in progress"; those already in concentration camps under the facade of labor service should "be assured of appropriate treatment (sufficient food, shelter, medical and religious care, respect for life)." They also asked for "full and loyal observance" of the rights of Jews under the protection of embassies accredited to Budapest. The memorandum included a veiled threat of retaliation by the countries at war with Hungary, including the possibility that "all Hungarians abroad would be exposed if the deportation and annihilation of the Jews is continued; not to mention the fact that in the event of an occupation of Hungary, the occupying bodies could apply the same methods to the Hungarian people." The note was signed by Rotta for the Vatican, Danielsson for Sweden, Harald Feller for Switzerland, Jorge Perlasca for Spain, and Count Pongracz for Portugal.[101]

The government ignored this protest, and the death march, which affected tens of thousands of people, continued. They were forced to cover 15 to 20 miles every day on foot—as far as Hegyeshalom, where SS officers took over from Hungarian gendarmes. Included were men and women of all ages, regardless of their state of health and capacity for labor, which was the ostensible purpose of this march. The roads were littered with the corpses of the many who collapsed exhausted by the roadside or were struck down by the gendarmes.

At this point, Rotta asked Sándor Ujváry of the Red Cross to provide signed blank protective letters for use in an attempt to rescue the most needy, ill, and exhausted people. When Ujváry replied that many of the people carried forged credentials and baptismal certificates, the nuncio, according to Ujváry, replied: "What you are doing, my son, is pleasing to God and to Jesus, because you are saving innocent people. I give you absolution in advance. Continue your work to the honor of God." Rotta then gave him a personal authorization that read as follows: "Budapest, 19th Nov. 1944. The apostolic nuncio in Budapest confirms that the nunciature has entrusted Mr. Sándor György Ujváry, the representative of the International Red Cross, with the task of inquiring after all persons of Jewish origin under the protection of the apostolic nunciature who have been removed from Budapest contrary to the agreements legally concluded between the apostolic nunciature and the Hungarian government and are on the way to the west, and to bring them home from the camps. Mr. Sándor Gyórgy Ujváry has also been empowered to intervene where necessary with the authorities in the name of the nunciature. We request the military and civil authorities to give the fullest support to Mr. Sándor Gyórgy Ujváry while he is carrying out these tasks. Nuncio Apostolico (Round stamp: Apostolic Nunciature of Budapest)."[102]

Rotta also enlisted Tibor Baránszky in the rescue effort. Baranszky was a 21-year-old seminarian who had come to see Rotta to plead for the Jewish Szekeres family. With Rotta's help, he succeeded in transferring the nine members of the Szekeres family into one of the Vatican's protected houses. During one of his visits to the nunciature, Rotta asked him whether he was prepared to immediately go to the nearby cement factory and extract persons who held Vatican protective letters. Baránszky agreed, but asked for the nunciature's Rolls-Royce in order to impress the Arrow Cross guards. Arriving at 10:00 p.m. with a list of 50 people, he managed to get 40 people released. His success pleased Rotta, who appointed him as secretary responsible for the department dealing with protected persons. In that capacity, Baránszky distributed hundreds of protective letters and took care of the 3,000 Jews in the Vatican protective houses. He also followed the death marchers to the Austrian border and was able to get many of them released. For this purpose, Rotta armed the young Baránszky with a document stating: "Budapest, November 20, 1944. Mr. Tibor Baránszky, a theologian, is assigned by the apostolic nuncio in Hungary to search in the various camps and bring back to Budapest persons of Jewish origin who are under the protection of the apostolic nunciature, and who in spite of the accords agreed with the Hungarian government, were picked up and taken to camps. The military and civilian authorities are asked to render Mr. Baránszky their support and all other facilities needed by him in the accomplishment of his work. (signed Angelo Rotta, apostolic nuncio)." Baránszky took along a batch of blank protective letters and filled them in with the names of those he encountered on the death march.[103]

On December 25, 1944, with Russian shells pounding Budapest, Rotta assembled the diplomats of the neutral powers in the nunciature for the last time to send one more petition to the Arrow Cross regime. The note presented to the government pleaded "on behalf of the persecuted and outlawed Jews," and especially against forcing the children into a special ghetto. "We hear it asserted that the Jews are Hungary's enemies, but even in wartime, justice and conscience condemn all hostile activities directed against children. Why, then, compel these innocent creatures to live in a place which in many ways is like a prison; where the poor little ones will see nothing but the misery, suffering, and despair of old men and women who are being persecuted simply because of their racial origin? All civilized peoples show consideration for children, and the whole world would be painfully surprised if traditionally Christian and chivalrous Hungary wanted to take action against these little ones." The petition was signed by Rotta, Danielsson, Feller, Perlasca, and Pongracz. Rotta followed this up with a message to the government stating that he would not abandon the city and accompany the government to its new location, but would remain in the capital city. In fact, he stayed there during the dreadful siege, which lasted until the city's full capture on February 12, 1945.[104]

From the documentation on hand, it is clear that Rotta went further than his superiors in the Vatican allowed him, bending the rules and giving a quite liberal interpretation of his diplomatic mandate, in order to exert pressure on the Hungarian government to temper its persecution of the Jews. His behavior especially stands out when measured against the lackluster attitude of the head of the Catholic Church in Hungary, Cardinal Serédi, who refused to budge and lend his great influence to stem the avalanche of anti-Jewish measures by a government claiming allegiance to the Catholic faith. It should be noted that Rotta's high position did not guarantee him against harm by the vicious Arrow Cross militia. With the approach of the Russian armies toward Budapest, they dropped all pretenses of respect for law and order, and were not beyond harming diplomatic representatives. They probably would not have attempted anything against Rotta himself, although they once raided his premises, looking for anti-government elements, but he could not be too sure of this, for he was well aware that the Arrow Cross leaders were well informed of the extent of his help to Jews.

Rotta urged his superiors at the Vatican to exert pressure on the Catholic Church in Hungary to take a more active stand against the anti-Jewish drive of the government. In a note to the Vatican secretary of state, Cardinal Luigi Maglione, on May 24, 1944, Rotta wrote of his disappointment that the Hungarian episcopate had not taken any steps. "Perhaps a direct action by the Holy See will be beneficial." Again, on June 18, 1944, Rotta informed Maglione that "the number of deportees has passed the 300,000 mark, serious people talk about extermination camps, and many die on the journey." He again complained about Serédi's compliant attitude, and asked for a direct intervention by the Holy See to stop the deportations. In a further message on November 27, 1944, this time to Cardinal Demenico Tardini, Rotta listed the efforts by the nunciature, including the 13,000 protective letters issued to many Jews (baptized and not), thus postponing their deportation. He also reported on the renewal of the deportations with extreme brutality and much cruelty. On December 11, 1944, Rotta informed the Vatican Secretariat of State that in light of the increasing arrests of priests, and the continuing persecution of Jews, the nunciature would not join the government in evacuating the city.

These and other documents demonstrate Rotta's personal and even emotional involvement, for he was fully aware of the practical implications of the Hungarian government's anti-Jewish measures. He did not merely comply with Vatican instructions, but issued thousands of protective letters, evidently on his own initiative. His memos to the authorities were written in direct, strong language, with frequent use of the term "protest." Twice he urged the pope to get involved, and in one communication (June 18, 1944) he insisted this was a necessary step. He tried to persuade Cardinal Jusztinián Serédi and the Hungarian episcopate to a more active stand, but with little success, to his disappointment. As the doyen of the diplomatic corps, and the senior member of the neutral countries, he acted as a catalyst and initiator of the three appeals to the government. As the apostolic nuncio he emphasized the plight of the baptized Jews (in line with standard Vatican policy), but his petitions always mentioned the plight of all Jews, and as time passed he no longer made distinction between the two categories. Bearing all this in mind, in 1997, Yad Vashem awarded the late Monsignor Angelo Rotta the title of Righteous Among the Nations.[105]

Chapter 8

Also Meriting Mention and Praise

The diplomats mentioned in the preceding chapters are persons on whom Yad Vashem bestowed the title of Righteous Among the Nations. As already alluded in our opening chapter, this honorific is based on a set of criteria formulated by a Yad Vashem-appointed public commission, known as the Commission for the Designation of the Righteous. Not all cases presented before this commission meet the conditions of these criteria. Some were denied the full Righteous title, while others received letters of thanks and appreciation. Still others are still in the investigative stage, since not all the elements of the story were or are present and fully known, and it is too early to predict. At the same time, the picture that emerges from the information already culled of these diplomats is of persons who extended aid and succor in one form or another. It is therefore appropriate in this study of diplomat helpers to mention their names and their deeds. This, as also in consonance with the Jewish traditional obligation of *hakarat today*, of acknowledging a good deed done. With the aforementioned in mind, the following diplomats will be described according to the countries in which they acted, and we begin with France.

France

This is rather a bizarre story, of a diplomat who sought to prevent the deportation of a group of Jews in France by supporting a claim advanced by them and others, that they were not really Semitic in origin, but rather Aryan—that is, paradoxically, a kindred ethnic group of the "master" race. **Abdol-Hossein Sardari** was the Iranian consul-

general in Paris during the war years. He supported the claim of the
Iranian Jewish community in France, based on spurious data, that far
from being Semitic by, they were in fact part of the Iranian racial stock,
thus Aryan by Nazi definition, who had many years before converted
to Judaism. They termed themselves Jugutis; in other words, Iranian-
Aryans of the Mosaic faith. Sardari supported this claim, and asked the
French and German authorities not to apply anti-Jewish measures on
this group of Iranian Jews, although some of them were in truth not at
all of Iranian origin, but had been born elsewhere. Sardari followed
this up with the presentation of a list of Iranian Jews then residing in
France. Sardari's action was mainly centered during the period of
1940-41, when Iran was neutral in the war. Following the German
invasion of the Soviet Union, in June 1941, Iran was occupied by both
Soviet and British troops, and Iran in fact lost its sovereign status. At
any rate, at this point it is not clear, to what extend Sardari's meritori-
ous action was limited to protecting all Iranian nationals, including
Jews, or went beyond that. That is, to himself having a hand in falsi-
fying records and including large numbers of clearly non-Iranian Jews
on a list which he presented to the authorities. This has not yet been
fully clarified. At the same time, it is clear that he was of help to Jews—
even a small and limited group, and this needs to be acknowledged and
appreciated.[1]

In Paris, as well, is the story currently under study of **Othon De
Bogaerde de Terbrugge**, originally from Belgium, who served as the
diplomatic representative of Liberia—at the time, the only independent country in Africa, below the Sahara. The information received so
far testify to his issuing a Liberian passport to Charles Mincberg, in
1942, at the urging of his ex-wife, Mrs. Kila Kugel, who worked as secretary in the Liberian legation in Paris. This made it possible for
Mincberg to leave France for Spain. In addition, when De Bogaerde
learned that Mrs. Kugel's brother, Jacques Kugel was in danger of
arrest, in Nice, 1942, he took the man in his car all the way to Portugal
(to where De Bogaerde was also accredited by the Liberian government), where Jacques was reunited with his close family. Upon crossing the Franco-Spanish border, De Bogaerde had Jacques Kugel hid-

den in the rear baggage section of his car, to dissimulate his presence. It is also claimed that De Bogaerde issued similar passports to other Jews, to facilitate their exit from the country, including Mrs. Kugel herself, but this has not yet been verified, and the case is still under examination.[2]

In Marseilles, we have a different quite extraordinary story, involving **Necdet Kent,** who served as the Turkish vice-consul. The story as told by him, but as yet not confirmed by witnesses or documentation, is that in 1943 he was alerted to the fact that the Germans had rounded up about 80 Turkish Jews, taken them to the train station and loaded them onto cattle cars, slated for deportation. Kent hurried to the train station, where he insisted that these persons be released on the strength of their Turkish nationality, a country with which Germany still entertained diplomatic relations. Not getting anywhere with the local commander, Kent claimed to have pushed his way through the guards and boarded one of the wagons. Not responding to the German request for him to get off, the train proceeded to Nîmes. There, a few German officers got on and gave him another chance to disembark, but he refused. "I explained to them... that more than 80 Turkish citizens had been loaded onto these animal wagons because of their Jewishness, and that as a representative of a government that rejected such treatment for religious beliefs, I could not consider leaving them alone and that was the reason for my presence here." After further consultations with their superiors, the Germans gave in and released the 80 persons in question, who were then returned to Marseilles. Kent furthermore stated that he tried to save Jews who claimed Turkish nationality, but had allowed their passports to lapse, as well as those with flimsy records, but still claiming to have once been Turkish nationals.[3]

Still in Marseilles, U.S. vice-consul **Hiram Bingham**, in 1940–41, in charge of visas—in contrast to other US consular officials in France, he displayed a friendly attitude to Jews applying for U.S. visas, on the basis of producing an affidavit when supported by a sponsor in the USA, and he tried to be of assistance as much as possible, within the framework of his country's immigration laws. In addition, he hosted

in his home the German-Jewish expatriate Lion Feuchtwanger, until
his visa for travel to the United States had come through. As stated by
Varian Fry, the American emissary of the Emergency Rescue
Committee, who worked out of Marseilles, Hiram Bingham had "a
heart of gold. He does everything he can to help us, within American
law."[4] It should be noted that the U.S. policy at the time was to dis-
courage immigration. As stated by Assistant Secretary of State
Breckinridge Long, consuls should be advised "to put every obstacle in
the way and to require additional evidence and to resort to various
administrative devices which would postpone and postpone and postpone the granting of the visas." Bingham's attitude was quite the oppo-
site; a friendly disposition, and an effort to come forward and help
within the confines of U.S. immigration laws and regulations. When
Bingham was reassigned to another post, his replacement, in Fry's
words, was a person "who seemed to delight in making autocratic decisions and refusing as many visas as he possibly could."[5]

In Marseilles as well, currently under study, is the story of **Gilberto
Bosques**, the Mexican consul-general in Paris, who after the fall of
France, moved his office to Marseilles, where he exerted himself to
assist refugees from the Spanish Civil War. His government, headed by
Lázaro Cardenas, followed a liberal immigration policy vis-à-vis former soldiers of the Republican army in the Spanish Civil War, who
were in need of protection after the Fascist victory. Under study are
claims that Bosques also gave out visas to Jews in need, an act not
allowed by his government, and when informed so, he stated he would
not annul the visas already handed out.[6] Also under examination is the
case of **Eduardo Proper de Callejon**, who served as secretary at the
Spanish embassy in Paris, in 1939. In June 1940, while in Bordeaux,
he reportedly issued visas to many Jews, wishing to cross into Spain,
after they had received Portuguese transit visit from the Portuguese
ambassador in Bordeaux, Aristides de Sousa Mendes. It is asserted that,
in February 1941, Proper de Callejon was reprimanded for this generous act by the Spanish Foreign Minister Ramón Serrano Suñer, and
the man was reassigned to a less prestigious post in Spanish Morocco.
This has yet to be established.[7]

Austria

Information received seemed to indicate that **Eero Harjanne** and **Kauko Sipinen**, both vice-consuls, who in the temporary absence of the Finnish consul in Vienna, in summer 1938, reportedly issued Finnish visas to Jews desperate to leave the city, presently in Nazi hands. Such as Fred Brand, who as an 18-year-old went from one consulate to the other in search for a visa, when he was referred to the Finnish consulate, where Harjanne and Sipinen validated a Finish visa on his passport, with which Brand was able to reach Finland by boat from Stettin, Germany, on August 12, 1938. According to Fred Brand, the two diplomats had handed out such visas to 150 people. As a consequence, the two diplomats were reportedly recalled home and either reprimanded or expelled from the diplomatic service, but so far no confirmation was received to this.[8] In Vienna, as well, **Rudolf Salek**, the Yugoslav consul gave out visas of his country, without prior clearance from his government, and was reportedly reprimanded for this and reassigned to another post. In 1947, the Rome office of the JDC (Joint Distribution Committee) sent Salek a letter of thanks and appreciation, for his help to "several hundreds" Jews, in 1938, by facilitating their travel to Yugoslavia. No confirmation of this had yet surfaced by beneficiaries of Salek's generous act.[9]

Switzerland

Moving to Switzerland, we briefly note the already mentioned **José Arturo Castellanos**, who was El Salvador's consul-general in Geneva during the war years. At the urgings of his first secretary, the Jewish George Mantello, Castellanos agreed to issue Salvadoran citizenship certificates to thousands of persons in Hungary, thereby hoping to protect them from deportation. Many of these certificates were delivered by the earlier-mentioned Romanian diplomat Florian Manoliu to Mr. Krausz, in Budapest. It appears that Castenadu Castro, president of El Salvador, consented to the issuing of Salvadoran citizenship ex post facto, after Castellanos and Mantello had already initiated this undertaking. Upon the further request of Castellanos, and his Foreign Minister, Julio Enrique Ávila, the Swiss agreed for its legation in

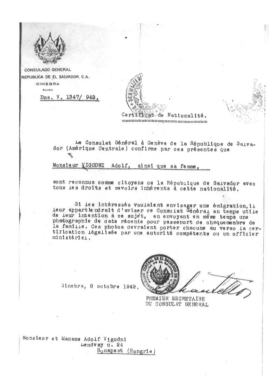

Citizenship certificate for a Hungarian Jew, issued by
José Arturo Castellanos, the San Salvadoran
consul-general in Geneva, Switzerland.

Budapest to also represent El Salvadoran interests, and in particular
the protection of Jews with Salvadoran citizenship certificates. It is not
known exactly, but it is assumed that thousands of Salvadoran citizenship certificates, most of them bound for Budapest, were issued in the
summer of 1944.[10]

Italy

Giuseppe Agénore Magno was a member of an aristocratic Italian
family and in 1934 was appointed honorary Portuguese consul in
Milan. In 1940, he reportedly issued Portuguese transit visas, mostly
to Jews of Spanish or Portuguese origin, making possible their passage
through Portugal on their way to overseas countries. Soon, orders from

Lisbon directed him to stop delivering transit visas, and in October 1940, the Portuguese government even ordered his replacement, but the information on this is a bit sketchy. Some reports show him to have continued at his post, but after being demoted to vice-consul on January 30, 1941. A further confusing note is the report that on February 2, 1941, the Portuguese Foreign Ministry announced it had no longer confidence in Magno, and recommended the closure of the Milan consulate; yet, the consulate apparently continued to operate, evidently with Magno still in place, and well into the postwar period. Magno's friend, Alfredo de Casanova, the Portuguese consul in Genoa, interceded on his behalf, in a special appeal to Portugal dictator Salazar. Casanova wrote that "Magno did indeed issue some passports which I suppose were not entirely regular, but, to understand such a decision, it is necessary first of all to be familiar with the great soul he possesses . . . to listen to him with the dignity and nobility he inspires . . . . If Mr. Magno has erred, it was surely because of his affectionate heart, his healthy and liberal ideas, and not because of dishonest motives." Faults should be forgiven because of the "tragic" circumstances that surrounded them, "such as those of Hebrew race, quite unhappy human beings, cruelly assassinated, robbed and persecuted for many years, as in a hunt for rabid dogs." Salazar remained unimpressed, and as stated he was demoted to vice-consul, but remained on the job in Milan.[11]

Hungary

Moving to Budapest, we note the activity of **Alberto Carlos de Lis-Teixeira Branquinho**, the interim chargé d'affaires in the Portuguese legation, from June 5 to October 29, 1944, when he was recalled to Lisbon. Branquinho began by issuing Portuguese visas on behalf of nine Hungarian Jews who had family or business relations in Portugal, based on his government's authorization to issue Portuguese passports to all Jews who could prove to have connections in Portugal or Brazil. By 1944, Portugal had changed its strict immigration policy of earlier years, and allowed its diplomats to be more lenient in issuing visas. After the Arrow Cross takeover, on October 15, 1944, Branquinho

also began to issue protective passes—and seven hundred were distributed. On November 15, holders of these certificates were ordered to
relocate into special diplomatically-protected buildings in the
International Ghetto. On August 26, 1944, Branquinho informed
Lisbon that he had issued 200 passports without mentioning the recipients' nationality and requested permission to issue a further 400 provisional Portuguese passports to about 400 Jewish families (1,200 people) who wished to continue to Palestine, and would therefore never
claim Portuguese nationality—a precondition demanded by Lisbon.
On October 29, 1944, Branquinho left Budapest to Bregenz, on the
Swiss border, upon instructions from Lisbon. From there, Branquinho
reported that on October 29, the Hungarian Government and the
German ambassador had undertaken to respect Jews sheltered in the
Portuguese Legation building in Budapest—a total of 50 persons; also
Jews employed at the Portuguese Legation, who numbered 35 persons,
as well as their families, for a total number of 200 persons. To this may
be added the 700 Hungarian Jews bearing Portuguese passports.
"Altogether about one thousand Semites who were saved will owe their
lives to the generous actions of the Portuguese government." Quite a
change from the stiff anti-humanitarian policy of Portugal of earlier
years.[12]

The work at the Portuguese legation was continued by Vice-Consul
Jules Gulden, who stayed on the job until December of that year. In
Geneva, on December 18, 1944, Gulden wrote to Salazar that "my
work protecting Jews has seriously compromised me in the eyes of the
country's dominant party. My case is all the more serious and could be
considered a 'crime of treason,' because I am an Hungarian: others
employed in this activity were all foreign diplomats. I have been getting threats, in the form of warnings, almost every day. On the 7th
inst., in fact, a functionary of the Foreign Ministry . . . also told me
that I should disappear as soon as possible. . . . The offices of the legation and the consulate are still functioning under count **François
Pongracz.**"[13]

Greece

According to a Spanish law, of 1924, persons claiming Spanish descent could acquire Spanish citizenship, without preferably actually setting foot in Spain—but enjoying protection by Spanish diplomats in the persons' countries of residence. As a result, when the Germans occupied Thessalonika (also known as Salonica) in April 1941, a number of Jews had in their possession official documents attesting to their Spanish nationality. The Jewish Solomon Ezrati, surprisingly headed the Spanish consulate in Thessalonika, and he drew up a list of 550 such persons. When the Germans began to deport the Jews of the city, in March 1943, they made an exception for Jews who were foreign nationals and could prove it by means of a valid passport. Spain was therefore requested to see to the evacuation of her Jews, and the deadline for completing this move was fixed for June 14, 1943; thereafter, the Germans threatened, Jewish nationals of Spain would be deported with other Jews. Spain, however, conditioned her acceptance of Spanish Jews that they would not stay on in Spain but immediately depart to another destination. Moreover, no group was to be allowed into Spain before the previous group had already departed from Spain. **Sebastian Romero Radigales** was the Spanish consul-general in Athens. His arrival in mid-April 1943 marked a turning-point in the protection of Spanish-claimant Jews. In the words of historian Haim Avni, "he devoted his best efforts to defending the rights and well-being of his Jewish wards; from the moment of his arrival he became their generous protector;" this without necessarily waiting for precise instructions from Madrid. The German ambassador in Athens, Altenburg, complained on April 30, that as a result of Radigales' interventions, he had been forced to postpone implementation of coercive measures against the Spanish nationals. Together with Solomon Ezrati, Radigales conferred with his Italian counterparts on the possibility of evacuating the Spanish Jewish nationals from Thessalonika to the Italian-occupied zone, centered in Athens. These efforts of Radigales and Ezrati were not in vain, and with Italian help about 150 Spanish nationals were removed from Thessalonika and reached Athens in an Italian military train carrying Italian troops on leave. Spain and

Germany continued to haggle whether these 150 persons were to be allowed to continue to Spain via ship, as the Germans demanded, or by land travel, as the Spanish suggested. There remained about 367 Spanish nationals in Thessalonika, whom the Germans sent to Bergen-Belsen concentration camp in Germany. After a long stay in that camp, they entered Spain in February 1944, but were made to continue to Morocco.[14]

Madrid's prevarications on this issue did not dishearten Radigales, and he multiplied his efforts on behalf of those under his protection in Athens—about 235 persons. Radigales was apparently informed that he could divide the persons into groups of 25 each, and that each group would be allowed to proceed when the previous one had already left Spain for another location. On October 7, 1943, the eve of Yom Kippur, when SS general Jürgen Stroop ordered Jews holding foreign citizenship to present themselves for registration with their papers on October 19, 1943 at the offices of the Jewish community, the Germans allowed the Spanish Jews to leave, on condition that Spain admit them. Spain agreed to this but asked for a postponement. Things continued without much further ado, when on March 24, 1944, the Germans arrested 350 Greek Jews, and at midnight of the same day a hunt was under way for foreign national Jews—Spaniards, Portuguese and Turks, who were taken from their homes and imprisoned in the Jewish community building—altogether 1,300 persons. They were taken to a concentration camp in nearby Haidari, and loaded on trains. Of the foreign nationals only the Turks and the Argentinians were removed from the transport. The 155 Spanish Jews were deported to Bergen-Belsen camp. Radigales attempted to intervene with the German ambassador, but without success. There remained about 80 Spanish Jews in Athens, and they managed to avoid capture. The 155 Spanish Jews in Bergen-Belsen remained there until that camp's liberation on April 13, 1945. Historian Avni's conclusion is that in Romero Radigales the Jews had found a man "with warmth and sympathy towards those dependent on his mercy."[15]

The deportation of Jews in Thessalonika, one of the most ancient Jewish communities in Greece, began on March 15, 1943, and was completed on August 7, 1943. Some 50,000 Jews were deported to the death camps in Poland, of which most were gassed upon arrival. **Guelfo Zamboni**, the Italian consul in the city, was able to save several hundred from this inferno. During his tenure there, he tried to spare from the deportations persons claiming Italian nationality, even those without proper documentary papers. This was in accord with Italian policy to protect persons claiming Italian ascendancy, who in Thessalonika numbered 281 persons. On March 29, 1943, Zamboni asked his superior in Athens, ambassador Gicci, how to act with regard to Jews who did not have the proper papers, but claimed Italian nationality. The ambassador referred this question to Rome, and on April 7, 1943, Under Secretary Bastianini responded that such persons were to be given a laissez-passer to Athens, in order to ascertain there their status. According to reports, Zamboni insisted that persons of questionable Italian nationality be allowed to proceed to Athens, then under Italian administration, as well as these persons' immediate family—who numbered 89 persons. Once released—to avoid their recapture, Zamboni placed them aboard an Italian military train heading for Athens. According to one report, a total of 350 persons were thus saved by Zamboni. True, it was the Italian policy to jealously guard the country's sovereign interests, including the fate of Jews claiming Italian nationality. But, it nevertheless took persons like Zamboni to insist on honoring this Italian policy, in a city filled with SS troops and sworn to destroy all Jews therein. Zamboni's replacement, Giuseppe Castruccio, June 18, 1943, reportedly continued his predecessor's policy of protecting Jews of Italian ancestry—the few Jews still left in Thessalonika.[16]

Turkey

We end with the story Archbishop **Angelo Giuseppe Roncalli** (the future pope John XXIII), who was the Vatican's apostolic delegate in Turkey, from January 1935 until mid-1944. From his base in Istanbul, he showed a great interest in the welfare of the Jews outside his immediate domain. At the request of Chaim Barlas, the Jewish Agency's representative in Istanbul, on March 13, 1943, Roncalli wrote to Cardinal

Luigi Maglione, the Vatican's secretary of state, passing on Barlas's request for the Vatican's intervention to allow the emigration of 22,000 Slovakian Jews to, as well as 2,000 children from Slovakia to Palestine, for whom there were British-approved certificates. On May 30, 1943, a similar letter went out by Roncalli to Maglione on effecting the release of a group of Jews in Slovakia and Croatia. Then, on September 4,1943, Roncalli wrote again to Maglione on the need to help Italian Jews. He then added an interesting statement, which brings to light the Vatican's position on the Zionist attempts to reestablish an independent Jewish state in Palestine. Roncalli noted that he felt uneasy about the attempts of Jews to reach Palestine, as if they were trying to reconstruct a Jewish kingdom. He did not think it proper that the charitable activity of the Holy See should be used in this way to help in the realization of any messianic dream that the Jews might have. Any notions of reestablishing a Jewish reign in Palestine were visionary and utopian. By this, Roncalli may have been using "politically correct" language to assuage the fears of his superiors on the migration of too many Jews to the expanding Jewish community in Palestine.[17]

Equally, with regard to Romania, in July 1943, Roncalli sent to the Vatican Secretariat of State a list of names of Jewish families in Transnistria who were deserving of help.[18]

The most urgent matter in mid-1944 was the plight of the Jews in Hungary. Ira Hirschmann, the War Refugee representative in Turkey, wrote after the war of his impressions of Roncalli in glowing terms. Meeting him in 1944, to ask for his intervention to stop the destruction of the Jewish community in Hungary, Roncalli was visibly moved by Hirschmann's description of the disaster that had befallen the Jews of Hungary. "Then he pulled his chair up closer and quietly asked, 'Do you have any contact with people in Hungary who will cooperate? . . . Do you think the Jews there would be wiling to undergo baptism ceremonies . . . I equivocated a bit and said that I could only guess or assume that if it meant saving their lives they would be ready to do so gratefully. . . . He went on to say that he had reason to believe that some baptismal certificates had already been issued by nuns to

C O P Y

Istanbul, August 1, 1944

Excellency:

In pursuance of Your Excellency's kind offer, in which you volunteered that you would be pleased to respond in writing to certain questions which we would be permitted to submit to you with refer ence to the rescue and relief activities of t he United States War Refugee Board, I have the honor to enclose for your co nsideration the attached list.

Permit me again, in the name of the Government of the United States of America, to express my gratitude for the audience which Your Excellency so kindly granted me, and to reaffirm to you how deeply moved I was by your great interest and efforts in the broad humanitarian aspects of the problem in which the War Refugee Board is actively operating.

With renewed assurances of my highest esteem, I am,

Your Excellency's most obedient servant,

Ira A. Hirschmann
Special Attache

His Excellency
Monsignor Ange Roncalli
Apostolic Delegate
Büyükada

Enclosures

IAH/b

*Letter of thanks by Ira Hirschmann to
Monsignor Roncalli for his readiness to help.*

Hungarian Jews. The Nazis had recognized these as credentials and had permitted their holders to leave the country. We agreed that we would communicate with his representatives in Hungary and that I would get in touch with our underground connections to arrange for either large-scale baptism of Jews, or at least certificates to be issued to women and children. . . . It was clear to me that Roncalli had considered this plan before my arrival . . . Operation Baptism."[19] According to unconfirmed reports, Roncalli followed this up by sending many baptismal certificates to the nuncio in Budapest.[20]

On August 18, 1944, Roncalli replied to a number of questions from Hirschmann with regard to help to Jews. Insofar as Hungary was concerned, Roncalli wrote that "the Apostolic Delegation has forwarded by diplomatic courtier several thousands of Immigration Certificates destined for Jews in Hungary. These were delivered to the persons concerned by the good offices of the Apostolic Nunciature in Budapest and the same Apostolic Nuncio later informed that those certificates had enabled their owners to escape transportation and to obtain the necessary permissions for emigration." Roncalli also added his willingness "to transmit by courier to Budapest Immigration certificates or other non-political documents which may be useful. It is also willing to recommend particular cases to the special care of the Apostolic Nuncio, as has been done, for example, in the case of Rabbi Salomon Halberstam." Roncalli then underlined that "I repeat that I am always ready to help you in your charitable work as far as in my power and as far as circumstances permit."[21]

Barlas was also deeply impressed by Roncalli. As he wrote later: "I realized that I stood before a man of lofty spiritual stature, who was truly interested in the sufferings that had befallen our people and who was prepared heart and soul to assist in whatever way he could. Whenever during my interviews he would hear of the news from Poland, Hungary and Slovakia, he would clasp his hands in prayer, tears flowed from his eyes." At the request of Barlas, Roncalli addressed an appeal to King Boris of Bulgaria to stay and withhold plans to deport the country's Jews. Luigi Bresciani, Roncalli's secretary related that when he wrote the letter to the king, "I had never before seen Monsignor Roncalli so disturbed." After composing the letter, he read the contents to Bresciani, who was impressed. "Even though calm and gentle as a Saint Francis de Sales come to life, he did not spare himself from saying openly that King Boris should on no account agree to that dishonorable action."[22]

Meir Touval-Weltmann, in a 1973 article in the *Jerusalem Post*, wrote of his meeting with Roncalli in Istanbul in 1943 as a representative of the Rescue Committee for European Jews. "When I visited Monsignor Roncalli from time to time, he always lent an attentive ear and expressed support and concern for the fate of the Jews under Nazi rule. One day I was pleasantly surprised when he turned with a request

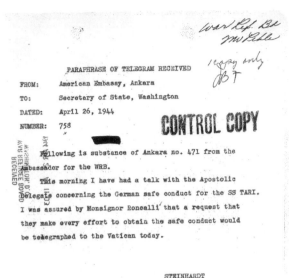

U.S. ambassador to Turkey, Laurence A. Steinhardt to the State Department on Monsignor Roncalli's readiness to help with the safe passage of a boat with Jewish refugees through the Dardanelles Straits.

to me. Two young Jews from Anatolia appeared at my hotel with a letter of recommendation from Monsignor Roncalli asking me to assist them to immigrate to Palestine. Subsequently Roncalli asked me to assist in the immigration to Palestine of other young Jews, and he also took an interest in arranging for them to continue their education here.[23]

Later, as Pope John XXIII, during the Second Vatican Council he welcomed a Jewish delegation with the words, "I am Joseph, your brother." Since Pope John's original given name, Giuseppe, actually was the Italian equivalent of Joseph, his utterance of these simple words from the book of Genesis (45:3–4) took on a special meaning. With one humbly spoken sentence, John XIII succeeded in establishing a familial bond between himself and the members of the Jewish delegation and thereby created an atmosphere that opened the door to dialogue. The result was the start of a process that would remove the anti-Jewish sting from Catholic liturgy and teaching and, later under John Paul II, lead to the dawn of dialogue and reconciliation between the Christian and Jewish faiths.[24]

Hopefully, when the Vatican releases for scholarly research the full wartime file of Pope John XXIII, a fuller appraisal will be made possible of the man's activity on behalf of Jews during the Holocaust.

*   *   *

The previous listed diplomats are hopefully an indication of other diplomatic colleagues from various countries who may have extended a helping hand to Jews in distress, either in compliance with instructions from above, or by going the extra mile in their humanitarian endeavors. The stories in this and previous chapters point to the possibility of similar stories coming to light in the coming years. If so, it would only add to strengthen our belief in the predominance of the human spirit.

Chapter 9

Conclusions

When the word "diplomat" is mentioned, what usually comes to mind is of a civil servant accustomed to think and act in accordance with what is considered "politically correct," and blindly obeying orders whether or not in agreement with the policies they embody. Governments may change, and with that their policies, and diplomats at foreign stations are expected to change course and adapt their actions to the new winds blowing from their chancelleries. When a diplomat steps out of line and voices his own opinion on an important issue, especially an opinion not consonant with the policy of his government, his superiors are deemed justified in meting out disciplinary punishment against the recalcitrant diplomat. There is a consensus among the public at large that this ought to be so, for otherwise pandemonium would reign and a country's policies would suffer damage in the eyes of other countries.

At the same time, since civilized life is based on the centuries-old accumulation of certain values of conduct and behavior, there are times when civil servants in high positions find themselves confronted with decisions of great moral dimensions. When they choose to distract their attention from these challenges, they unwittingly place in jeopardy the moral values upon which all civilized societies are based. During the Nazi period, the sanctity of life of all humans was the principle under challenge. Diplomats had the weapon on hand to meet this attack head-on by offering the innocent victims of the Nazi terror an escape hatch, a bridge over stormy waters, with a scrap of paper or a seal—in the form of a visa or other protective document. The diplomats in our study were able to pass this moral test and simultaneously overcome the obstacles placed in their way by their own governments, whose orders they were forced either to disobey or to find loopholes that permitted them to help the victims pounding at their doors.

Diplomats like the Portuguese Mendes, the Brazilian Dantas, the Dutch Zwartendijk, the Japanese Sugihara, the Chinese Ho, and the German Duckwitz—as well as the others in our study—were able to grasp the human dimension at stake and find ways to overcome the obstacles in their effort to save human lives threatened with destruction through no fault of their own. These courageous officials braved the risks to themselves, and some were made to pay a stiff price for their disobedience or for their actions that were not in accordance with the spirit of their countries' immigration laws. As some of them have stated, they felt that they had no alternative but to act as they did, even if it meant the prospect of crippling their diplomatic career and losing the financial emoluments that went along with it.

The thousands of people spared from death thanks to the benevolence of these courageous diplomats were able to pick up again and recreate new lives, while at the same time reflecting on the goodness of their rescuers. The saving action of these rescuers leads us to think that people, in whatever station of life they find themselves, may at times be called, by certain actions, to reconfirm their attachment to basic moral values. The diplomats in this study, and those who may still be discovered, point out the lesson that a potential for goodness, of whatever measure and quality, is an attribute shared by most people. It is the spark of light in our souls that makes life worth living.

The goodness displayed by these diplomats during the Holocaust is proof that even civil servants, trained to obedience, may find themselves in situations where they have to make moral choices, some of which may be at variance with the policies of their governments. The diplomats studied in this book are also proof that the human dimension was not lacking even among those who represented non-democratic systems of government. They all represent models of behavior that can serve as beacons for future generations.

Bibliography

Afonso, Rui. "Count Giuseppe Agénore Magno." *Portuguese Studies Review* 5, no. 1 (Spring–Summer 1996): 12–21.

Anger, Per. *With Raoul Wallenberg in Budapest.* New York: Holocaust Library, 1981.

Avni, Haim. *Contemporary Spain and the Jewish People* (Hebrew). Jerusalem: Hebrew University Press, 1974.

———. "Spanish Nationals in Greece and Their Fate during the Holocaust." *Yad Vashem Studies* 8 (1970): 31–68.

Barlas, Chaim. *Hatzalah Bimei Hashoah* (Rescue during the Holocaust). Tel Aviv: Hakibbutz Hameuchad, 1975.

Bennett, Jeremy. "The Resistance Against the German Occupation of Denmark 1940–45." *The Strategy of Civilian Defence*, ed. Adam Roberts. London: Faber & Faber, 1967.

Bertelsen, Aage. *October 1943.* New York: Gross Brothers, no date (1980s).

Blet, Pierre, Robert Graham, Angelo Martini, and Burkhart Schneider, eds. *Actes et Documents du Saint Siège Relatifs à la Seconde Guerre Mondiale.* Vatican City: Libreria Editrice Vaticana, 1965–75; IX, SSVG, 361–362; VIII, SSVG, 647; IX, SSVG, 87–90; 272, 327–328, 337, 469.

Braham, Randolph L. *The Politics of Genocide: The Holocaust in Hungary.* Condensed ed. Detroit: Wayne State University Press , 2000.

———. *The Politics of Genocide: The Holocaust in Hungary.* New York: Columbia University, 1981, vol. 2.

Brustin-Berenstein, Tatiana. "The Historiographic Treatment of the Abortive Attempt to Deport the Danish Jews." *Yad Vashem Studies* 17 (1986): 181–218.

Deaglio, Enrico. *The Banality of Goodness: The Story of Giorgio Perlasca.* Translated from Italian by G. Conti.. London: University of Notre Dame Press, 1998.

Fralon, José-Alain. *A Good Man in Evil Times: Aristides de Sousa Mendes—the Unknown Hero Who Saved Countless Lives in World War II.* London: Viking, 1998.

Franco, Manuela, and Maria Isabel Fevereiro. *Spared Lives: The Actions of Three Portuguese Diplomats in World War II.* Lisbon: Ministry of Foreign Affairs, 2000.

Friedlander, Saul. *Nazi Germany and the Jews.* New York: Harper Collins, 1997.

Fry, Varian. *Surrender on Demand.* Boulder, Col.: Johnson Books, 1997.

Hirschmann, Ira. *Caution to the Winds.* New York, David McKay, 1962.

Ioanid, Radu. *The Holocaust in Romania.* Chicago: Ivan R. Dee, 2000.

Kranzler, David. *The Man Who Stopped the Trains to Auschwitz.* Syracuse, N.Y.: Syracuse University Press, 2000.

Kulka, Otto D., and Esriel Hildesheimer. "Germany." *Encyclopedia of the Holocaust,* ed. Israel Gutman, vol. 2. New York: Macmillan, 1990; 557–575.

Lesser, Jeffrey. *Welcoming the Undesirables: Brazil and the Jewish Question.* Berkeley and Los Angeles: University of California Press, 1995.

Lester, Elenore. *Wallenberg: The Man in the Iron Web.* Englewood Cliffs, N.J.: Prentice-Hall, 1982.

Lévai, Jenö. *Abscheu und Grauen vor dem Genocid in aller Welt.* New York: Diplomatic Press, 1968.

———. *Black Book on the Martyrdom of Hungarian Jewry.* Zurich: Central European Times, 1948.

Levine, Hillel. *In Search of Sugihara: The Elusive Japanese Diplomat Who Risked His Life to Rescue 10,000 Jews from the Holocaust.* New York: Free Press, 1996.

Lewin, Isaac. *Remember the Days of Old: Historical Essays.* New York, 1994.

Meyer, Ernie. "The Second Wallenberg." *Jerusalem Post Magazine,* September 29, 1989.

Milgram, Avraham. "The Jews of Europe from the Perspective of the Brazilian Foreign Service, 1933–1941." *Holocaust and Genocide Studies* 9, no. 1 (Spring 1995): 94–120.

Morley, John F. *Vatican Diplomacy and the Jews During the Holocaust, 1933–1943.* New York: Ktav, 1980.

Morse, Arthur D. *While Six Million Died: A Chronicle of American Apathy.* New York: Ace Books, 1967.

Paldiel, Mordecai. *The Path of the Righteous: Gentile Rescuers of Jews during the Holocaust.* Hoboken, N.J.: Ktav, 1993; 252-255.

―――. *Saving the Jews.* Rockville, Md: Schreiber, 2000; 59-62; 252-255.

Pollack, Hubert. *The Human Personality.* Yad Vashem Archives, 02/340.

Rautkallio, Hannu. *Finland and the Holocaust: The Rescue of Finland's Jews.* New York: Holocaust Library, 1987.

Runberg, Björn, *Valdemar Langlet: le Sauveur en Danger.* Le Coudray-Macouard: Cheminements, 2003.

Smith, Michael. *Foley: The Spy Who Saved 10,000 Jews.* London: Hodder & Stoughton, 1999.

State of Israel; Ministry of Justice. *The Trial of Adolf Eichmann.* Jerusalem: Keter, 1992, vol. 2.

Strauss, Herbert A., *In the Eye of the Storm: Growing up Jewish in Germany, 1918–1943: A Memoir.* New York: Fordham University Press, 1999.

―――. *Uber dem Abgrund: Eine jüdische Jugend in Deutschland 1918–1943.* Frankfurt a.M.: Campus, 1997.

Strauss, Lotte, *Over the Green Hill: A German Jewish Memoir.* New York: Fordham University Press, 1999.

Swedish Ministry for Foreign Affairs, *Raoul Wallenberg: Report of the Swedish-Russian Working Group.* Stockholm, 2000.

Tschuy, Theo. *Dangerous Diplomacy.* Grand Rapids, Mich.: William B. Eerdmans, 2000.

Warhaftig, Zorach. *Refugee and Survivor: Rescue Efforts During the Holocaust.* Jerusalem, Yad Vashem, 1988 Translation of *Palit Vesarid Bimei Hashoah.* Jerusalem, Yad Vashem, 1984.

Yahil, Leni. *The Rescue of Danish Jewry: Test of a Democracy.* Philadelphia: Jewish Publication Society, 1969.

———. "Raoul Wallenberg: His Mission and His Activities in Hungary." *Yad Vashem Studies* 15 (1983): 7–53.

———. "Denmark." *Encyclopedia of the Holocaust,* ed. Israel Gutman, vol. 1. New York: Macmillan, 1990; 362–365.

All references to YVA are to Yad Vashem Archives followed with the appropriate file number.

Notes

Chapter 2

[1] Hilberg 5–6. In 1935, a Dutch motorcyclist on his way to Berlin took photographs of antisemitic signs in the towns he passed, such as "No Jews wanted," "The local residents want nothing to do with Jews," "Jews enter at their own risk," "The Jew is our misfortune. Let him keep away," "Hyenas are scum and so are Jews," and "Jews get out!"; Kulka/Hildes 563.

[2] Captain Foley's story is based principally on testimonies by beneficiaries of his aid, listed in his file, and Hubert Pollack's postwar testimony—both stored in the Yad Vashem Archives; YVA, M31-8378 and 02/340. A fuller account of Foley's life and activity appears in Michael Smith, *Foley: The Spy Who Saved 10,000 Jews.*

[3] Gill Bennett, chief historian, at the British Foreign and Commonwealth Office, in a communication to Yad Vashem in 1999, stated that Foley, in common with other passport control officers, did not have diplomatic immunity during his time in Berlin and well after the outbreak of the war in September 1939. That may be so from a formal point of view, but it is uncertain whether the Nazis knew of this, for they allowed Foley to operate freely on the premise that as a diplomat he did enjoy diplomatic immunity.

[4] YVA, M31-8378.

[5] YVA, M31-3984.

[6] Ioanid, 259; YVA, M31-10472.

[7] Ioanid, 260–261, 263–265.

[8] Ibid., 267–268.

[9] Ibid., 269.

[10] YVA, M31-10472.

[11] Strauss (German ed.), 102–103.

[12] Ibid., 270–273.

[13] Comité International de la Croix-Rouge, Histoire Orale; Interview de M. Jean Edouard Friedrich par Philippe Abplanalp, 8 décembre 1997; Gèneve, 29 avril 1998; 21. In YVA, M31-8206.

[14] YVA, M31-8206.

[15] YVA, M31-2305. Also read Milgram's article.

[16] Friedlander, 241–248.

[17] Norbert's parents elected to stay behind, and perished in the Holocaust together with their brothers and sisters.

[18] All quotations and statements in this story are taken from the Yad Vashem file of Feng Shan Ho; YVA, M31-8688.

[19] Ibid.

[20] Paul Grüninger was tried by the Swiss police in 1941 for allowing over 2,000 Jews free entry into the country against regulations and was dismissed from the police force with all pension benefits forfeited. Yad Vashem also awarded him the Righteous title. YVA, M31-680.

[21] YVA, M31-2393.

Chapter 3

[1] Warhaftig, *Palit*, 104.

[2] After Zwartendijk left, people who wished to jump on the Curaçao bandwagon wrote to the Dutch consul A.M. de Jong in Sweden, asking him to issue similar Dutch visas for Curaçao, and he responded favorably, issuing some 400 such documents. In 1968, Yad Vashem awarded de Jong a letter of thanks. YVA, M31-110. The Dutch consul in Kobe, Japan, N. A. J. de Voogd, similarly helped the refugees when a group arrived in Tsuruga, near Kobe, with Japanese visas, but no Curaçao ones. The Japanese sent them back to Vladivostok, Russia. Nathan Gutwirth, who had a legitimate Curaçao visa issued by Zwartendijk, showed it to de Voogd. After reading it, de Voogd

allowed a Jewish refugee named Gelernter to fill in the names of the stranded refugees on official Dutch stationery, including transit visas and end-visas to Curaçao. These documents were then turned over to the Japanese authorities, who deemed them satisfactory. It stands to reason that de Voogd also deserves credit and acknowledgment for his role in enabling stranded Jewish refugees to enter Japan without asking permission from his ambassador in Tokyo.

3 YVA, M31-7793. In fact, none of the Curaçao visa people ever reached the island. If they had, as foreigners they would probably have been refused entry to a place where crude oil was being refined for war purposes. In any event, the Curaçao visa was merely a ploy with which to get as far as possible from the Nazis. Once out of their reach, the refugees moved to various temporary and permanent locations in Japan (Kobe), China (Shanghai), Canada, the United States, and Israel. See also Lewin, *Remember the Days of Old*, and Warhaftig, *Refugee and Survivor*, 102–111.

4 Warhaftig, op. cit.

5 As told by Warhaftig to Dov Levin in 1965. YVA, M31-2861.

6 Teruhisa Shino, "The Longest Travel to the Promised Land" (manuscript); YVI, M31-2861.

7 Ibid., 249–250.

8 Ibid., 251.

9 Ibid., 252.

10 Ibid., 253.

11 Ibid., 246–247.

12 Ibid., 257.

13 There are hardly any Lithuanian Jews on Sugihara's list because he was unable to help them. As Soviet citizens once their country was annexed, they were unable to obtain Soviet exit and transit visas.

14 Levine, 267. Warhaftig was minister of Religious Affairs in the Israeli government for many years.

15 Ibid., 273.

16 Ibid., 240–242, 244.

17 Ibid., 259; YVI, M31-2861.

Chapter 4

[1] Milgram, 98, 104, 107, 110–111. Even Brazilian diplomats who favored immigration of Jews to their country could not refrain from injecting anti-Jewish invective into their otherwise positive evaluations of Jewish immigrants. Consider, for instance, the strange and convoluted ideas expressed by Ildefonso Falcão, the Brazilian consul in Cologne, who in mid-1933 reported on Jewish applicants for visas: "Even though they are of Semitic origin they do not display the reproachable features of the race: they continue to be German politically, and they personify the Aryan mentality and work ethic at its best;" Milgram, 96.

[2] Milgram, 95, 102, 108–109. Foreign Minister Aranha reportedly instructed his representative at the Evian Conference that at the most only individual Jews could be allowed entry into Brazil, not large groups, since "when [they come] en masse, [the Jews] constitute a menace to Brazil's future integrity"; Milgram, 106.

[3] Milgram, 111–112; Lesser, 137.

[4] Lesser, 139–141; Milgram, 112, gives a larger number of Jewish refugees aboard the *Cabo de Hornos*. The *Time* story reads in part: "When the ship (*Cabo de Buena Esperanza*) reached Rio de Janeiro, the refugees found that their visas were good for only 90 days— 90 days they had spent at Dakar—and the Brazilian authorities would not let them ashore. A few days later, the boat sailed again, on a forlorn chance that perhaps Argentina would admit them. . . . The Argentine government gave the refugees 90 days grace. Perhaps in that time they would find a country that would let them in. . . . They were bundled aboard another of the 'White Sepulchres' the *Cabo de Hornos*. The *Cabo de Hornos* turned her white bows north and east again toward Rio and Hitler's Europe. . . . All night long a police launch cruised the far side of the ship to pick up anyone who might jump overboard. Next day, the *Cabo de Hornos* started the long voyage back to Europe. . . . Finally the passengers of the *Cabo de Hornos* landed at Curacao."

[5] Lesser, 138. When the Vichy government in July 1941 announced measures to dispossess non-resident Jews of their property, including

Brazilian Jews, as part of its "Aryanization" program, Dantas threatened similar action against French citizens in Brazil unless the decree was annulled; Milgram, 112.

6 YVA, M31-9667.

7 His full name was Aristides de Sousa Mendes do Amaral e Abranches.

8 Fralon, 47; Franco, 37, 82, 106.

9 Fralon, 56.

10 Ibid. 54, 57–60.

11 Ibid., 61–63.

12 Ibid., 66, 69; Franco, 39. A French diplomat reportedly threw himself on his knees and begged Mendes to grant him and his family visas. Transit visas were also granted to the Belgian politician Albert de Vleeschauwer and Archduke Otto, the claimant to the Habsburg throne; Fralon 68, 70.

13 Franco, 86–88, Fralon, 86–87.

14 Fralon, 95; Testimony of Rabbi Kruger, YVA, M31-264.

15 Franco, 85; Fralon, 90–92.

16 Franco, 91–92.

17 Fralon, 106–107.

18 Franco, 93, 96–97; Fralon, 110, 112–113.

19 Franco, 95–96, 98–99.

20 Franco, 103–104, Fralon, 1008.

21 Fralon, 105.

22 Franco, 110–111; Fralon, 114.

23 Fralon, 115, 119.

24 YVA, M31-264.

25 Fralon, 33, 153, 155.

26 Fralon, 159. The children of Aristides de Sousa Mendes (1885–1954) and his wife Evangelina (1888–1948) were: Aristides César (1909–1961), Manuel Silverio (1911–1934), José Antonio (1912–1969), Clotilde Augusta (1913), Isabel Maria (1915), Feliciano Artur Geraldo (1917–1969), Elisa Joana (1918), Pedro Nuno (1920), Carlos Francisco Fernando (1922), Sebastian Miguel Duarte (1923),

Teresinha do Menino Jésus (1925), Luis Felipe (1928), John Paul (1931), Raquel Herminia (1933–34). At the time of his demotion, he had 12 living children.

[27] Franco, 113.

Chapter 5

[1] Duckwitz to Yahil, January 1948, YVA-027/14.

[2] Ibid.

[3] David Melchior, at the Eichmann trial, May 10, 1961.

[4] Ibid.

[5] Alfred Joachim Fjischer, *Ein Volk Rettet Seine Juden.* YVA, M31-679.

[6] Fischer.

[7] Duckwitz to Yahil.

[8] Ibid.

[9] Ibid.

[10] Ibid.

[11] N.E. Ekblad, 1958, YVS 027/14.

[12] Fischer; Ekblad; Ibid.

[13] Ekblad, 11; Fischer; Ibid. Duckwitz to Yahil. In his postwar account, Duckwitz stated that the SS commander in Denmark, Rudolf Mildner, although a loyal Nazi, was also opposed to the planned action due to the lack of manpower at his disposal. As for Foreign Minister Ribbentrop, he too was not enthusiastic, but dared not cross Hitler's will.

[14] Ekblad; Ibid.

[15] Ibid.

[16] Hedtoft-Hansen was prime minister of Denmark in 1953–1955.

[17] Hedtoft, in Bertelsen, 16–19.

[18] Ekblad; Ibid.

[19] Ibid.

[20] Fisscher; Duckwitz to Yahil; Ekblad; Ibid.

[21] Hedtoft, Fischer.

[22] Melchior.

[23] Yahil, *Rescue,* 305–308.

[24] Melchior.

25 Duckwitz to Yahil.

26 Ibid.

27 YVA, M31-679. Some 30 years after the war, two historians questioned Duckwitz's account. They claimed that Duckwitz and his Social Democratic friends were all actually engaged in collaboration politics with the German occupiers. Also, that Duckwitz engaged in espionage for the Germans. Villhjalmur O. Vilhjalmsson, 2003. See Brustin-Berenstein's critique of Duckwitz's postwar account of his role in sabotaging Hitler's order to deport the Danish Jews.

28 YVA, M31-679.

Chapter 6

1 According to one unconfirmed account, Puncuch represented the Croatian government during that country's short-lived independence as a German vassal state in 1941–1945.

2 YVA, M31-10287.

3 YVA, M31-8860.

4 *Encyclopaedia Judaica*, vol. 14 (1971): 145–148.

5 YVA, M31-4128.

Chapter 7

1 Braham, *Politics* (condensed ed.), 21, 23, 29.

2 Ibid., 24, 32.

3 Anger, 44–45.

4 Braham, *Politics* (condensed ed.), 32–34, 36, 96. The Labor Battalions were a uniquely Hungarian phenomenon. Jewish workers commanded by non-Jewish officers were deployed for road building, mining, rail line construction, and fortification work for the military within Hungary and in Hungarian-controlled areas of Ukraine and Yugoslavia, Braham, 37.

5 Anger, 17–19, 24.

6 Braham, *Politics* (condensed ed.), 13, 55, 64.

7 Ibid., 13, 56–57, 66.

8 Ibid., 13, 31, 77, 89, 95, 97, 213–214. Earlier, in September 1943, Gisi Fleischmann of the Slovakian Jewish community reported: "We

know today that Sobibor, Malkyne-Treblinki, Belzec, and Auschwitz are annihilation camps." Ibid., 90–92.

[9] Ibid., 100–103, 106.

[10] Ibid., 111–114.

[11] Ibid., 134–136. In his June 26, 1944 memorandum, Prime Minister Sztójay told the diplomatic representatives that the Jews were being deported to Germany for labor purposes, and their families were going so that worry about their loved ones would not affect their work performance; Ibid., 61.

[12] Ibid., 74–77.

[13] Ibid., 117, 122–123, 127, 130, 133, 137, 153. Some 20,000 Jews were sent to Strasshof, a camp near Vienna, for labor in industrial and agricultural enterprises in a number of communities in eastern Austria, including Gmund, Weitra, Wiener-Neustadt, and Neunkirchen. Ibid., 149.

[14] Ibid., 152, 161–166.

[15] Ibid., 155–158, 167–169, 171.

[16] Ibid., 184, 196, 289.

[17] Ibid., 167, 185–188, 190–192, 195.

[18] Ibid., 252–253.

[19] Ibid., 213–214, 233.

[20] Ibid., 214, 230, 234. The Allied nations, at war with Hungary and Germany, were not very generous, to say the least, about the prospect of a sudden mass influx of Jews to Palestine, should the Germans have agreed to such a plan. This anxiety was reflected in a British Foreign Office memorandum on July 20 suggesting that instead of sending the Jews to Palestine, "camps should be established . . . somewhere in the Mediterranean area, but not Palestine and preferably not too near Palestine" (Ibid., 296). The attitude of the other countries was no less promising. On June 9, 1944, President Roosevelt allowed only 5,000 refugees to be housed in the former army post at Oswego, New York. Brazil expressed on September 6 its readiness to admit 500 children as long as it would have no financial responsibility in regard to transport and upkeep; Ireland (September 8) indicated its willingness to include Hungarian Jewish children among the 500 children it had earlier

agreed to admit; Australia was deterred by the "unpromising shipping position"; New Zealand "decided for the time being they were unable to help; South Africa indicated that it already had "its hands full" with war refugees and evacuees; Canada shut its doors. Ibid., 296.

[21] Yad Vashem Archives (henceforth YVA), M31-46; also for the rest of the Lutz story.

[22] Ibid.

[23] Anger 109–110.

[24] YVA, M31-8575

[25] YVA, M31-8233 (Zürcher), M31-9044 (Vonrufs).

[26] Braham, *Politics* (condensed ed.), 192, 243–245, 293. Also Braham, *Politics of Genocide*, Volume 2, 1062–1063.

[27] YVA, M31-3560.

[28] Braham, *Politics* (condensed ed.), 235–236, 228–229. By establishing the War Refugee Board, the U.S. government was in no way detracting from its restrictive immigration policy of non-admittance of Jewish refugees. The WRB was instructed that its rescue operations could in no way be inconsistent with British and American immigration policies.

[29] According to historian Leni Yahil, Wallenberg knew that one of his forebears on his mother's side, Michael Bendicks, had been among the first Jews to settle in Sweden at the end of the eighteenth century and had his children baptized. Yahil, *Yad Vashem*, 23–24.

[30] Ibid., 27, 29, 30.

[31] Ibid., 31. Also, Swedish Ministry of Foreign Affairs, *Raoul Wallenberg* (Uppsala: Swedish Institute,: 1988), 7.

[32] Yahil, *Yad Vashem*, 32; Anger, 50, 51, 57; Braham, *Politics (Condensed)*, 236–237, 297.

[33] Anger, 49–50.

[34] YVA, M31-31.

[35] Braham, *Politics* (condensed ed.), 237; Yahil, *Yad Vashem*, 38.

[36] YVA, M31-31.

[37] Anger, 69, 91.

[38] Ibid., 59–60.

[39] Ibid., 91–93.

[40] Yahil, *Yad Vashem*, 40.

[41] Anger, 74, 163, 165; Yahil, *Yad Vashem,* 37.

[42] Braham, *Politics* (condensed ed.), 188, 197, 237, 297; Braham, *Politics,* 872–874..

[43] Swedish Ministry, 33–34, 46–47, Anger, 86.

[44] Swedish Ministry, 8.

[45] Ibid., 9–12.

[46] Ibid., 15–18, 51; "Raoul Wallenberg: Report of the Swedish-Russian Working Group," Ministry for Foreign Affairs, Stockholm 2000 (hereinafter SR), 111, 115.

[47] SR, 123.

[48] SR, 7.

[49] SR, 49, 50, 57, 81.

[50] SR, 88, 91–92, 94, 96–97, 103.

[51] SR, 63–72.

[52] Anger, 140, 162; SR 43, 59–61, 75; Swedish Ministry, 13.

[53] Anger, 152, 157–159.

[54] SR, 173–174.

[55] YVA, M31-31.

[56] Anger, 46–48, Yahil, *Yad Vashem,* 28.

[57] Per Anger file, YVA, M31-1915.

[58] Anger, 40–41.

[59] Ibid., 67–69.

[60] Ibid., 90.

[61] Ibid., 71, 110–111.

[62] Ibid., 73, 77–80.

[63] Ibid., 81–82.

[64] YVA, M31-1915.

[65] Yahil, *Yad Vashem,* 25, 27.

[66] Yahil 34, based on Braham, *Politics,* 791–797.

[67] Anger, 75.

[68] Ibid., 52; YVA, M31-1915a, 1915b.

[69] Runberg, 12, 51, 54.

[70] Ibid., 56, 65–66, 74.

[71] Ibid., 81, 83–84. Nina Langlet gives the figure for protective letters issued at between 4,000–6,000. Runberg, 83.

72 Ibid., 22, 34–35.

73 Ibid., 57, 74, 85–86, 120.

74 Ibid., 98–117; Anger, 56, 73.

75 YVA, M31-101.

76 Runberg, 46, YVA, M31-101.

77 Kranzler, 82, 97; Tschuy, 124.

78 Kranzler, 83, 86.

79 Lévai, *Abscheu,* 31.

80 Kranzler, 88.

81 Tschuy, 134.

82 YVA, M31-9160.

83 Braham, *Politics,* vol. 2, 1093–1093.

84 YVA, M31-121.

85 Deaglio, 19–20; YVA, M31-3911.

86 Ibid., 31–32, 60, 67, 69–70.

87 Ibid., 76–77, 80.

88 Ibid., 69, 78–79.

89 Ibid., 82, 84, 87–88, 93–95.

90 Ibid., 102–103.

91 YVA, M31-3911; Deaglio 132–133.

92 Levai, *Black,* 358–359, 387–388; Deaglio,, 90.

93 YVA, M31-3911; Deaglio, 11–12, 110–111.

94 YVA, M31-3911; Deaglio, 4–5, 69, 78, 142.

95 Braham, *Politics* (condensed ed.), 241–242.

96 Rotta file, YVA, M31-3110.

97 Braham, *Politics* (condensed ed.), 243.

98 Rotta file, YVA, M31-3110.

99 Levai, *Hungarian Jewry,* 63.

100 Ibid., *35.*

101 Rotta file, YVA, M31-3110.

102 YVA, M31-3110.

103 YVA, M31-1548.

104 Ibid.

105 YVA, M31-7690.

Chapter 8

[1] YVA, M31-2054.

[2] YVA, M31-10778.

[3] YVA, M31-5289.

[4] Fry, 10.

[5] Fry, 215. Yad Vashem sent the Bingham family a letter of thanks and appreciation. YVA, M31-10404.

[6] YVA, M31-10715.

[7] YVA, M31-13252.

[8] YVA, M31-10998.

[9] YVA, M31-8283.

[10] YVA, M31-625.

[11] YVA, M31-3459.

[12] Franco, 68-77.

[13] Franco, 120, 122-125.

[14] Avni, *Yad Vashem*, 40-41, 43, 47, 52-53, 57, 63.

[15] Avni, *Yad Vashem*, 58-62, 66, 68.

[16] YVA, M31-5351. In appreciation of Zamboni's humanitarian endeavor, Yad Vashem sent him a letter of thanks and appreciation.

[17] Morley, 94.

[18] Morley, 43, 45, 91-92.

[19] Hirschmann, 181-182.

[20] Morse, 294-295.

[21] War Refugee Board Records, at the Franklin D. Roosevelt Library, Hyde Park, New York; in YVA, M31-1773. Also, Blet et al., Vol. 10, 390-393.

[22] Morse, 259-260.

[23] Meir Touval-Weltmann, "How Pope John Helped Rescue European Jews," *The Jerusalem Post*, June 26, 1973.

[24] YVA, M31-1773.

Index

235